VANISHING FLORIDA

A Personal Guide
to Sights Rarely Seen

David T. Warner

To Lydia
A fellow
Florida
Fanatic
Love
DTW

RIVER CITY PUBLISHING
Montgomery, Alabama

Library of Congress Cataloging-in-Publication Data:

Warner, David T., 1948-
 Vanishing Florida : a personal guide to sights rarely seen / by David T. Warner.
      p. cm.
ISBN 0-913515-49-3 (alk. paper)
 1. Florida—Description and travel. 2. Florida—Guidebooks. 3. Florida—Biography Anecdotes. 4. Warner, David T., 1948—-Journeys—Florida. I. Title.
 F316.2 .W36 2001
 2001001496

Designed by Lissa Monroe.
Edited by Jim Davis.
Printed in the United States of America.

Also by David Warner: *High-Sheriff Jim Turner: High Times of a Florida Lawman*, published by River City Publishing under our Black Belt Press imprint.

Vanishing Florida

Acknowledgments

The author and publisher express deep and sincere gratitude to Ed Baatz, Keith Bollum, and Debra Force.

Thanks also to the Sam and Robbie Vickers Florida Collection of Jacksonville, Florida, for the use of the cover art, *The Champion, Florida East Coast* by Leslie Ragan (born 1897). The original, in watercolor and gouache, measures 21 x 17.5 in.

Some of the material in this book previously appeared in these distinguished publications:

Body, Mind, and Spirit —"Looking for Atlantis"
Cimarron Review—"Key West Writers," "Cedar Key," and "Borden Deal"
Gulfshore Life—"Host of Fridays," "Everglades City and the Ten
    Thousand Islands," and "John D. MacDonald: A Remembrance"
Marjorie Kinnan Rawlings Newsletter—"*The Yearling* Revisited"
New Business—"Adventures in the Skin Trade"
Sarasota Magazine—"The Secret Life of Borden Deal," which won a
    statewide award.
Zelo—"The Other Hemingway"

This book is dedicated to Ed,
without whose help it would not have been possible.

Introduction

1. Yesterday

2. The Oyster Coast

A wood pier at Fernandina Beach on Amelia Island. A man fishing at the end of the pier and a large seabird midway on the railing, both enjoying a quickly vanishing empty stretch of beach.

Photo by Debra Force.

. . . In an amnesiac world, where ghosts were figments and graves lay forgotten under lawns, where newspaper archives and historic papers became intentionally or accidentally bonfires but were not mourned, where churches fled from tennis courts and unique linguistic cultures from a pandemic of fairways and putting greens, where people strode past the monuments of their heritage not caring what they meant, but only what they were worth, where worth was measured by the acre and the square foot and not by cubic volume of accumulated experience, [he] belonged to another way, the old way, the culture of memory.

—Russ Rymer in *American Beach*

. . . at any given moment of universal time each human being is in the proper place which he earned for himself . . .

—Manly P. Hall in *The Mystical Christ*

INTRODUCTION

Florida, for most people, consists of palm trees, beaches, and Mickey Mouse. Restaurants are either fast-food or gourmet, and nightlife is urban and sophisticated. Miami and Palm Beach, not Cedar Key and Apalachicola. Orlando and Naples, not Cross Creek and Crescent City.

But there is another, more timeless, Florida. A Florida with roots closer to the nineteenth than the twenty-first century. A Florida of time-worn blacks and whites with cane poles, seated on the banks of muddy, slow-rolling rivers; of weathered fish-houses on barnacled wooden pilings, perched like ancient gulls above a pale-gray sea; of century-old inns with winding stairwells, muted candelabrums, and elaborate gardens; of forests of live oak, pine, and palmetto, where the only sound to be heard is the steady chirrup of crickets and the whisper of the wind.

This is my Florida. *Vanishing Florida . . .*

A crew at work, laying pavement to make a nine-foot-wide road in Polk County, east of present-day Tampa. Photo taken May 9, 1917.

Part 1
YESTERDAY

Entrance to Marineland, one of Florida's first theme parks.

Yesterday

Yesterday is my vision of Florida. Having passed the half-century mark, I live more in the Eternal Now, which encompasses past, present, and future. Old friends and new. The living and the so-called dead, including persons heard about secondhand or read about in books, inhabit my being with an equal urgency. My grandfather . . . Les Hemingway . . . Tennessee Williams . . . John D. MacDonald . . . Borden Deal . . . Jack Kerouac . . .

Who says you can't go home again?

Florida's Highway A1A, riding 2,500 miles along the Atlantic coast from Kent, Maine, southward to Key West, age-old refuge of rebels and renegades.

Photo by Debra Force.

Highway A1A

I'm drinking a beer in Pete's Bar at Neptune Beach, thinking back on my wild and wooly youth at the Jacksonville beaches and Ponte Vedra where I visited my grandparents. As my grandfather, the honorable Senator J. T. Butler, used to say with a deep sigh and a shake of his stately silver-maned head, "Jacksonville Beach is where the good go bad, and the bad get worse." Well, maybe, but my sainted grandfather was a bit of a prude, though one with a sense of humor regarding the foibles of mankind. In his day, Pablo (later Jacksonville) Beach was home to roistering sailors from the nearby naval base, bootleggers, illegal gambling joints, and assorted pimps and prostitutes. During my checkered youth in the '50s and '60s, there were numerous beer and strip joints, a raucous boardwalk, and the *possibility* of getting laid—though it seldom if ever happened. Well, once . . .

Pete's Bar was established in 1933, the first bar in Duval County to be issued a liquor license following Prohibition. Except for the addition of an extra room, it hasn't changed much in the thirty or so years since I first entered. There's an art deco blue neon sign over the entrance flashing *Pete's* and a lot of WWII memorabilia, including army helmets and weapons, on the wall behind the long wood bar. There's smoke and pool tables. And the *same* customers are arguing the *same* barroom arguments they have been arguing for over seven decades. In other words, it's an old-timey, politically incorrect, *bar* bar, not some yuppie fernery with pricey fancy-named drinks and cell phones where everyone is trying to impress everyone else. A breath of fresh air in this era of conformity.

Running through this neon and concrete jungle is Highway A1A, a black-tarred vein connecting the pulsebeat of honky-tonk Florida, 470 miles south to the Keys, and finally to that tropical honky-tonk of honky-tonks, Key West. The 2,500 mile highway, stretching from Kent, Maine, to Key West, was established in 1925 as part of the Federal Highway Act to unify the nation's roads. Since then it has become synonymous with Florida vacations.

Just south of Neptune and Jacksonville Beach is Ponte Vedra, where I was the first surfer. Ponte Vedra was built around the Surf Club, an exclusive resort founded in the '20s. Today it has mushroomed into clubs, condos, and exclusive homes. But back then the Surf Club—world-famous golf course, restaurant, and swim club—was the only game in town. Sam, the tanned and gnarled bachelor patriarch of the swim club—zinc-ointmented nose, silver-metal whistle about wrinkled neck, and a starting pistol—was a time-honored fixture, the bane of us naughty children until the day (Who knows why? Did Sam have a personal life?) he blew his brains out.

Then, there was the beach house, solid, gray with heavy red wood shutters and a semicircular red brick walkway leading down to a saw-grass yard. Beyond that, the hard sand beach and the turbulent blue Atlantic. Mariah—starched gray uniform, white apron, and ample middle—was my grandparents' black maid, and the finest cook ever. Her masterpieces— steaks, chops, chicken, summer vegetables, and fresh-baked rolls—were displayed on a lazy susan in a large, airy, sea-breeze-cooled room.

There was Grandpops in his three-piece pin-striped suit and weathered navy blue fedora. Once, having finished reading the Sunday papers

(New York Times, Miami Herald, Florida Times-Union), he was lying down on the couch with the funnies over his face when his younger sister Mary came to visit. Though now a charming dowager, Aunt Mary had been a bit wild in her youth, when Grandpops served as her custodian following their parents' untimely death. And all these many years later, there was still rancor between them. When Aunt Mary finished chatting with the rest of the family, she strode over to Grandpops lying on the couch and kicked him hard in the rear. "Dammit, Turner, I know you're not really asleep!" When he was dying, Grandpops called his cousin, friend, and hunting/fishing partner, Jim Turner, and asked him to drive the 150 miles from Levy County, so he could watch him enjoy one last scotch and water before passing on.

Twenty miles south of Ponte Vedra is St. Augustine, the nation's oldest city, with a turreted coquina fort and the Bridge of Lions. As teenagers, a friend and I were arrested here for reckless driving and spent the better part of a night in the same cell where Mrs. Malcolm Peabody— of the distinguished Peabodys of Boston—had been incarcerated the night before for sitting at a "whites only" lunch counter with Rev. Martin Luther King, Jr., and the Freedom Marchers. On hearing of our dilemma, Grandpops contacted his old friend Sheriff L. O. Davis, who arrived in a drunken haze to release us.

Later my ex-wife and I lived in a rented house on Marine Street, a few doors down from the house where, in 1974, a thrice-married former Powers model and girlfriend of Joe Kennedy, Jr., was hacked to death in broad daylight in her front yard by an irate neighbor before a teenage witness. But the frightened teenager refused to testify against him in the Oldest City's most notorious murder trial—the murderer walked free.

BUT ENOUGH of the past . . . Life should be lived in the Eternal Now.

I leave Pete's and begin the 350-mile drive south down A1A to Miami. First, Ponte Vedra with luxurious homes and condos . . . Then St. Augustine and Marineland, Florida's first theme park, where parts of *The*

Creature from the Black Lagoon trilogy were filmed, and Flagler Beach with '50s-style "Mom and Pop" motels . . . Pink sand beach . . . Last clear view of pale blue Atlantic . . . '20s-style Topaz Hotel, former home of architect Dana Fuquay and a bootleggers' rendezvous during Prohibition (they unloaded the stuff underneath the stone-supported house), with nostalgic bric-a-brac-filled lobby and Bix Beiderbecke–style jazz cornetist Bobby Branca. He's a silver-haired Argentinian elf with a Bela Lugosi accent, dressed in all brown ensemble—shirt, tie, pants, and shoes—in the award-winning restaurant and bar. Branca once accompanied Josephine Baker, Lana Turner, Gene Tierney, and Hollywood greats too numerous to mention . . .

On past Pegasus Bookstore, with an extensive collection of Florida and metaphysical titles . . . Snack Jack on the roaring Atlantic, where Frieda Zamba, two-time winner of the World Woman's Surfing Championship (1985–1986) developed her style. The original surfer bar, wind-cooled year-round with good seafood, sandwiches, and cold draft beer . . . Ormond and Daytona Beaches with concrete, honky-tonks, race cars, and motorcyclists . . . New Smyrna with its ancient sugar mill ruins, the spot where the hapless travelers in Stephen Crane's famous short story "The Open Boat" met their fate . . . Melbourne and Cocoa Beaches with more concrete and honky-tonks . . . Cape Canaveral with the space program . . . Fort Pierce, Jupiter Beach, and Stewart where tall, phallic condos have replaced hotels and motels . . . North Palm with blacks and Hispanics to serve their elegant neighbor to the south . . . Palm Beach with castle-like estates known as "cottages," owned by descendants of robber barons . . . Delray and Deerfield Beaches with elegant resorts and beautiful blonde hookers in skin-tight tiger-skin pants . . . Boca Raton, Lauderdale, and Hollywood with more concrete and condos, creeping traffic, and scattered glimpses of bikinied flesh . . . Finally, Miami and South Beach, fashion capital of the world, with hip celebrities, world-famous resorts like the Fontainebleau, and art deco architecture . . .

As I drive, I note the incredible number of "third ears" (cell phones) held to vacuous heads—people driving through life with one foot on the brake, constantly preoccupied with what is behind, in lieu of surfing the Cosmic Curl! Like much of modern technology, the cell phone makes one constantly *elsewhere*, not *here*.

He who believes in statistics becomes one. Mystic/writer Joel Goldsmith states in *Realization of Oneness*:

> Every morning of the week, safety engineers forecast approximately how many accidental deaths will occur that day. They can't tell who will be the victims, but those casualties could be you or me or anyone else. Man has become a statistic, but no one wants to be a statistic. . . .
>
> Remember that temptation, whatever its form (accidents, sickness, tornadoes, hurricanes), has to be consciously rejected. This is not easy to do because the one thing the world is suffering from is mental inertia. It will not wake up and think. It wants to look at pictures. It does not want to give voice to specific truth. It does not want to live with truth . . .

ON ARRIVING at Coconut Grove, I spot more third ears. Lazing by the pool, I watch as a matching couple of swimsuited blue-eyed blondes, the perfect advertisement for AT&T, mindlessly chat to third and fourth parties in lieu of each other. And people on the beach are listening to third ears, instead of wind and sea. That night at Taurus, the oldest steakery and saloon in Coconut Grove, two would-be high-powered executives fire bogus stock quotations back and forth via the third ear, in a vain attempt to impress the local lovelies. In the future, newborn babes will arrive with this evolutionary mutation dangling from the appropriate ear.

Then there's that sinister device, the car alarm, which negates silence and solitude with an obnoxious screech, crying wolf to an already over-anxious public. We are a country besieged by loudness—car, fire, and burglar alarms, dust blowers, the ubiquitous sound of heavy machinery constantly backing up. It goes with the mentality that claims he who makes the biggest noise and carries the biggest stick wins the most attention and the biggest prize. When, in reality, it's often just the opposite.

Coconut Grove, like all of south Florida, has grown astronomically in the last two decades. The old Coconut Grove Hotel, where once I conducted a long-distance love affair with a married lady from Key West, is now a Doubletree Inn, and the Grove's romance and distinctive nightlife have been replaced by Disneyese—Planet Hollywood, Sloppy Joe's—with dozens of TVs soundlessly blinking hockey and women's basketball to a spectator sports–saturated public. Beautiful blondes (holograms of light and sound, I suspect) gaze across crowded dance floors with vaguely distracted expressions, awaiting the perfectly featured, evenly tanned, gold-chained, and Rolex-watched mate who never arrives. Like cardboard cutouts posing before the backdrop of technological eternity, a smokescreen of perfectly coifed and muscled beautiful people dance to an otherworldly ethereal beat that only they can hear. In rural Florida, men try to impress women with how tough they are; in urban Florida, it's how rich and powerful you are.

In other words, I didn't get laid.

A1A stretches ever southward across the blue, green, and turquoise waters of the Florida Keys to the southernmost tip of the United States at Key West—age-old refuge of rebels and renegades. And, like Key West, A1A typifies the best and worst in American society.

The Other Hemingway

I heard of Leicester Hemingway for the first time thirty years ago. I was drinking at a joint called Opel's, in Bimini, when a character named Cap'n Dick walked in and bought a round for the bar.

"Les Hemingway is twice the man his brother was," slurred Cap'n Dick. "Twice the sailor, twice the fisherman, twice the drinker, twice the brawler, *and* twice the writer!"

No one disagreed. After all, he was paying for the drinks.

Ten years later I met the infamous Les himself.

This time, I was drinking at the Compleat Angler, Ernest Hemingway's home base on his trips over to Bimini from Key West during the 1930s, when a man who resembled the ghost of Papa drew up the stool beside mine.

"You *have* to be Leicester Hemingway."

"At your service."

Les looked like a more genial version of his older brother, with the same bearlike build, grizzled white beard, and professorial glasses Papa hated wearing, though he was nearly blind without them.

"I suppose you get awfully tired of strangers wanting to talk about your brother."

"Not at all," he replied in a too-genial tone of voice.

So we talked about Ernest: about his wars, his women, and his family in Oak Park, Illinois. Inevitably, his suicide, and their father's, came up. Dr. Hemingway, suffering from ill health and a series of financial setbacks, shot himself in the head in 1928. Grace Hemingway, the boys' mother, sent Ernest the gun her husband used to kill himself. Thirty-two years later, Ernest, too, shot himself in the head.

"Dad should have shot our bitch of a mother 'stead of himself," said Les when he finished the story.

The conversation turned to other writers. "Mailer thinks he's being macho and following in Papa's footsteps. But so far as I'm concerned, he's just another bullshitter. And as for Truman Capote [Les pronounced Capote so that it was a two syllable word rhyming with *toot*], he's a bullshitter and a faggot to boot."

Next Les began explaining about a project he had been working on for years. "Some friends and I are forming our own commonwealth off the coast of Jamaica. It's called 'New Atlantis' and we're building it from scratch with scrap metal and sand. Once we're finished, we'll issue our own stamps and commemorative coins and sell them to collectors for a fortune."

Then he began talking about counterfeit one-dollar bills. "Right now, they're passing 'em like crazy in Key West. All a fellow would need is a small press in his basement. He could make a fortune."

I told Les about a novel I'd written about hauling cocaine from Bimini to Birmingham, Alabama.

Les seemed interested. "I've always wanted to write a book about Bimini, like Papa's *Islands in the Stream*. But I know if I told the truth I'd never be welcome here again. And I love this island. It's like another world. So calm and peaceful." He paused to gaze wistfully about the darkened bar. "You get the feeling that if the rest of the world succeeds in blowing itself

26

up, folks on Bimini will just shake their heads and say, 'We always knew the bastids was crazy.'"

WHEN I GOT home to Sarasota, I mailed Les a copy of my manuscript. A week later he phoned from Miami. He liked the novel and wanted me to drive down to talk to him about it. The next day I drove to Miami.

Les lived in a two-story Spanish-style house on Star Island overlooking Biscayne Bay. I parked my car behind a beat-up Volkswagen with Illinois license plates and walked up to the front door. Les's daughter Hilary answered my knock and told me her father would be down in a second.

A barefoot Les came down the stone staircase in a pair of beige shorts. He was throwing on a faded khaki shirt. Following the introductions, he led me over to a heavy plank table in the den and went off to mix us drinks. I had a gin and tonic. Les, a diabetic, was drinking Tab. He brought out my manuscript and flung it down between us on the table.

Les wanted to print up a thousand copies of the novel on his basement press. It was all very complicated, but it boiled down to this: I was to work on a percentage, which increased for every thousand copies sold. Les was hurriedly scribbling figures on a piece of white butcher paper. I was hurriedly slamming down gin and tonics.

He said, "I've got connections. For one thing, we can sell it at the Hemingway house in Key West. Meanwhile we'll retain the copyright ourselves. That way, we can sell it to the movies for a nice piece of change."

Something about the deal didn't strike me as kosher. I tried to change the subject. Les suggested I spend the night. The next day, the two of us would fly over to Bimini and discuss the matter further. Then we began talking about Bimini.

"It's getting rough over there," warned Les. "People are being fed to the sharks off South Bimini. Girls walking past a certain point on the King's Highway are disappearing forever."

Around five, we took my car and drove to Jackson Memorial Hospital to pick up Les's wife, Doris, a nurse, and their son-in-law, an orderly. On the way over, Les pointed out the sights in Indian talk, like Colonel Cantwell in *Across the River and into the Trees*, Ernest's least successful novel.

"Long time ago, good; now, no good," he remarked about a particular section of town.

Les continued his monologue after we picked up our passengers and started the drive back. But no one, except me, was paying any attention. It was as though they had heard it all too many times before.

Back at Les's house, I felt ill at ease, as though I wasn't the first stranger whose presence Les had imposed on his family. Excusing myself to go to the bathroom, I climbed out the window and escaped to the sanctuary of my car.

All the way back home, I thought about Les sitting in the Spanish-style house by the bay, estranged from family and friends, alone with the legacy of his famous brother.

LEICESTER HEMINGWAY was born on April 1, 1915, the youngest in a family of two brothers and four sisters. Ernest was sixteen when Leicester was born. By the time Leicester was three, Ernest had come home a hero from the Great War in Europe. One of Leicester's earliest memories was of Ernest, in his Italian uniform, posing for pictures in the front yard of their Oak Park, Illinois, home.

Their mother, Grace, has been described by both Leicester and Ernest as a cold, unfeeling woman who dominated her physician husband. Her two interests in life were art and music. Both boys were forced at an early age to practice the cello until it became apparent, even to their mother, that neither possessed the slightest talent.

When Leicester was five, Ernest broke with the family and moved to Kansas City, where he began work on the *Kansas City Star*. While

Leicester was growing up in Oak Park, Ernest was making a name for himself writing.

On December 6, 1928, when Les was thirteen, Dr. Hemingway shot himself behind the ear with a Smith & Wesson revolver. Ernest hurried home to take charge of things. While there, Ernest asked his brother to visit him and his second wife, Pauline, at their home in Key West.

Four years later, Les took him up on his offer.

Jake Kilmo, author of *Hemingway And Jake*, recalls his first meeting with Les at Mobile, Alabama. Les had built a sailboat and was preparing to sail down the Gulf coast to Key West.

According to Jake, "[Les] kept talking about this older brother of his. Said his older brother was always putting him down. But Les was going to show him. This older brother couldn't have sailed across the bathtub, much less the Gulf. But *he* was going to."

Following twenty-three days at sea, Les and a friend arrived at Key West, where they were enthusiastically greeted by Ernest. Each day, weather permitting, Ernest, Les, and several of Ernest's cronies would fish the edges of the Gulf Stream in Ernest's new boat, the *Pilar*. One day, according to Les in *My Brother, Ernest Hemingway*, Ernest asked if Les was serious about wanting to become a writer. Les admitted he was.

"You've got a hell of a road ahead. Everything you do, they'll say you're riding on my reputation. You know that, don't you?"

Les nodded.

"If you really want to write, Bo, then, go ahead and write . . . I'm not going to help you if I can avoid it. I've helped a lot of guys, and will again. But mainly it weakens them."

Jake Kilmo recalls Les feeling highly competitive toward his famous brother. One afternoon, according to Kilmo, Les asked Ernest if an aneroid barometer used mercury.

"I guess it works that way."

"No, it doesn't. It works on a spin basis with a coil."

"For Christ sake, Les, stop trying to be a big shot over a *blanking* barometer."

IN 1935 LES WAS twenty and married to his childhood sweetheart when he began working for the *Chicago Daily News*. Over the next five years, he worked as a reporter or editor for several publications in Chicago, Philadelphia, and New York. During this period, he sent samples of his fiction to Ernest, who felt Les was overly concerned with what actually happened. According to Ernest, Les needed to turn loose his imagination and make up things if he intended to write fiction.

In December 1939, Les headed south to Key West for a month's cruising. He ran into a young Englishman named Tony Jenkinson. Jenkinson had obtained a naval intelligence assignment and was looking for someone to navigate. Les fit the bill. Their assignment was to sniff out Nazi refueling depots in the western Caribbean. Les later used the information they gathered to write a series of syndicated newspaper articles and a piece in *Reader's Digest*. He was just coming into his own as a freelance writer when World War II erupted.

Les entered government service a week before Pearl Harbor as an information specialist with the War Production Board, and later served as a field correspondent in London for the Foreign Broadcast Service. In September 1943, he enlisted in the U.S. Army and was assigned, along with writer Irwin Shaw, to a special motion picture unit that covered the D-Day invasion and the campaign in northern Europe. Shaw later used Les and his famous brother as unsympathetic characters in *The Young Lions*, his first novel.

Following the liberation of Paris by the Allies, Les ran into Ernest, who had personally liberated and was now bivouacked at the Ritz Hotel. In his novel, *Sound of the Trumpet*, Les describes a party at the Ritz that he and a friend attended at the behest of his famous brother:

They heard the laughter and watched the people they both knew well, but in the dark and at the side they were neither seen nor heard. The food became dull, and the wine had no effect . . . "It wasn't intentional," Dan said. "He didn't realize the big table couldn't hold everybody until he saw it."

Following the War, Les freelanced articles on boat building and big-game fishing. In 1953 his novel was released to hopeful reviews. It wasn't up to Ernest's work, claimed most critics, but Leicester Hemingway was a writer worth watching. It would be Les's first and only novel.

Hal Hennessey, a fellow writer, remembers Les around this time. "I was living in Brooklyn trying to make it as a freelance. Les and his wife, Mouse, used to drop in for drinks and dinner. One night Les asked if I'd ever read his novel. When I told him no, he said not to waste my time 'cause it was bullshit."

Another time, Hennessey got an assignment from *Argosy* magazine to go down to Havana and interview Ernest. According to Hennessey, "When I told Les about it, he just grinned and said, 'You and my brother are going to tangle.' Les knew I had my own opinions on things, and he figured Papa wouldn't stand for it. He was right. Papa and I tangled, and I came back to New York sans interview."

During the '50s, Les worked as a charter captain out of Jamaica. In his spare time, he penned articles and short stories published under pseudonyms in magazines like *Adventure* and *Sports Illustrated*. He was working on a biography of Ernest when Ernest committed suicide on July 2, 1961, at his home outside Ketchum, Idaho. *My Brother, Ernest Hemingway* was published later that year. It was an instant success. Les and his second wife, Doris, along with their two small daughters, set out on a cruise of the Caribbean.

IN 1964 LES SURFACED in Miami with an idea for forming his own island nation. The idea had originally come to him in 1943 as the plot for

31

an unwritten novel. Les's nation, New Atlantis, consisted of twelve square miles of shallow ocean bottom 6.5 miles off Bluefield, Jamaica. A raft was anchored to mark the site of New Atlantis. Using royalties from his biography of Ernest, Les planned to form an artificial island with large rocks and steel girders.

"All you need is a hundred feet of land," he told reporters gathered at Miami. "On a hundred feet, you can sleep. You can live."

According to Les, New Atlantis would serve as a mecca for lovers of out-of-the-way places. Letters of credit could be issued, marriages performed, and New Atlantian stamps and coins issued and sold to collectors around the world. Future plans included a post office, a quaint island hotel, and a self-supporting marine experimental station. By 1965, New Atlantis had seven citizens—along with citizenship, one was granted the honorary title of Duchess or Earl—none of whom resided on the still-nonexistent island. Les, as acting president, began issuing stamps which he printed at home in Coconut Grove, Florida. Those commemorated by the stamps included Lyndon Johnson, Hubert Humphrey, Winston Churchill, Ernest Hemingway, the provisional government of the Dominican Republic, and the American military in Vietnam.

Dr. John Martin, a dentist in Coconut Grove, remembers discussing New Atlantis with Les. According to Martin, "Most of our talks centered around the New Atlantian constitution, which was a hodgepodge of the best parts of constitutions from around the world. Les was a big fan of a Frenchman named Frederick Bastiat who lived around the time of the French Revolution. Bastiat believed the sole purpose of any government should be to provide equal justice to all its citizens. In other words, the less government, the better."

Les became increasingly obsessed with the concept of New Atlantis. He spent countless hours boning up on maritime law and the rights of newly formed nations. He appointed, only half in jest, a New Atlantian cabinet composed of friends. The unit of exchange on New Atlantis would be called a "scruple" because, according to Les, "A man can never have too many scruples." Hurricanes in '64 and '65 destroyed the raft that floated above New Atlantis. But Les's dream died hard. Having exhausted his own funds, he sought in vain to interest other investors in the project. Weeks prior to his death, he was still poring over maritime law books, researching possibilities.

In 1964 Les began publication of the *Bimini News*—printed on 7 by 8.5–inch paper, he referred to it as the smallest newspaper in the world. Bimini is a tiny island forty-eight miles due east of Miami, on the eastern edge of the Gulf Stream. Ernest helped introduce big-game fishing here in the '30s, and over the years Bimini has come to be known as the Big-Game Fishing Capital of the World. Given its easy access to the States, it's also known as a haven for drug smugglers.

Manny Rolle, owner of Manny's Market on Bimini, remembers Les hawking his papers. According to Manny, "He had that gray beard and he looked just like his brother. Whenever a new boat would dock in de harbor, he'd run over and snap pictures of the captain and crew. He called the gentlemens 'Sire' and the womens 'Your Ladyship.' If anyone on de boat bought a year's subscription, he'd put their pictures in de next issue of the *Bimini News*."

Only with the drug traffic, a lot of people didn't want their picture taken.

FREQUENT VISITORS to Bimini recall seeing Les strolling the Queen's Highway wearing dirty trousers and a ragged t-shirt. Often he would bring his lunch over from Miami in a paper bag and stay overnight with friends. As he aged, his resemblance to Ernest became uncanny. He even spoke like his brother in short monosyllabic utterances. "Confusion to the enemy!" became his favorite barroom toast.

Phil Brinkman, a Miami muralist, remembers an incident that occurred in 1974. According to Brinkman, "Les and some friends discovered a fresh-water spring among the mangroves on east Bimini. Les claimed the spring had healing powers. It healed the skin cancer on his forearms and another guy's lumbago, according to Les. He carried samples of the water over to the University of Miami to be analyzed, and the stuff had an extremely high lithium content. Since lithium's used for manic-depression, Les figured he was on to something.

"I have a friend named Skipper Hill who owns the Shell Liquors chain. Les wanted Skipper to bring a barge in and begin pumping up the water from the spring. Claimed they'd make a fortune selling his water for twenty dollars a quart in the supermarkets. Skipper flew over one weekend so the two of 'em could take a skiff out to the spring. But there was a big nor'easter that weekend. By the time it blew over, Skipper had left for home.

"Later Les wanted to start a spa for wealthy sick people on Bimini. But nothing came of that idea either."

When New World Publishing ceased publication of *My Brother, Ernest Hemingway*, Les began printing copies on his own press. He made frequent trips to Key West, where he autographed copies for visitors to the Hemingway House. Later there was talk of a movie based on Ernest's life for which Les was to have served as consultant. Though Les was hired to write a treatment, the project was eventually shelved.

Les had been suffering for years from diabetes and a recurring circulatory ailment when he made his final trip to Bimini to sell the *Bimini News*.

Bonefish Willie, a local fishing guide, remembers seeing him step off the Chalk's Airline seaplane. According to Willie, "He handed me a *Bimini News* and I led him over to a bench. He looked terrible, all gaunt and haggard. There was a paper bag with his lunch in it, and he told me to take the bag and make use of it. Then he asked me to make a reservation for him on the next flight back to Miami. Ten minutes later another plane flew in, and I escorted him up the metal steps and through the hatchway."

Ernest Hemingway home and museum in Key West. Photo taken in 1966 by Charles Barron.

Back in Miami, Les underwent an arterial bypass operation on his left leg similar to one performed earlier on his right. The doctors feared they would have to amputate eventually.

"To do what I have to do, you have to be able to go places," Les told Andy Taylor, a former UPI reporter and family friend.

On September 13, 1982, at approximately 2 P.M., Les put the barrel of a .38 Smith & Wesson revolver to his temple and fired off a round. His wife found him sprawled in the foyer, naked except for a pair of beige shorts. There was no note.

Bonefish Willie remembers Les as a man who was "always reaching for something great . . . [but] he never quite grasped it."

My Brother, Ernest Hemingway has been republished by Pineapple Press of Sarasota. Hilary Hemingway and her husband, Jeffry Lindsay, are writing books together, as is Leicester's niece Loren.

Key West Writers

It's 1982 and I'm down in Key West researching a piece on Key West writers. The ghost of Papa Hemingway is present, along with that more recent, still-living phantom, Tennessee Williams. Also there's Ralph Ellison, Phil Caputo, John Hersey, Ramona Stewart, Peter Taylor, James Kirkwood, Nancy Friday, Bill Manville, John Ciardi, Shel Silverstein, Richard Wilbur, Evan Rhodes, James Merrill, David Kaufelt, Allison Lurie, Norman Rosten, Howard Sackler, John Williams, Joe Lash, Phillip Burton, and John Brinnin. Thomas McGuane and Jim Harrison are former residents and visit often, as does Hunter Thompson, who keeps a cigarette boat docked at Stock Island. James Herlihy lived here for years and still owns a house he visits occasionally, and through the years Elizabeth Bishop, Carson McCullers, Wallace Stevens, Hart Crane, Gore Vidal, Truman Capote, and Robert Frost have put in time here.

What is it about the island that attracts them? Perhaps it's the ambience. Key West's population consists of an eclectic mixture of "conchs" (native Key Westers), Cubans, West Indian blacks, shrimpers and fisher-

Conch tour "train" full of sightseers passing through a residential area of Key West.
Photo taken in 1960 by Charles Barron.

men, cocaine cowboys, petty criminals, rednecks, hippies, gays, the military (active and retired), high society, low society, assorted wackos, artists, actors, and writers. Here, too, are "Mom and Pop" tourists, attired in mismatched Hawaiian outfits and knee socks with dress shoes, Instamatics strung about their necks—people who Captain Tony, owner of the famous saloon bearing his name, describes as "pieces of meat with eyes in them." Add a sprinkling of "carpetbagger" businessmen and smooth-talking Southern lawyers out for the tourist dollar, stir well, bake till brown, and one has the human casserole known as Key West.

My first night in town, I'm seated at The Bottlecap Bar on Simonton Street when I eavesdrop on the conversation of the couple next to me. The man is discussing writers. He approves of Hemingway, but blames Tennessee Williams for the influx of gays and society types and the corresponding rise in prices.

"Fifteen years ago, a man could get a good meal at a Cuban restaurant for less than a dollar. Today the same meal will run him closer to ten."

Still, he admits Williams has talent, and soon he and his lady friend are discussing *A Streetcar Named Desire*. This is no literary saloon, mind you. It's a neighborhood bar frequented by fishermen, cab drivers, restaurant help, and construction workers.

The next morning I'm in a realtor's office. When I mention I'm working on a piece about Key West writers, the realtor pulls out his little black book and rattles off the names of about thirty writers, publishers, and agents, along with their addresses and phone numbers. Apparently the town is nuts about writers.

The first writer I call on is Bill Manville. Bill has written several novels and has recently published *Saloon Society* from articles published in the *Village Voice* during the early '60s. He's at work on a thriller, a portion of which takes place in Key West. I ask why he and his wife, Nancy Friday, author of *Men in Love* and *My Mother, Myself*, chose to settle in Key West.

"Neither of us set foot here till five years ago. We drove down from Palm Beach looking for balmier weather and were staying at the Pier

House when we met the owner, David Wolkowski. David showed us around town and it wasn't long before we were looking for a house to rent. Now we *own* three of them. What appeals to us is the island's cosmopolitan atmosphere, the way different levels of society mingle. You go to a party here, and you're liable to meet anyone from the mayor, to a drug smuggler, to Tennessee Williams. There's no country club, really. The local yacht club is open to anyone with a boat, and the Stock Island golf course is going bankrupt for lack of paying customers. Once when the heat was on, the mayor water-skied to Havana behind a power boat, only to return a week later when things quieted down. I mean it's America, yet it's not America. It's Key West."

I LEAVE MANVILLE and walk back to my motel room in a light drizzle. I've walked these same streets many times before, but each time I notice something different, a narrow alleyway or flowering tree. Today it's a turbaned hippie wearing a long flowing white robe like the one worn by Peter O'Toole in *Lawrence of Arabia*. There's a gaping wound in one side of a house that exposes the living room to anyone passing by on the street. Later I learn this is one of three houses and two bars violated this way in the past month by dope- and alcohol-crazed motorists who missed a turn.

The next person I visit is Howard Sackler. Sackler wrote the play *The Great White Hope* and the screenplays for *Jaws*, *Jaws II*, and *Saint Jack*. He is currently at work on a screenplay about a bigamist who keeps separate homes at Palm Beach and Key West and commutes between the two in a cigarette boat. Sackler has a home on the Spanish island of Ibiza, but spends a part of each year in Key West. During the '50s he hung out in New York's East Village with Anatole Broyard, Seymour Krim, Chandler Brossard, Jack Kerouac, Carl Solomon, Allan Ginsberg, Neal Cassady, William Burroughs, and other writers of the Beat Generation. I ask about those days.

"Well, everyone was more than a little neurotic, you know. Kerouac

40

was a good writer, but I can't recall his saying anything memorable. Just hovered in the background taking mental notes. Ginsberg was the one kept the whole thing going. It really wasn't happening for them in New York. So he moved the act out to 'Frisco. The West Coast has always had a chip on its shoulder about not being New York, and it wasn't long before it hugged the group to its bosom.

"The thing that finished me with them was Carl Solomon tossing a refrigerator door out a fifth floor window trying to nail me on the sidewalk. I have no idea why he wanted to kill me. Anyway, Kerouac and Ginsberg talked me out of issuing a warrant for his arrest. They said he was a genius. Maybe he was, but since then I've avoided writers. They're all so self-absorbed and competitive. Now I prefer the company of actors."

I ask how he came up with the idea behind the Jack Johnson play, *The Great White Hope.*

"I was living in Havana during the late '50s and met a woman who was Johnson's girlfriend while he was training for the Jeffries fight. You know the famous photograph of Johnson shielding his eyes from the sun while he's taking the count? Everyone assumes that meant he threw it. But from what this woman told me, Johnson trained as hard for the Jeffries fight as he did for any of the others, and in the tropical heat, too. Why do that if he was going to throw it? That set me to thinking and eventually led to my writing the play."

"What draws you to Key West?"

"I'm an avid skindiver and water sports enthusiast, and Key West offers all that, and is convenient to New York or L.A. by plane. But the main reason I like Key West is for the great 'B' movies they screen at the theaters here. Honest to God, some of them are shown nowhere else in the country."

THE NEXT MORNING I see Peter Taylor, one of America's finest short story writers. Over the phone he sounded hesitant about meeting me, but in person he's a cordial Southern gentleman. Immediately he explains his reluctance to see me.

"A woman from the *Paris Review* has been conducting a series of interviews about my writing. She's a charming lady, but I feel such a pompous ass discussing my working techniques."

I ask why he winters in Key West.

"My doctor advised me to seek out a tropical climate for my arthritis. Since my old friends John Ciardi and Dick Wilbur were already living down here, I chose Key West."

"Ever write a short story that takes place here?"

"Finished my first this morning. It's about Key West dogs. The way they laze about, belly up, in the daytime, then go marauding for food at night."

I tell Taylor about an experience on the island of Bimini. It was late at night and I was walking the island's main road when I spied a pack of about a dozen dogs scouting for food. Two or three would tilt a garbage can over with their forepaws just far enough to get at food lying on top. Ever so silently, they would return the can to its original position—to avoid being kicked in the ribs by a surly Bahamian, had the can tipped over and rattled on the pavement.

When I finish my story, Taylor takes a notebook out of his shirt pocket and jots down my anecdote for possible inclusion in his story. That's a writer for you . . .

My next stop is a bookstore on Duval Street. The proprietor is a lanky young man wearing hornrimmed glasses. When I ask for books by Key West authors, he launches into a diatribe against the lot of them.

"They're all riding Tennessee Williams's coattails! Most aren't worth the paper and ink their books are printed on. When I moved down from Boston, I thought there might be a market for good literature here, but I learned different. Look at the books on my shelves. Seventy-five percent of them are junk. Another twenty percent are mediocre. In supposedly literary Key West, I'm selling popular romances to housewives."

"But the library is pretty good for a town this size, don't you think?"

"Are you crazy? The library here stinks. Look, I graduated from Harvard with a degree in Library Science. Don't you think I know a good library when I see one?"

I skulk away with an armload of books . . .

THAT AFTERNOON I meet with poet and biographer John Brinnin in his studio apartment overlooking the pale-blue Atlantic. Brinnin has written biographies of Dylan Thomas and Gertrude Stein and has recently completed *Sextet*, a book dealing with, among others, Truman Capote, Cartier-Bresson, the Sitwells, and T. S. Eliot. Beneath us on the beach belonging to the Sands Restaurant, owned by literary enthusiast David Wolkowski, are youthful bathers, some topless, most scantily attired, and a few openly smoking joints.

I ask Brinnin to fill me in on Key West and Key West writers.

"When I first came here eight or nine years ago, Key West wasn't nearly the 'in' resort for writers it is now. Truman was staying at the Pier House when two people who resembled armored guards arrived to carry a portion of *Answered Prayers* up north to Esquire. But Truman was down here on a visit, not to live.

"Now people from the media and fashion worlds are moving down. Roy Scheider, the actor, recently purchased a home here. So did Calvin Klein. He reportedly paid over a million dollars for his house, and prices hereabouts are rising accordingly. Soon many writers won't be able to afford to live here. They'll have to move elsewhere."

I ask Brinnin if Key West writers might be divided into different camps.

"Well, you have everyone here from commercial writers to poets. America's foremost playwright lives here. Then you have the 'Hemingway' school, consisting of Tom McGuane, Jim Harrison, Phil Caputo, and the publisher Sam Lawrence. There are good commercial writers like David

43

Kaufelt and Jamie Kirkwood, and such noted poets as Norman Rosten, Richard Wilbur, John Ciardi, and James Merrill. Poets aren't striving for earthly success. They're after immortality."

I LEAVE BRINNIN and walk past the Hemingway house on Whitehead Street. In the old days a conch named Toby Bruce worked for Papa, looking after the house, skippering the boat. Today these functions are performed for a number of Key West writers, including Harrison and McGuane, by Toby's son, Dink. Dink's mother, Betty, works at the Monroe County Library and has invited me to a reception this afternoon for Key West writers.

When I arrive, Wilbur, Ciardi, and Hersey are standing in the center of the room surrounded by little old ladies drinking iced coffee. One of the ladies, a widow, asks Hersey if she might visit his home sometime to discuss his work. Hersey makes a noncommittal reply. It's obvious he's used to this sort of opportunism by lonely people. I take a seat at the rear. A lady draws up the chair next to mine. She's Ramona Stewart, author of any number of thrillers, including *The Possession of Joel Delahny*. One of the little old ladies strolls over and asks Ms. Stewart if she didn't once write a book of recipes. Ms. Stewart replies politely that she didn't. The lady acts offended and vanishes back into the crowd.

I meet Evan Rhodes, novelist and playwright, author of *The Prince of Central Park* and *The Children's Crusade*, and we drive to his house on Catholic Lane across from the cemetery. Rhodes is at work on an eight-volume paperback opus tracing the history of the White House and its occupants from its construction up through the Nixon era. It's fiction based on fact, in the manner of John Jakes's novels.

"I'm guaranteed three-quarters of a million dollars for eight books. A half million copies of the first book have already been printed, plus fifteen thousand 'giveaways' for promotional purposes. If the first book doesn't sell over four hundred thousand copies, the entire series will be dropped, and I'll only receive four hundred thousand dollars. If the series flies, I'm committed to turning out a book every three months till the series is completed. That's to keep the momentum going. Otherwise, the housewives who buy these books forget you exist."

We discuss other Key West writers and I mention James Leo Herlihy, author of *Midnight Cowboy* and *All Fall Down*, a novel in which much of the action takes place in Key West.

Rhodes mixes me a drink. "In 1971 Jamie Herlihy and I were planning to collaborate on a book about the 'peace and love' generation of the '60s. We had a contract with a publisher and combed the country attending peace rallies, visiting communes, and doing all the things considered fashionable then. But by the time we came home to Key West, the movement had ended and no one was interested. The last holdouts of the 'peace and love' generation drifted down to Key West. It's sad. They're like dinosaurs who fail to realize their time has ended.

"Jamie Herlihy hasn't written a book in eight years. What he really wants is to be a movie star. He's in L.A. running an acting school. He recently appeared in Arthur Penn's new movie, *Four Friends*, and got rave reviews. Jamie Kirkwood [is] the same way. They *all* want to be movie stars."

Before I go, Rhodes hands me a paperback original by a young Key West writer named Fred Balland. It's entitled *Flesh Wound*. On the cover there's a lurid picture of a bloody dagger poised above a shrimp boat. It looks awful, but I carry it back to the motel and read it anyway. I'm only a few pages into the text before I realize I'm reading something good. It's a labor novel dealing with the seafood industry of Key West and reads something like early Steinbeck. The cover is extremely misleading, and anyone who picked it up looking for something light and sexy was, I'm afraid, disappointed. It's the sort of book that should have been printed in hardcover and seriously reviewed, and I wonder how many other similar books are floating about unread by the literate public.

THAT NIGHT I attend a cocktail party at the restored conch home of James Merrill, Pulitzer Prize–winning poet and son of the Merrill in Merrill Lynch, who has recently completed a long poem entitled *Changing Light at the Ballroom at Sandoval. Sandoval* is going to be compared to Eliot's *Wasteland.* Also present are writer/critic David Jackson, James Boatwright, critic and editor of the *Shenandoah Review*, Peter Taylor, John Brinnin, three lady professors from Vassar down to collect the papers of deceased poet Elizabeth Bishop, and five or six young men in bikini swim trunks splashing about in the tiny circular pool. I'm standing next to the bar on the patio when I approach one of the Vassar professors with romantic ulterior motives. It doesn't take me long, however, to realize she, like Bishop, is not heterosexually inclined. Following my subtle overtures, she says in typical academic fashion, "I realize all writers are neurotic. But really, I don't see how they *ever* get any work done down here! Since we arrived, it's been one party after another."

David Jackson overhears and walks over. "Artists are driven persons. They're always working. Even when they're partying, they're working. That's something you academics fail to understand."

"Maybe so, but I'm New England enough to think everyone needs a schedule."

Jackson sighs and draws me aside. "Ralph Ellison will be down tomorrow. I hear he's just completed a thousand-page novel, and it's excellent." (The manuscript was later destroyed in a fire.)

I ask about Allison Lurie, author of *The War Between the Tates.*

"She's down in Australia attending a government-sponsored writers' conference. Have you read her new book on fashion? It's about how what a person chooses to wear reflects his or her personality. She and I spent hours at the Sears mall studying various styles."

But enough literary chitchat . . . I spend the rest of the evening getting seriously drunk. Around midnight I find myself seated beside the pool with Merrill and Jackson discussing heaven. Merrill, who conducted a long series of seances with departed friends and historical persons for *Sandoval,* thinks it's become overcrowded recently, and those of us wishing to gain entrance better hurry up and die. I agree. Next thing I know a cab magically appears to whisk me back to my motel.

I spend the following morning trying to set up an appointment with Tennessee Williams, but Williams is headed for Europe the next day and doesn't have time for an interview.

So I pack my bag to leave, but before I do, I call Fred Balland and tell him how much I enjoyed his book. Balland tells me he's recently completed another novel dealing with the Key West of the '20s, and I wish him the best of luck with it.

I catch my plane. As we circle Key West and point toward the Gulf Stream, I'm reminded of what Liz Lear, friend to McGuane and Harrison, and a soon-to-be-published novelist herself, told me a few evenings before over cocktails. When she and Harrison are out on the Gulf Stream fishing, Harrison often wonders aloud if they mightn't at that instant be passing over the salt-encrusted bones of Hart Crane. It was somewhere in this vicinity the great poet chose to slip over the railing of a passenger ship rounding the Keys, headed to New York from Mexico.

For some reason, I feel strangely comforted . . .

Williams and Capote died untimely deaths during the 1980s. Herlihy committed suicide. Ellison, Hersey, Taylor, Ciardi, Ellison, and Silverstein, along with several others, have since passed on.

Novelist Alison Lurie has recently written a book, *Familiar Spirits*, dealing with James Merrill and his lover David Jackson's obsession with the Ouija board and the heavenly realm.

Tennessee Williams: A Cry of the Heart

Playwright Tennessee Williams always wrote about the wounded and dying . . . physically and spiritually. Laura, Blanche, Brick, Chance—all of his heroes and heroines are drifting toward the inevitable with a grace that contradicts their *apparent* fragility. In the words of Blanche DuBois, "I have always depended on the kindness of strangers." And Williams himself, according to all reports, was a lifelong hypochondriac. In other words, he was always dying or about to die, physically and spiritually.

Once in Key West, I met a relative of Williams, who was occupying his house while Williams was in Europe.

"Poor Tom [Tennessee], he hasn't long for this world!" he exclaimed. "The doctors give him a few months—a year at most."

The nature of Williams's fatal ailment was vague, but it had something to do with his heart.

Later I met people who knew Williams intimately. The poet James Merrill, poet and biographer John Malcolm Brinnin, a Key West society matron . . . They all told the same story: Williams was ill. He was experiencing palpitations of the heart. Always the heart! Williams, in both his life and work, was *all* heart. A thin fragile membrane capable of hemorrhaging at any instant.

One night I was seated at the bar in the Hog's Breath, a rough Key West nightspot, when I glanced over my shoulder and saw Williams seated alone at a table.

"That's Tennessee Williams," I whispered to the friend beside me. "Maybe I ought to go over and say hello. Tell him how much his work means to me."

But when I turned back around, it was apparent from the haunted, intent look on Williams's face he wanted to be left alone. He was observing. Writers never quit, I thought. Even when they're world-famous like Williams, there's something in their makeup that makes them loners. "The eternal kid with his nose pressed against the window peering in at the party," as novelist Scott Fitzgerald put it.

A couple of years later I was dancing on the Sands's patio, a popular Key West nightclub owned by Williams's friend, the ubiquitous David Wolkowski, when I again spied Williams seated at a table with two young men.

"That's Tennessee Williams," I told the girl with me, a space cadet I'd picked up hours earlier on Duval Street.

"Oh yeah!"

Next thing I knew the girl was seated at the table across from Williams and his friends and I was standing behind her.

"You're Tennessee Ernie Ford, the singer, aren't you?" she exclaimed. "My parents just love your music!"

"No," replied a smiling Williams. "But people often mistake the two of us."

Thus ended my first literary conversation with Tennessee Williams.

SHORTLY THEREAFTER, I was researching an article on sado-masochistic gay murders in Key West when Williams's name came up. If my informant was right, he'd been running with a rough crowd. Something in Williams needed to be hurt, I thought. Hurt to the point of death. It was crucial to his writing. And like most artists, he was willing to do anything to get the work accomplished. Poor, doomed Tennessee Williams. Then I caught myself. Williams *chose* his path of pain and suffering. Without the suffering, there wouldn't have been the work.

My last encounter with Williams was, again, at the Sands. He appeared out of nowhere at my side shaking his doomed head. "I can't go anywhere anymore. People are always trying to pick me up!"

So much for literary conversation with my idol.

Not long after that, he was dead.

Ironically, it wasn't Williams's heart that killed him. It was a plastic pill-bottle cap that lodged in his throat. There was a brief flurry of rumors that Williams was murdered. Then, silence . . .

Hopefully, in the end, Williams, like his best characters, realized, in the words of mystic/writer Joel Goldsmith: "When we understand the nature of God as love, we shall understand Grace. Then we shall understand . . . our good comes by Grace, not by deserving it or being worthy of it . . . "

One night after Williams's death, I awoke in the middle of the night with the feeling that his spirit was in the room. For a fleeting instant, I caught a glimpse of his haunted, intent face the night I saw him at the Hog's Breath. When I switched on the bedside lamp, the room was empty.

The Crescent Club on Siesta Key, the oldest saloon in town and the author's "office" in the days when he owned the infamous South Trail Cinema of PeeWee Herman fame.

Photo by Ed Baatz.

Siesta Key

I'm drinking a beer at the fifty-year-old Crescent Club on Siesta Key, the oldest saloon in town, thinking back on my life in Sarasota. The Crescent Club—hardwood paneled and red-lit interior, swinging wooden doors, and charcoal portraits of beautiful long-term bartenders—is a cool, other-worldly haven away from the white-hot glare of the sun. Like every *good* saloon, it's the sort of place where one expects a mysterious blonde to stride through the entrance at any second.

The Crescent Club, the prototype for the bar in John D. MacDonald's book *Condominium*, served as my office in the days when I was a reluctant businessman. I was the owner of the Eightball Lounge, a working-class bar where fights and rowdiness were an everyday occurrence, as well as the infamous South Trail Cinema, a XXX movie house, the very theater where Pee-Wee Herman was arrested. The wooden telephone booth in the corner of the Crescent Club was the conduit to my sleazy empire. Not that I ever *consciously* intended becoming a porn king, or even a bar owner.

But I'm getting ahead of my story . . . In those days, before the influx of too many New Yorkers (for some reason, Midwesterners are alright) and the European hordes, when Sarasota and I were young together, I drank copiously, smoked incessantly, and chased wild women. (I no longer smoke cigarettes unless I'm drunk, and I never *ever* chase wild women.)

My best pals were Ed and Andrew, who also worked for me in an informal fashion—they told me what they were going to do, then did it— with Ed running the theater and Andrew the bar. Ed was our rudder, with strong left-brain logic, and Andrew was the loose cannon every business needs if you're going to have any fun. Once he bailed a steady customer out of jail on a charge of grand theft auto, using the bar's weekly receipts, then hired the customer as a bartender so he could repay the debt. When the register came up short fifty or a hundred dollars following the felon's nightly shifts, Andrew couldn't believe anyone would be so obvious a thief. He was busy playing Sherlock Holmes when the felonious bartender simply walked off with an evening's receipts and never returned.

And there was the time Andrew and I were cruising south down I-75 and spotted two green signs. One read Business Route, the other South. "Given the choice between Business and South, I've always headed South," announced Andrew.

THEN THERE WAS my literary mentor, Borden Deal, in his guayabera shirt; or else his western vest, Stetson hat, and string tie. A feisty Southern novelist with a ferocious thirst for Jack Daniels and endless packs of menthol cigarettes. Borden and I would cruise Sarasota nightly, hitting the "in" spots like St. Georges with the suave and sophisticated owner-manager, Jean Claude, and dapper Carl at the piano bar. The place "to see and be seen," as Borden dubbed it. At the close of a long, drunken evening, when all the bars had closed, we'd wind up at Borden's place with a case of cold Miller bottles in the freezer and Borden stripped down to his shoes and socks and jockey shorts, his buddha belly hanging out, strumming blues on his twelve-string, discussing books and the literary life. Borden, like his close friend and nemesis, noted Florida mystery novelist John D. MacDonald, is gone now, but memories of them both live on in my heart.

Borden introduced me to the liars' lunch, a group of writers, cartoonists, and artists, including Deal, MacDonald, and cartoonist Dik Browne of *Hagar the Horrible* fame, who met every Friday afternoon for lunch to play three rounds of liar's poker for drinks.

There was a girl, too, or rather several. But my favorite was Linda, a willowy auburn-haired Midwestern beauty and former English teacher with sensitive blue eyes—the sweetheart of Sigma Chi and homecoming queen at Albion College, who sold multimillion-dollar real estate, dressed beautifully, loved animals, had perfect taste in food, music, art, literature, and everything else, and knew everybody who was anybody. It was from Linda that I learned the secrets of swanky restaurants and luxurious hotels. The more expensive the restaurant, the less food you get; the more luxurious the hotel the fewer TV channels are available. She even attended the ballet, while I drank at a bar across the street.

According to her mother, who promised her a trip to Europe if she didn't smoke or have sex until she reached twenty-one, she was a virgin when she married her first husband—a monumental feat in today's era of loose morals.

Women are always mad at me, but most hide it until the final explosion. At least with Linda I knew when she was mad at me and why she was mad at me. It was up to me whether I wanted to do something about it. You tell me, Linda, have I left anything out?

THEN THERE WAS Lew Harper, an old-time projectionist from Fort Wayne, Indiana, who was in his eighties when I bought the theater. He taught me everything I know—which was never enough for him—about running a movie house. And, as my country cousin Jim Turner would say, *more besides . . .*

And Barb, Lew's thrifty wife, who bought cleaning supplies and kept the theater—eventually, a porn palace—as spic and span as her own home. Well, almost. The Harpers adopted me as their unruly child. When I misbehaved—throwing late night parties and drinking beer in the projection room, messing up the curtain mechanism so they opened and closed continuously through a screening of *Pinocchio*, with hundreds of angry mothers and bawling offspring demanding their admission back—they were my stern, but forgiving, surrogate parents.

During this time, I was a contributing editor for *Sarasota Magazine* and came to appreciate the brilliant, raven-haired editor-in-chief, Pam, the only person I know who scored perfect 800s on her SAT test, and "Sarasota's Resident Genius," the worldly, ultra-sophisticated, and terminally hip Bob Plunket, author of *My Search for Warren Harding* and *Love Junky*, and *Sarasota Magazine*'s gossip columnist, *Mr. Chatterbox*. Bob is also a playwright and part-time movie star, close personal friends with everyone who is anyone in New York and L.A.

Once Bob and I took a trip to Key West and toured the gay bars. At one bar, a man in a g-string was shooting both a game of pool and the moon (at the same time), and I asked Bob how the guy got to the bar in a g-string. Bob sighed one of his exasperated Mr. Chatterbox sighs and said, "He wore a raincoat, of course." At the Pleasure Chest, surrounded by bikinied Arnold Schwarzenegger lookalikes with gold rings in their nipples, I was a bit nervous. Bob once again sighed exasperatedly. "David, you're not at the Tuscaloosa Country Club now!"

Touché.

The next day I hooked up with a space-cadet girl named Nanette who fascinated Bob. He couldn't ask me enough questions about her personal life. Sure enough, several years later, she turned up as one of the main characters in *Love Junky*. The fink didn't even bother to disguise the fact she had picked *me* up while I was eating oysters at the Pier House's swimming pool bar. He didn't even change her name.

But let's return to the Crescent Club . . .

My first night in Sarasota, I was brought here by a blind-date from Long Island who exclaimed, "In New York, it's Jones Beach. Here it's Siesta Key. I guess that says it all." And she was right. Sarasota, with its history of tolerance and sophistication and its wealth of writers and artists, is still, in spite of relentless traffic and rampant development, a subtropical paradise. And Siesta Key, with its wide, powder quartz, blindingly white sand beach and blue-green Gulf, is the jewel in Sarasota's crown. The best and most beautiful beach in Florida, the United States, and possibly the world.

To get to the Crescent Club, follow Stickney Point Road west from the Tamiami Trail (U.S. 41) across the South Bridge to Siesta Key and turn south. The Crescent Club is a block down on the left.

A Host of Fridays

It's one o'clock on a Friday afternoon in 1985 and the group is seated around a long formica table in a dimly lit corner of Merlin's Restaurant (since torn down).

"Does anyone know if Dik Browne is coming today?" asks writer and radio personality Tim Kantor.

"He's got the flu," says cartoonist Ralph Smith.

"Too bad. Dik's usually good for at least one round of drinks," quips radio-TV writer Irving Vendig.

The table is nearly full by the time novelist John D. MacDonald arrives carrying a shopping bag filled with booby prizes for the losers at liar's poker.

"What's in the bag today, John?" asks Vendig.

Prizes donated by MacDonald in the past have included a badly translated tome on the Ecuadorean economy and an African elephant's ear. In addition to receiving a prize, the loser of each of the three games must buy a round of drinks.

MacDonald eases onto the chair beside Vendig's. "Why not lose a round and find out?"

Novelist/playwright Joe Hayes tells a story. "The preview for *Desperate Hours* was in Chicago. Paul Newman was the Dillinger character and Karl Malden played the father whose family was abducted. Five minutes into the first act, Newman's prop gun misfired and Malden dropped to the floor as if he was shot. The actors froze. If Malden's character was dead, the play was over before it really started! Finally, one of Newman's two henchmen—the big, dumb one, naturally enough—went over and kneeled beside the body. He rolled him over and dropped his ear to Malden's chest. 'He's dead, alright!' "

The group roars with laughter.

"What happened after that?" someone asks.

Hayes smiles. "The curtain went down and the director came out and explained what had gone wrong. Believe it or not, the audience loved it and we got rave reviews!"

By 1:15 those who are going to arrive have arrived, and it's time for the first game. As players are eliminated from the competition, conversations spring up around the table, ranging from a twenty-year-old series of murders, to the latest ecology disaster, to a story about Welsh poet Dylan Thomas relieving himself on his hostess's couch. Everything under the sun is discussed except literature with a capital L.

THE IDEA BEHIND the lunch originated in November 1952 when Pulitzer Prize–winning novelist MacKinlay Kantor hosted a luncheon at the Orange Blossom Hotel for writers Norton Weber, Joe Millard, and Dick Glendinning.

Sarasota was known as an artists' colony but it was quietly becoming a good place for writers. According to Glendinning, writers "dreaded the thought of anything that smacked of being an 'authors' club' made up of hopeful writers in search of panaceas, magic formulae, and the name of

60

a good agent . . . Yet the lunch at the Orange Blossom went so smoothly that those present . . . decided . . . what made this lunch different was the fact . . . they met primarily as friends who also happened to be in the same profession."

A later discussion between Glendinning and novelist John MacDonald turned the notion of "a loose assemblage of kindred souls [meeting] without plan, purpose, or program for lunch" into reality. According to Glendinning: "John shared [his] enthusiasm for a broader meeting and [the two of us] decided to put out a quiet and selective call for lunch at the Plaza Restaurant on Friday, December 19, 1952." The Plaza's atmosphere suited the group perfectly since it was "more like a club than a restaurant . . . with its pseudo-Spanish theme and ill-assorted frills . . . and its food, chosen from a menu that may not have seen a change since opening day in 1928."

An undated letter sent out around this time contains a couple of paragraphs that come as close to a definition of the group as anything ever attempted:

> All talk of bylaws, constitutions, and baskets to needy writers will be discouraged. Anyone proposing a Story Laboratory for mention in *Writer's Digest*, or chatty papers on Helpful Hints to Writers, or little talks and book reviews, or anything else which has no proper place in a gathering of this sort will be hooted into the men's room where he will please flush himself down the drain
> . . .
>
> Attendance would indicate that you are probably there. Absence tends to suggest the opposite. In any case, no one will be altogether sure.

In a letter to Kantor in Spain, Glendinning described what happened. "I know you will be glad to know that the spadework you did was not in vain. On January 2, those of us who follow the tin-cup existence of writing and are forced through dire straits to remain in Sarasota met in semidrunken conclave at the Plaza. Aside from a few raw stories and pro-fanities directed at editors, nothing at all was accomplished—which is, of course, as it should be."

When he returned from Spain, Kantor became the unofficial leader of the group. "He was the grand guru, and pretty much set the tone in the old days," says Joe Hayes. A tall trim man with a military bearing, Kantor was an unabashed patriot who cherished old-fashioned values like integri-ty and valor. A quick man with a story or joke, he could recite the lyrics of most of the popular songs written since 1900 and could tell five or six ver-sions of the same joke. Though his ultraconservative views often clashed with the more liberal ones of his friends, they adored him. According to Hayes, "In his presence one felt amused, warmed, sometimes irritated, often exhilarated, but always alive."

From the beginning, the gathering was an all male enclave for rea-sons described by Glendinning.

> The idea . . . [that women] should be invited never came up. It was still possible at that time to have an all male lunch without feeling guilty about it and without a picket line quickly forming . . . What's more, the women in our lives were delighted to have us out from underfoot for a change, but it was a guarantee . . . delight would not [occur] if there were any strange women [involved].

Eventually this unwritten rule led to the barring of playwright Lillian Hellman.

"Lillian was in Sarasota with S. J. Perelman," recalls Hayes. "[Perelman] was invited to attend, and he asked if he could bring her along. When the circumstances were explained to him, he said if that was the way things were, he wouldn't come either. I understand Lillian was quite miffed."

AS THE YEARS PASSED, the lunch became increasingly popular with out-of-town visitors. To quote Glendinning, "Sarasota was a pleasanter place for conferences than the slosh of New York. Editors, publishers, agents, authors from other areas, people from pictures, radio, television, and stage, newspaper feature writers, and columnists from around the country all seemed to wind up at the Friday lunch."

Out-of-town writers attending over the years included Erskine Caldwell *(God's Little Acre, Tobacco Road)*, James T. Farrell *(Studs Lonigan)*, Buckminster Fuller (philosophical and scientific writer who invented the geodesic dome), William Inge *(Come Back, Little Sheba* and *Picnic)*, Budd Schulberg *(On the Waterfront, What Makes Sammy Run)*, William Manchester *(Death of a President, An American Caesar)*, Thornton Wilder *(Our Town, The Skin of Our Teeth)*, Larry L. King *(The Best Little Whorehouse in Texas)*, political satirist Art Buchwald, Watergate conspirator E. Howard Hunt, author of a series of thrillers, and best-selling novelist Stephen King.

At one lunch, when the subject of productivity came up, it was determined the eight people present had written more than three hundred books. Sarasota writers Dick Glendinning and Borden Deal were low men on the totem pole with less than twenty-five books between them.

Sometime in the late 1950s, liars' poker—a game played with the serial numbers on currency instead of cards—was introduced to Sarasota via Manhattan, and promised to be a solution to the problem of guests who felt politeness demanded that they buy a round of drinks. Following the suggestion of a visiting editor who thought it might be interesting to see how imaginative minds fare against the law of averages, a record of wins and losses was kept.

At first, the records—illegible chicken-scratchings scribbled on the backs of cocktail napkins, canceled checks, or whatever else was at hand— were stored behind the bar. According to Glendinning, "[A]fter they had been used a few times by absent-minded bartenders for bar rags or drink coasters, after they had served as note paper for phone numbers and cryptic messages, after a few heavy sloshings to serve as a fixative for cigarette shreds, cigar ashes, lipstick smears, squashed olives, and salted peanuts . . . deciphering them became a real challenge." The records were moved to the molding of a frame containing a photo of group member Jim McCague. But "as . . . the wad of weekly playing sheets became bulkier and heavier, Jim's picture developed a pronounced list to the right." One morning a cleaning woman was straightening the frame when the paper slips came tumbling down. Figuring them to be dinner orders that never made it to the kitchen, she cleaned up the evidence and dumped it in the trash with the intention of saving some poor waiter his job.

SINCE THAT TIME, the records have been kept by Glendinning (later Kantor, then Peter King, author of the gourmet detective novels), and an inscribed plaque is presented at the end of each year to the worst liar. Winners over the years have included novelists MacKinlay Kantor (*Andersonville*, *Taps for Bugle Annie*), Borden Deal (*The Least One*, *The Winner*), and Richard Jessup (*The Cincinnati Kid*); historians Phillip Van Doren Stern (*The Day Lincoln Was Shot*) and Carl Carmer (*Stars Fell on Alabama*); songwriter Nick Kenny (*Love Letters in the Sand*); and cartoonist Dik Browne (*Hagar the Horrible*).

Over the years, contenders for the plaque have included Browne, Joe Hayes (*The Desperate Hours*, *The Happiest Millionaire*), Bob Plunket, Irving Vendig (creator of *The Edge of Night* and *Search For Tomorrow*), Ralph Smith (*Captain Vincible*), Tim Kantor (*Hamilton County*), Roy Bassler (*A Short History of the Civil War*), Bill Steven (former editor-in-chief of the *Chicago Daily News* and the *Houston Chronicle*), Dick Glendinning (*Terror in the Sun*, *Carnival Girl*), Ted Irwin (former editor of *Look* magazine), Ray Troyer (*Father Bede's Misfit*), and Rob Roy Buckingham (former UPI reporter and manager of *The New York Times* wire service).

Though the overwhelming majority of the lunches have passed without incident, there have been exceptions. MacDonald liked to recall the time he was bitten on the ear by a Pulitzer Prize winner (no, it wasn't

Mack Kantor). Then there was the excluded war novelist who used to occupy the table next to the group's and make his presence felt by glaring ominously in their direction. Clifford Irving showed up fresh from being sentenced to a jail term for his fake autobiography of Howard Hughes, only to find that the forewarned members had gathered elsewhere.

As Glendinning puts it, "There had been crises and stormy scenes . . . bruised egos and punctured balloons. There had been table thumpings and inner furies . . . emotional walkouts and irritated boycotts. But all of these things were inevitable in a group of unreconstructed individuals who refused to be anything but themselves."

For more than fifty years now, these "unreconstructed individuals" have met once a week for lunch. As members of a group without constitution, minutes, or bylaws, they share two things in common: love of good conversation and hatred of pretense.

Today, though most of the original group has passed away or moved on, and the Plaza has long since closed, the Writers' Lunch still meets on Friday afternoons at a different location for four rounds of liar's poker and conversation.

The Main Street Bookstore in Sarasota has an excellent selection of inexpensive, remaindered books on practically any subject.

John D. MacDonald: A Remembrance

When I first started reading John D. MacDonald's novels, I never in my wildest imaginings dreamed we would someday be friends.

MacDonald was perhaps the best known of our Florida novelists. Unlike Hemingway, who wrote only one book, *To Have and Have Not*, that takes place in the state. Or Marjorie Kinnan Rawlings, who wrote solely of Florida crackers. Or MacKinlay Kantor, who wrote mostly historical novels. MacDonald was the first of note to examine present-day south Florida. (Today many noted mystery novelists, including Carl Hiaasen, James Hall, and Elmore Leonard, cover the same territory.) Kantor once labeled MacDonald "a modern-day Sinclair Lewis." Like Lewis or Faulkner, MacDonald created a world of his own, inhabited by such easily recognizable Florida types as the fly-by-night land speculator, the pretty-boy stud, the murderous sociopath, and the fading beauty nursing her regret with sunshine and the bottle. In other words, the dark underbelly of the Florida Gold Coast, whose tawdry facade is held up in the unrelenting glare of a Florida summer's noon.

I began reading MacDonald's novels many years ago, following the breakup of my marriage. MacDonald's brand of cynical humanism was just the antidote for a bad case of postmarital guilt. His was an amoral world characterized by greed, lust, and environmental rape. A world of politicians on the take, businessmen on the make, and crooked cops. The only saving grace is usually a world-weary romantic with an overwhelming need to set things right.

MacDonald's most famous romantic was that Don Quixote of beach bums, Travis McGee. The protagonist of twenty-two novels, McGee is everything a sensitive twentieth-century male yearns to be: successful with women in a nonpredatory way, knowledgeable in many unrelated fields (mariner, detective, connoisseur of food and wine), and caring without being a wimp. Unlike the investigators in other series, McGee's character evolved over the years as his inner life took precedence over the violent physical action of the early books. In the final McGee novel, *The Lonely Silver Rain*, he even undergoes a midlife crisis.

McGee was my role model at the time, and I expected his creator to be a carbon copy of his creation. Only, I was mistaken . . .

EXCEPT FOR a similar philosophy of life, they were total opposites. McGee, despite his liberal philosophy, was something of a womanizer. MacDonald was married to the same woman for fifty years. McGee was tall, dark, and handsome. MacDonald, though hardly unattractive, was not conventionally handsome. McGee led a flamboyant lifestyle, living on a houseboat and driving a uniquely modified Rolls Royce "pick-up truck." MacDonald strove for anonymity and drove a Toyota station wagon. McGee had few if any ties. MacDonald's life was filled with familial and other obligations. Finally, McGee was athletic. "Why, John D. can't even swim, much less captain a boat," claimed my friend, Southern novelist Borden Deal. "If he resembles anybody in the McGee books, it's Meyer."

In the series, Meyer is an economic consultant who lives on the

Maynard E. Keynes, the boat in the slip next to McGee's at the Bahia Del Mar boat basin in Lauderdale. Meyer serves as a sounding board for McGee's ideas and dispenses a few theories of his own—a sort of intellectual Dr. Watson to McGee's more active Holmes.

Borden was right. If MacDonald resembled anyone, it was Meyer. Stoop-shouldered, with horn-rimmed glasses and a pinkish pale complexion, John D. was a ringer for the absent-minded professor. His conversation, too, was professorial in knowledge, and his fund of arcane lore—the best French restaurant in Bangkok, where to get the highest rate of exchange in Mexico City, the inside workings of a multinational corporation (John D. had a master's degree in business from the Wharton School of Finance)—was inexhaustible.

THE FIRST TIME I met John D. was at the liars' lunch. During lunch, he kept cocking his head to listen to the sound of a video game being played in an adjoining room. Its futuristic *ping-ping-ping* fascinated him.

"That's the sound of the future, John," commented someone at the table.

And I could sense John D. making a mental note of the comment.

"John D. is nothing if not an intellectual magpie," said Borden later.

Sure enough, a year or so later, the comment about video games was put in the mouth of a character in a McGee novel. It was one of my first experiences with how a *real* writer works. Any chance comment was grist for the mill, filed away for future use.

Once John D. gave me the only literary advice he ever volunteered. "Never use *very*," he said. "Something either is or it isn't. Something is either blue or it isn't blue. Nothing is *very* blue."

During the liars' lunch, John D. awarded the loser of each game a prize. The nature of the prize depended on the recipient. For instance, a particularly needy writer was given a set of big-band records, along with a stereo. A longwinded writer was given a weighty tome on the Ecuadorean economy. A disheveled writer (myself) was given his choice of three brand-new billfolds to replace his, which was falling apart at the seams.

Except for the liars' lunch, events to raise money for environmental causes, and Sarasota's prestigious New College (MacDonald's favorite charity), John D. seldom made the social rounds. "It angers up my blood," he said once, quoting black baseball star Satchel Paige. Or again, "Literary cocktail parties are my idea of hell."

Like most writers, John D. had the aura of a loner. Maybe it was due to long hours spent in solitude worrying over his craft. Maybe it was his disdain for the trivial subject matter of most conversation. Or maybe it was because he found it easier to deal with imaginary rather than real-life characters. "Real people have a habit of disappointing you," he told me once. "Whereas, imaginary characters never let you down. They're consistent."

When I mentioned I was working on a novel, John D. suggested I send the first hundred or so pages to his agent, along with an outline. Eventually the manuscript came back with some pertinent comments as to how to improve it.

When John D. read the letter, he turned to me and said, "What do you think?"

"He's right," I grudgingly admitted.

John D. smiled. "You're learning. Only difference between a pro and an amateur is an amateur disregards constructive criticism."

John D. was a *pro*.

"HE WORKS TWICE as long as you and me," said Borden. "Four hours in the morning, four hours in the afternoon. Seven days a week, holidays included." Whenever John D. went on cruises around the world, he took his word processor and worked his regular schedule unless they were in port. The liars' lunch was his only regular interruption, and even then he worked nights to make up for it. This professionalism is reflected in the amount of work he turned out. Sixty-odd novels, two nonfiction books, numerous novellas, and more than five hundred articles and short stories.

There were rumors John D. had already completed the final novel in the McGee series—the one in which he would meet his demise—to be published posthumously.

"It's called *Black is the Color*," insisted Borden.

A favorite pastime of McGee fans was to speculate if and when he would be killed (McGee's fans are as rabid in their devotion as trekkies). But no final McGee novel was uncovered after John D.'s death, and Travis, unlike his creator, proved immortal.

A couple of days before John D. was due to report for surgery at the Mayo Clinic in Minnesota, he attended the liars' lunch. His prizes were unusually lavish that day, and after lunch he bid us good-bye for what he hoped would be only a few months. A pro to the end, he made arrangements with his doctor to recuperate at the Milwaukee Athletic Club and hoped to get a book out of his experiences there.

On December 28, 1986, John D. MacDonald died of complications following bypass surgery. At his request, there was no funeral.

That week, at the liars' lunch, we lifted our glasses in a toast to our departed friend. His great good heart would be sorely missed.

Fifteen years after John D.'s death, his sixty-odd books are still selling like hotcakes, and the classic 1958 movie *Cape Fear* was remade in 1991 with Nick Nolte and Robert DeNiro in the Gregory Peck and Robert Mitchum roles.

Borden Deal's home in Sarasota, where he lived from the mid-70s until he died in 1985.

Photo by Ed Baatz.

The Secret Life of Borden Deal

I was a little nervous as I knocked on Borden Deal's door one sunny afternoon in 1981. In the short time I had known the Sarasota author, we had
managed to become good friends in spite of our differences. I was young,
unpublished, eager for advice about writing and the world in general. He
was a famous best-selling author, a local celebrity as well known for his
hard-drinking, outrageous ways as for his literary output.

But this afternoon, after I hadn't heard from Borden for a while, I
was worried. He came to the door in his ragged yellow bathrobe, looking
old and tired, as though he hadn't slept for days. Now I understood. He was
working on a new book.

He confirmed my hunch. "It's a secret project," he said, smiling
devilishly. It was as if he were dying to tell me more. "It's being written
under a pseudonym."

Knowing something of this Southern novelist's work, I figured the
book might deal with country music. "Could it be you're ghosting a biography of Elvis with Colonel Parker?"

Borden laughed. "Not even close."

I could tell by Borden's animated expression that he was excited about it. He ushered me inside the house and we sat down with a bottle of Jack Daniels. "The myth of the cynical writer is just that, a myth. There isn't a writer in the world, from Harold Robbins to Norman Mailer, who doesn't feel that everything he writes has the potential for becoming a masterpiece. Else why bother?"

What was Borden getting at? Was there something about the book that required an apology? I felt a special moment had come, that Borden was finally going to tell me something important—a secret bigger than just the nature of his new book.

He lit a cigarette and looked at me, his mind made up. "I'm the author of the 'Anonymous' books."

"Really?" I was unsure what the Anonymous books were.

If Borden noted the uncertainty in my voice, he didn't mention it. Instead he strode over to a wooden chest in one corner of the room. Raising the lid, he made a sweeping gesture to indicate its contents. Stacked up inside were dozens of paperbacks with sexy covers.

Now I understood. The Anonymous books. That series of popular paperbacks—*Her, Him, Me*, and a half dozen other pronoun titles—that were bringing soft-core fiction to the middle-class reading public. A cover blurb coyly described the author as a best-selling novelist who preferred to remain anonymous, and everyone was wondering who it was.

"I wrote these!" exclaimed Borden in the manner of a proud parent showing off a comely brood of children. "But don't tell anybody. I want it to remain a secret. When I die, there's a provision in my will revealing Anonymous's identity. Everybody will know I not only wrote books dealing with the New South, I also wrote some of the sexiest damn books around."

BORDEN DEAL DIED in Sarasota on January 23, 1985. True to his wish, two days later his widow, Pat, released the news he had authored the "Anonymous" series that had sold millions of copies over the last fourteen years. The story ran on the front page of the *Sarasota Herald-Tribune* and was the talk of the town.

As it turned out, I wasn't the only one to whom Borden had confided his secret. All told, there must have been at least a dozen of us. It's hard to expect a writer to keep a secret when the nature of his business involves confessing all he knows and some things he doesn't. Unfortunately, Borden's secret became the most salient fact about his life's work as a writer. At a recent meeting of the liars' lunch, someone said, "Borden Deal? Isn't he the one who wrote those dirty books?"

I doubt this would have bothered Borden a great deal, or that he would have admitted it if it did. He rarely seemed to mind what people thought. He displayed a reckless, often abrasive, obstinacy in both his writing career and his personal style. I remember sitting with him on the beach shortly after his second heart attack, watching him blow cigarette smoke at the joggers who passed before us. Stretched tight across his pot belly was a t-shirt with an illustration of a hand shooting a bird; underneath was the word *Joggers*.

And he was proud of the books. As he states in the preface to *Her*, the first book in the series:

> I have tried to tell . . . a true and simple love story—the truth as
> real as the simplicity. It seems to me . . . in these recent years since
> the censorship bars have been lowered, the language of love, fol-
> lowing Gresham's Law, has been debased into a coarse coinage,
> with neither tenderness nor love—nor, indeed, any true emotion
> at all. It has been my ardent desire to new-mint these words, this
> language, by writing them in the context in which they are most
> often spoken. For this, the earthy language of love is the best and
> truest tongue in the world.

Her is a story of a recently divorced man and a recently divorced woman, both professors at a Southern university. In an effort to avoid painful emotional involvement, they decide to make themselves available to one another on a strictly sexual basis at any time of the day or night. Naturally, things don't work out as planned . . .

But read the book for yourself.

EVENTUALLY THE series grew to nine novels—each involving a different type of sexual relationship (older man/younger woman, older woman/younger man, etc.). In keeping with his desire for simplicity, Borden gave each book a one-word personal-pronoun title. He was working on the tenth when he died, though by then the sexual combinations were becoming anything but simple.

Doubleday, which for many years had published Borden's serious works, rejected *Her* as too explicit. Borden's attorney, Maury Greenbaum, sent the manuscript around to various publishers under the Anonymous pseudonym—a cautionary measure Borden had used before to keep thrillers and a Gothic novel from detracting from his reputation as a serious novelist. After numerous rejections, Bantam decided to bring *Her* out as a paperback original. When it sold close to a million copies, Bantam went to Greenbaum to ask that the author write a sequel.

By then the pseudonym had become a selling point. In the prefaces to the books, Anonymous takes pains to let the reader know he is a well-established writer in his own right. It was a tantalizing gimmick. But as the books became the most lucrative project of his career, he must have been aching to take credit for them—particularly as his "serious" career failed to keep pace.

Following the relative failure of *Adventure* in 1978, Borden decided to write a sequel to an earlier novel of his that dealt with country music. In order to research the novel, he crisscrossed the country on the tour bus of singer/songwriter Tom T. Hall.

When the book was completed, Borden sent it off to a new editor at Doubleday, only to have the editor recommend drastic changes in the text. Infuriated, Borden flew up to Manhattan where he proceeded to inform everyone in the Doubleday offices—from the office boy on up—he had been writing books for more than thirty years and wasn't about to change one word of his novel for anyone, especially some recent Vassar graduate who up to that time had been assigned to children's books. Doubleday refused to publish the novel. After 1979 Borden was forced to rely almost entirely on the Anonymous books for income.

As novelist Kurt Vonnegut, a good friend of Borden's, once put it to me, "It was the bravest and most foolhardy act I've ever seen any writer commit." But it was pure Borden—proud, independent, colorful, and, finally, self-destructive. For the rest of his life, he would find success only behind the "Anonymous" mask.

BORDEN DEAL WAS born in 1922 in Pontotoc, Mississippi, and grew up on a tenant farm halfway between New Albany and Oxford—as he put it, "about fifteen miles northeast of William Faulkner." While in high school, he wrangled a job maintaining the school typewriters so he could learn to type. He read indiscriminately, anything he could lay his hands on, from *Screen Romances* to *Huckleberry Finn* (the owner of the drugstore would give Borden leftover issues of magazines, after he had torn off the covers and returned them to the distributor for a refund). Borden knew he'd be a writer.

At sixteen, after his father died in a truck accident coming home from an itinerant job picking cotton, Borden left home to join FDR's Civilian Conservation Corps and was sent to Oregon to fight forest fires. He kept five dollars a month spending money; the rest of his wages he sent home to help support his family. It was around this time Borden began riding the rails. Once, as he watched, a friend lost his grip on the boxcar ladder and was cut in two by the train's wheels. Fearing the consequences, Borden did not report the incident.

During World War II, after flight training as a naval aviation cadet, Borden was an instructor at a fire-control school in Fort Lauderdale. The closest he came to combat was a round of buckshot aimed at his fleeing backside by a jealous husband (Borden claimed he hadn't even known the lady was married). Throughout this period he was writing an overwrought novel in the style of Thomas Wolfe, the manuscript of which he later abandoned in Mexico City when forced to leave the country and his wealthy Mexican wife in a hurry—but that's another story.

FOLLOWING THE WAR, Borden attended the University of Alabama solely to enroll in Hudson Strode's creative writing class. *Time* had recently run a cover story on Strode's class, and hopeful writers—mostly veterans on the G.I. Bill—were arriving at Tuscaloosa in droves. With his redneck origins, Borden was never, as he put it, "one of Strode's fair-haired boys." Still, Strode recognized Borden's talent and encouraged his literary ambitions.

While still in college, Borden entered a short story contest sponsored by *Tomorrow* magazine and won a first prize of $500 and publication in the magazine. This story was Borden's first publication. He immediately sent $450 home and blew the remaining $50 on a beer bust for friends.

The story later appeared in *Best American Short Stories of 1949*, an annual collection edited by Martha Foley. As the first member of Strode's postwar writing class to achieve publication, Borden became a campus celebrity. Little did he realize it would be six long years and numerous jobs later before his first novel, *Walk Through the Valley*, was published.

In 1954 Borden was working as a copywriter for a radio station in Mobile, Alabama, when Charles Scribner's Sons offered him an advance on the novel. By then, Borden had married Babs Hodges and fathered two children. Armed with the advance and what little money they had managed to save, he quit his job and moved the family north to Scottsboro, Alabama, Babs's hometown, to work on his second novel, *Dunbar's Cove*. Luckily, once published, *Walk Through the Valley* proved a critical success, and Borden was awarded a $5,000 Guggenheim Fellowship for the new book.

Dunbar's Cove, a novel dealing with the birth and growth of the Tennessee Valley Authority, was sold to Twentieth Century Fox for, as Borden put it, "a nice piece of change," and became the classic movie *Wild River*, directed by Elia Kazan and starring Montgomery Clift and Lee Remick. The book was a worldwide success translated into more than twenty languages.

At about this time, Borden's wife, Babs, began to write. Over the next twenty years, they separately produced more than thirty novels and 150-odd short stories. As Borden often stated, he never held another honest job again.

In 1964 Borden moved his family to Sarasota, where he continued to write novels celebrating what is now known as the New South. He wrote novels like *Interstate*, about the drama of constructing the national highway system, *Bluegrass*, about the breeding of thoroughbred horses, *The Spangled Road*, about the circus, *The Least One* and *The Other Room*, about his childhood and early adolescence in rural Mississippi, and *The Insolent Breed*, about country music.

Borden and Babs were divorced in 1975.

THAT THE *ANONYMOUS* BOOKS turned out to be such a financial success was, in my opinion, a much deserved reward for a writer who, over the course of his life, worked long and hard and produced many good books. "Being a writer has its ups and downs," he once said. "But it sho' as hell beats pickin' cotton."

Owing to his origins, Borden always lived with the fear of poverty, and a writer's life did little to relieve it. Perhaps as a way of demonstrating his sophistication, he could indulge in some rather embarrassing behavior. I remember once having lunch with Borden and Greenbaum at Le Cirque in New York. Sipping his usual Jack Daniels with a splash of soda, he motioned the headwaiter over.

"This is not Jack Daniels," said Borden with a sullen expression. "It's Jim Beam."

"But sir, I watched the bartender pour it myself, and it was poured out of a Jack Daniels bottle," protested the headwaiter with more than a trace of hauteur.

"I don't care what kind of bottle it came out of, it's Jim Beam," declared Borden.

The headwaiter left and returned with an unopened bottle of Jack Daniels. Deftly slashing the seal with his knife, he poured the bourbon into a glass filled with freshly shaved ice and added a dollop of soda.

Borden took a cautious sip. "Just as I thought. The liquor distributors in this city are pouring Jim Beam bourbon into Jack Daniels bottles to make a few extra bucks."

If it was an act, it was a damn good one. I got the feeling it was a familiar routine.

Borden liked to attract attention. Though he didn't get any recognition for the Anonymous series during his lifetime, he obviously delighted in imagining the scandalous revelation that would hit Sarasota and the publishing world after his death. Still, the books provide a troubling close to Borden's career. He may have been proud of the writing when the series began, but by the end the novelty was wearing thin. The last book in the series had been slated for an overhaul due to its overly fantastic plot. In the end, he must have felt trapped by the series' success.

Even though publishers were no longer interested, and despite the health problems that plagued him, he continued to write serious fiction along with the Anonymous books. The talent was still there, and a lifetime of discipline and craft took over. He was, if nothing else, a born storyteller.

Six months before he died, Borden's luck at last changed. New Horizons agreed to publish *There Were Also Strangers* and *The Platinum Man*, the book Doubleday had earlier turned down. *Greenfield County*, another novel written during this period, is still unpublished.

Borden invented the Anonymous pseudonym to protect his reputation as a serious novelist; as a final irony, there are those who would say that it did just the opposite—"Borden Deal. Isn't he the one who wrote those dirty books?" But anyone who knew Borden could easily picture his reaction. A sip of Jack Daniels. A drag on his cigarette. And a long last laugh.

There Were Also Strangers, a Jungian novel about Borden's sharecropping youth, was published shortly after his death. In the late 1980s, *Bluegrass* was made into a TV miniseries starring Cheryl Ladd and Mickey Rooney.

Adventures in the Skin Trade

This is the confession of a man who grew up loving the movies. In the Alabama town where I was reared, there were three theaters. Two featured first-run films; the third was the Ritz (nicknamed the Ratz by us kids), and it screened double and triple bills of dubious quality—westerns and horror pictures mostly. Sometimes the projectionist, who was invariably drunk, would get his reels mixed. The end of the movie was in the middle and the beginning at the end. It didn't matter. The action was all that mattered, not what passed for a plot.

During the '80s, I owned a theater for adults and the same principle applies. It was the South Trail Cinema, the triple-X place down past Gulf Gate with the steady stream of elderly men ghosting in and out. Most likely, you envision it as a regular Sodom and Gomorrah. It was the sort of place where the projectionist, eager to get home on time, could simply leave out the middle reel of an especially long feature, and hardly anyone would notice.

These films leave nothing to the imagination. Most involve male fantasies like the one about the plumber in a sorority house full of available girls, and the plot is a flimsy excuse for the action. In one of them, a wicked husband fakes a fatal heart attack, then pretends to come back as a ghost to scare his buxom wife to death and inherit her fortune. Nice plot, but it wasn't really introduced until the last few minutes of the movie.

Occasionally I ran across a fairly decent film. There was a gangster porn film, for example, that was more realistic than anything in the regular theaters, simply because the actors spoke real street talk as opposed to Hollywood-ese, and the hoods really looked the part, which they probably were.

But these were the exceptions. Most of my films were the farthest thing imaginable from the quality I hoped to offer when I bought the theater in 1979. I wanted to screen "classics" and foreign films, but the market for these was nearly nonexistent.

So I decided to go "first-run" with films starring actors like Clint Eastwood, Robert Redford, and Burt Reynolds. But these movies cost big bucks. The theater owner must guarantee the distributor so much money against a percentage of the take. For instance, I once screened a bomb entitled *The Fifth Musketeer*. The guarantee was $10,000 against 70 percent of the week's gross, 60 percent of the second's, and so on down the line. Columbia, cognizant the film was a loser, canceled all TV and radio spots and left me holding the bag. The first week's receipts totaled a little over $600. The second week, I pulled the film and brought in another. Columbia kept the ten grand. If advance word indicates the film is a winner, the distributor will most likely award it to a chain-owned theater rather than waste it on an independent like me.

Next, I screened second-run flicks at a buck a head, the advantage here being I could pick them up for a flat percentage of the take, usually 25 percent. But by the time a film has run long enough to be considered second-run, it's probably already been shown on cable TV or, nowadays, released on videocassette.

Then I tried free beer and pretzels with a $3 admission and blew $1,000 on newspaper and radio advertising. I even hired a security guard to patrol the aisles for rowdies, then bought four kegs of draft beer and enlisted the aid of three friends to help pour. The big night arrived and six people showed up, two bikers and four teetotalers.

SARASOTA IS WHAT they call a "retirement market." The local sports arena is named after the founder of a chain of funeral homes. As it turns out, the elderly comprise about ninety percent of the Sarasota market for porn films.

Since I knew of a fellow in St. Petersburg who was screening porn for an elderly audience, I decided to give him a call. Fred Hand (not his real name) is an independent theater owner from Buffalo, New York, who owned three theaters—two up north and one in St. Pete. All three were screening porn. Hand had the same problems dealing with the major distributors I did and switched to porn ten years before. To this old-time theater man who had been screening films since the 1930s, porn—like "talkies," "3-D," or "Dolby sound"—was simply the latest in a long string of developments.

Hand gave me the phone number of a distributor in Miami. When I dialed the number, the man on the other end of the line claimed to know nothing about dirty movies; in fact, he'd never seen one. I called Hand back. When I finished explaining what happened, he said: "Tell him Fred told you to call and ask to speak to Sally." Sure enough, the second time I got through.

Within a week, a car drove up to the theater and a man got out to deliver two hour-long features for a double bill. The man wasn't my idea of Mafia at all. As a matter of fact, he was quite polite with a soft Southern accent and a quiet, unassuming manner. We went next door to the Red Lobster. Over drinks, he explained the legal ramifications of what I was getting into.

First, each film had to be tried separately on its own merits for obscenity. In other words, a police detective had to sit through an entire showing, then confiscate the film and arrange for a trial during the course of which the film would be screened before a judge, It was a long and costly procedure. During the interim, I could be showing other films.

Two things to watch out for were prostitutes and minors. An advantage a theater has over, say, a bookstore is there's nothing a customer can carry home where it might be viewed by children. "Run a clean operation, and the law won't bother you," he advised.

Another advantage of porn was that the distributor doesn't want an arm and a leg for his product. A $500 guarantee against 25% of the gross. Other distributors wanted even less, but Hand insisted that the reliability of this particular outfit made it worth the extra money.

THE FIRST COUPLE of days I worked the box office myself. The majority of men attending the matinees, including those whose wives dropped them off at the entrance prior to going shopping, were elderly. Some were nervous about entering, but an equal number were matter-of-fact. As the weeks rolled by, I noticed some attended daily. Most attended at least once a week. The films changed every Friday.

I can make these generalizations about the clientele. Quite a few parked next door, then snuck around the corner to the box office. Some told the cashier, week after week, that it was their first porn flick. Others walked briskly along the sidewalk as though passing by, then veered sharply at the last instant, hand extended with exact change. The evening crowd and the matinee crowd differed a little, with the matinee drawing mainly old men; at night some couples attended. Most of the evening patrons were attractive and well dressed, the sort you'd expect to see at the country club. The crowd was steady throughout the day. Hardly anyone worried about starting times, since pretty much the same thing was always happening on the screen.

86

At least 80 percent of the patrons attended one or more times a week. In this way, the theater resembled a neighborhood bar. Most came alone (in more ways than one), so the parking lot was usually jammed with cars. Fridays and Saturdays were the best days; Sundays were by far the slowest. A surprising number of cars in the parking lot on weekdays sported religious decals. Although there was a seasonal variation, weekly receipts were remarkably consistent, seldom varying by more than a few hundred dollars. The title was irrelevant so long as the movie was Triple-X. In fact, the same film would sometimes run under three different titles over the course of a year. The exception was any film with the word *teen-age* in the title. *Teen-age Hitch-hikers* was the biggest grosser ever, though the women portraying the teenagers were in at least their thirties.

Some customers didn't mind being recognized, like one particular elderly couple who attended every Friday afternoon. They remained seated throughout both features, and on the way out the man signaled his opinion of the films with a thumbs-up or thumbs-down gesture. Others preferred anonymity. Once an elderly man suffered a stroke inside the auditorium. When the projectionist started to phone an ambulance, the man insisted he be carried next door to the Red Lobster first.

By talking with steady customers, I discovered most of them believe that women are the aggressors in any relationship, and a woman's sole criterion in choosing a mate is the size of his instrument, not his wallet.

The first couple of weeks, I charged $3 admission. Sally, the booking agent, phoned from Miami and suggested I charge at least $5. Eventually, I charged $7 with no appreciable drop in attendance.

THINGS ARE a little different today than when I screened porn. With the advent of videocassette recorders, the audience dwindled, just as it has for movies in general. But my audience was an elderly one, and they were the last to purchase VCRs. Besides, most wouldn't have screened films of this sort in the sanctity of their homes, and many liked the neighborhood-bar sociability of the place.

My business and others like it evolved out of a sense of desperation. Consider, for example, the "Mom and Pop" motels along U.S. 41 that have to compete with Hiltons and Holiday Inns. Is it any wonder some of them turn to closed-circuit Triple-X videos, and a market that allows them to turn their rooms over two or three times a day?

Things have changed in Sarasota over the last few years. There are more theaters, several film societies, and a much better market for the kind of films I had hoped to screen. So if I had to do it over again, would I still screen porn?

Given the profits and the few hassles involved with running a porn theater, if it were a simple business decision, the answer is *yes*.

ON JULY 26, 1991, at 8:30 P.M., Paul Reubens, AKA PeeWee Herman, was arrested by three undercover deputies, working vice, for allegedly masturbating in the darkened auditorium of the South Trail Cinema . . . and all hell broke loose. The media were on the case like piranha on a bleeding carcass.

I was in New Mexico, living in an old mission building, away from phones and news coverage, and it wasn't until a week or two later, during a long-distance phone conversation with my former Sarasota girlfriend Linda that she said jokingly, "Aren't you ashamed for corrupting that clown?" When I asked what she meant, she suggested I turn on a TV. When I finally located one in a friend's house, a panel of so-called experts were discussing the effect that Reubens's arrest would have on the nation's children. I could hardly believe my ears. If the media hadn't blown the affair all out of proportion, there wouldn't have been any ill effects to worry about.

The rest is trivia history—Reubens's name was besmirched in the tabloids for practicing a form of safe sex, and the South Trail Cinema graced the cover of a national news magazine—surely a first for a porn theater. (I was later amused to read in an issue of *Vanity Fair* that PeeWee's downfall took place in a sparsely attended, run-down movie house. In fact, the theater was well attended and recently renovated. So much for accurate reporting!) The local paper was rife with rumors that I, the owner of this den of iniquity, must be at least a Mafia don, since no one had been able to contact me for comment. The truth was, I was unavailable for comment because I was blissfully unaware of what was going on.

Eventually the South Trail Cinema was picketed, boycotted, twice bricked through its plate glass windows, fire-bombed, and legislated to death—*must not be within 500 feet of a residential area*—by a special act of the Board of County Commissioners.

Today an excellent restaurant, the Manhattan Bar & Grill on U.S. 41, occupies the property where once stood the theater, and there's a downtown theater, Burn's Court, screening art and foreign films, my original goal for the South Trail.

Paul Reubens is making a much-deserved comeback after a long career lull.

O'Brisky Books in Micanopy, one of the many antiquarian bookstores in Florida.

Jack Kerouac: The End of the Road

Jack Kerouac is the quintessential late-twentieth-century American writer.

His classic novel, *On The Road*, describes a spiritually constricted America in which the speed of the automobile has replaced the leisurely traversing of the continent by covered wagon. As Kerouac's friend, poet and oriental sage Gary Snyder, put it:

> My vision of Cassady [the novel's hero] is of the 1880s cowboys . . . with no range left to work on . . . reduced to pool halls and driving back and forth across the country . . .
>
> Cassady . . . like . . . many Americans . . . inherited that taste for the limitless . . . [Y]ou can get hooked on that, if you don't know how to translate it into other regions, since when the sheer physical space disappears you go crazy . . .
>
> What was intended . . . was . . . you should step forth into wild space; what you ended up doing a hundred years later is driving back and forth in a car as fast as you can . . . Space becomes translated into speed . . . Cassady is the cowboy crashing.

Is it so strange, then, that Kerouac, King of the Beats, chose to finish out his life in a drunken haze with his ailing mother and nursemaid third wife in America's Elephant Graveyard—St. Petersburg, Florida? After all, he had already traveled many different roads to self revelation—from pure ecstasy to Buddhism and back again to his native Catholicism—during his brief 47-year life, only to find them all somehow lacking.

Kerouac was born on March 12, 1922, in Lowell, Massachusetts. His parents, Leo, a printer and sometimes bookie, and Gabrielle, a factory worker, were French-Canadians, and Kerouac's first language was French. When he was four, his sainted brother Gerard died, and Kerouac felt guilt the rest of his life for having survived him. A high school football star, Jack got an athletic scholarship to Horace Mann Prep and later Columbia University in New York, where he mingled with sons of the upper class. An injury and a later determination to become a writer ended his football career prematurely, and he became a wanderer working at different jobs—and writing—for the rest of his life.

Kicked out of the Navy during World War II as a result of a mental breakdown, he joined the Merchant Marines and hung out with a decadent New York crowd of intellectuals, writers, and criminals—Allen Ginsburg, William Burroughs, Herbert Hunke, Edie Parker, Lucien Carr—who later became known as the "Beats," as in "beat down" or "achieving beatitude." Though briefly married twice and the father of a daughter he never publicly acknowledged, Kerouac continued to travel and write autobiographical books, mostly in "spontaneous prose," or "first thought, best thought," a concept of his own making. His first novel, *The Town and the City*, was published in 1950 to lukewarm reviews, and it would be seven long grueling years and many rejections later before *On the Road* was published, to national acclaim.

Kerouac's story is in the tradition of the search for the Holy Grail or enlightenment. Only, in the end, instead of finding what he sought, he burnt himself out like one of his own characters in *On The Road* "who never yawn or say a commonplace thing. But burn, burn, burn like fabulous yellow roman candles exploding like spiders across the stars and in the middle you see the blue center light pop and everybody goes 'Awww!' "

MY OWN SEARCH for Kerouac began more than twenty years ago after I read Ann Charteris's groundbreaking biography and learned that Kerouac died in St. Pete. I had just broken up with my wife of five years, moved to Sarasota, sixty miles south of St. Pete, and was searching for some kind of identity as a writer. Kerouac was a newfound idol.

I drove to the St. Pete library and looked up his obituary in the *St. Petersburg Times*. It was a short listing among many. "John Kerouac, writer, born Lowell, Massachusetts, March 12, 1922. Died St. Petersburg, Florida, October 21, 1969 . . . " His final address was given and the name of the funeral home where he was embalmed. The brevity of the obituary amazed me. After all, he was one of America's premier writers, a man who had almost single-handedly created the Beat Movement, which led to the social upheavals of the 1960s and beyond. But in 1969 he was a forgotten man.

I scribbled Kerouac's last address and left the library. As it turned out, his house was a '50s-model single-story brick bungalow in a subdivision of similar bungalows. I didn't have the nerve to ring the doorbell and confront his widow. After all, I was only one of many fans of the dead writer's work. So I went in search of the nearest bar, where I felt certain he had put in time. It turned out to be in one of a chain of liquor stores known as ABC Liquors. I ordered a vodka and soda and asked the bartender if she had known a writer named Kerouac. She hadn't. The bar wasn't open at the time of his death.

Then I noticed the funeral home across the street. Sure enough, it was the one mentioned in the obit. I downed my drink and walked over. When I asked the receptionist if she remembered a writer named Kerouac who was embalmed there, her face lit up. Of course, she remembered *Mr.* Kerouac. Before he died, she would see him sitting on a green bench in front of the local A&P grocery store in grease-stained jeans and a ragged t-shirt, chugging from a paper-sacked bottle which, she assumed, held wine. She had figured him for a wino. Imagine her surprise when AP, UPI, and *The New York Times* descended like a flock of vultures at his death. She was still talking when the head mortician came out of a back room. When he heard us discussing Kerouac, his face lit up like a jack-o'-lantern and he brought out a scrapbook of newspaper clippings about Kerouac's death. He even remembered the amount of blood Kerouac had lost as a result of alcoholic hemorrhaging!

Apparently Kerouac was the only semi-famous person ever embalmed there.

FOUR YEARS LATER I was down in Miami working on an article when I ran into a freelance writer named Jack McClintock. McClintock was a reporter for the *St. Petersburg Times* when Kerouac lived there. Later he published a piece in *Esquire* about Kerouac's last days. According to McClintock, Kerouac used to drink at the Boar's Head, a hangout for the University of South Florida crowd. Once, a pompous English professor publicly berated him for the run-on quality of his prose, but he refused to defend himself, drawing solace from the Buddhist dictum that argument is futile in the world of *maya*, or illusion.

A month or so before his death, Kerouac went to a black bar where his drunken philosophizing got him badly beaten. The complacent '40s and '50s were over, and a drunken white man wasn't going to get away with anything during the racially conscious '60s.

During the last months of his life, Kerouac would phone his old friends long-distance late at night. But his drunken, rambling monologues were annoying. Carolyn Cassady—Neal's widow and Kerouac's former lover—pretended that they had a bad connection and hung up on him a week before he died.

McClintock recalled his last meeting with Kerouac. Between sips of straight bourbon, he talked of life and literature. McClintock asked him to name his three favorite American writers, and without hesitation he replied, "Thomas Wolfe, Herman Melville, and me. In *that* order."

Kerouac's estimation illuminates the essence of his writing. Thomas Wolfe was his boyhood idol, and their long-winded, lyrical styles share much in common. Like Kerouac, Melville was a philosophical and religious writer who wrestled with the concept of good versus evil. Finally, like most good writers, Kerouac had enough ego, following years of struggle, to include himself among his idols.

And he should be included . . .

In a letter to Scott Fitzgerald, Thomas Wolfe divided writers into "Putter-inners" and "Taker-outers." Kerouac, like Wolfe and Melville, was a "Putter-inner." "Memory Babe," they nicknamed him as a child. Many people have a photographic memory, but blessed few share Kerouac's ability to take memories, sprinkle liberally with imagination, and create art.

POSTSCRIPT: A dozen or so years after my search for Kerouac, I went to Ybor City, the old Cuban section of Tampa, to read this piece before a gathering of aficionados at an art gallery. It was the twentieth anniversary of his death, and the crowd resembled that of a Beat poetry reading of the '50s and early '60s. I read to a tittering of appreciation. Then a black woman poet skillfully recited a "Kill Whitey" poem in the tradition of Ginsberg's Old Testament–judgment–sounding "Howl." At its conclusion, there was a long moment of stunned silence from the mostly white audience, followed by a thunderous ovation. Later a group of us readers hit the bars in newly restored Ybor City. As it turned out, the black woman wasn't nearly as intimidating as her poem. In fact, she was downright friendly to this Southern white boy. Like the Beats, her work was designed to intimidate the status quo, not the individual.

Tampa's Ybor City is a miniature Key West, with several blocks of turn-of-the-century shops, restaurants, and saloons.

Established in 1933, Haslam's Bookstore at 2025 Central Avenue in St. Petersburg is Florida's largest, with 300,000 new and used books. During the '60s, Kerouac often visited Haslam's. Like many authors, he would move his books to eye-level locations so they could be more easily seen. Recently Haslam's experienced a rash of poltergeist phenomena in which Kerouac's books, among others, were moved to different locations while the store was unoccupied. However, a well publicized exorcism by a local psychic has apparently put to rest Kerouac's uneasy spirit.

Finished in 1928, the Don Cesar on St. Pete beach is a huge pink-and-white-trimmed Moorish palace of a hotel with minarets and cupolas—a pink castle against a pale-blue Florida sky—which has hosted the likes of writers Scott and Zelda Fitzgerald, attorney Clarence Darrow, baseball greats Babe Ruth and Lou Gehrig, and gangster Al Capone.

Part 2
THE OYSTER COAST

The Captain's Table Restaurant at Cedar Key, where the sheepshead were biting on this chilly November day.

The Oyster Coast

Yankeetown . . . Cedar Key . . . Suwannee . . . Horseshoe Beach . . . Steinhatchee . . . Dekle Beach . . . St. Marks . . . Panacea . . . Lanark . . . Carrabelle . . . Eastpoint . . . Apalachicola . . . Cape San Blas . . . Port St. Joe . . . Mexico Beach . . .

The very names recall an earlier era, a quieter, more contemplative time. B.C.—Before Condos and bumper-to-bumper traffic.

Running along a 175-mile arc from Yankeetown in the south to Mexico Beach in the northwest, the Oyster Coast is as different from the rest of coastal Florida as night and day. Mostly beachless, except for a few tiny, white, cypress-root studded inlets like Alligator Point or Carrabelle Beach, and offshore islands like Dog or St. George. Rural. Oyster-blessed. Often resembling New England with weathered clapboard houses and pearl-gray harbors, these sleepy fishing villages have only recently awakened to the modern day.

To tour the Oyster Coast, follow U.S. 19 north of Crystal River to Perry. Then take State Road 98 west across the Panhandle to Mexico Beach.

Whither Goeth Yankeetown

If Key West has become a condensed Greenwich Village, and Cedar Key resembles old-time Key West, whither goeth Yankeetown?

I'm seated at the bar in the Island Hotel at Cedar Key surrounded by peaceniks discussing nuclear power and the latest peace march. An hour before, I was in Richburg's Diner where native conversation centered around the encroachment of blacks and the slaughter of sharks. How did these dissimilar groups come to coexist? I wonder . . . Not to mention the hordes of realtors and fast-buck artists making a selling point of peace and serenity? For an answer, I head south to Yankeetown.

Yankeetown is a pleasant community of rambling wood houses on either side of Riverside Avenue, a broad, oak-lined boulevard running parallel to the Withlacoochee River. Here, as in all the Big Bend area, which extends from just north of New Port Richey to just south of Tallahassee at Alligator Point, there are no sizable beaches. This is due to a shallow bottom that is seldom deeper than six feet and extends miles into the Gulf, allowing for little wave action.

Yankeetown was christened by a disgruntled mail carrier who transported tourists from the train stop at Dunnellon. Whenever anyone asked to be taken to Knotts (it was founded in 1923 by A. F. Knotts, an attorney for U.S. Steel who named the community after himself), the cracker would snort derisively, "You mean Yankeetown, don't ya?" The name stuck.

During the '20s and '30s, "See Yankeetown" signs on sawed-to-a-point boards were as common along north Florida and south Georgia roads as "See Rock City." In the summer of '61, United Artists filmed an Elvis Presley movie here based on Richard Powell's novel, *Follow That Dream*. Presley stayed at nearby Crystal River for two months. Fans came from miles around to see Elvis, and extra traffic-police were brought in by my cousin Jim Turner, the High-Sheriff of Levy County. Jim saw Elvis wrestling with his "double," whom Jim assumed was Elvis's brother, so alike were they. The main set was at the bridge where County Road 40 crosses Bird Creek, a mile from where it dead-ends into the Gulf. County Road 40 from U.S. 19 West has been renamed Follow That Dream Parkway.

The poorer section of town, east of Yankeetown proper, is called "Crackertown" and the local crackers have dubbed the ritzy section of Yankeetown "Beverly Hills." Compared to most parts of Florida, however, sixty years of so-called progress has had little effect on Yankeetown and environs. Knotts avoided the rampant land speculation common to other parts of the state by insisting that, to get a deed, land purchasers build within a year. Other reasons include the prevalence of sand fleas and the absence of a beach. The sand fleas prefer to dine in the cool of early morning and during the serenity of sunset—"Just like us," according to locals. As for the beach, there isn't one. Unless you count a narrow, fifty-foot spit of rock-hard sand and sand spurs at the end of a delightful drive past acres of marshy grasslands. Island-like oak hammocks give way to ever smaller grass islands before melting into the Gulf on Follow That Dream Parkway.

There are, however, compensating factors.

First, there's the fishing, salt and freshwater, on the Gulf and river. Then there is the beauty of an unspoiled semitropical setting and the peace and quiet. Take a walk along Yankeetown's shaded main street any time of the day or night and experience a tranquility denied most twenty-first-century mortals.

But things are changing . . .

THREE MILES EAST of Yankeetown, in Inglis, is a restaurant called December's that stands out amid its surroundings like a pimple on Miss America's nose. On a recent evening, the parking lot of this yuppie eatery was jammed with Mercedeses and Jaguars. Inside, it was wall-to-wall business people and realtors from Crystal River.

Crystal River, a Florida version of Anyplace, USA, with fast-food restaurants and chain motels, is ten miles south of Inglis on U.S. 19. It didn't have a beach either until the county built a manmade one. As for sand fleas, Crystal River can afford to spray for bugs regularly.

Yankeetown, Cedar Key, Crystal River: three stages in the evolution of a Florida village.

Stage one—the locals make a marginal living, farming and fishing, with a sprinkling of tourists coming in (Yankeetown).

Stage two—people longing to get away from it all are attracted by the quaintness of the surroundings. They move in and restore old buildings for business and private use. Tourism increases dramatically (Cedar Key).

Stage three—business people, smelling money, buy up all available land from the locals. Condominiums and chain restaurants go up, and the place becomes Anyplace, USA (Crystal River).

The bottom line is money. Offer a person enough money and he is likely to sell his birthright. The remedy is restrictions on building.

In Yankeetown, people like Wayne and Linda Harrington, owners of the rustic Izaak Walton Lodge, are trying to retain the charm of a village setting and still provide a steady stream of tourist income for themselves and the locals. Founded by Knotts, the eighty-year-old lodge was named after English writer Izaak Walton (1593–1683), author of *The*

Compleat Angler, a classic treatise on the serenity of fishing as opposed to the violence of hunting. The lodge features stained cedar siding, brick chimneys, and white and green window trim. Columns made from fat palm trees support the roof over the broad front porch. Inside, a walnut-paneled gourmet restaurant and bar with a huge fireplace overlooks the slow rolling Withlacoochee River. Otters, manatees, alligators, and an occasional dolphin may be spotted. Upstairs are ten small rooms with shared baths, and out back are two studio apartments.

The Harringtons have owned the lodge for about fifteen years. Before that, it was run by a reclusive fellow who seldom unlocked the front door, much less received guests. In July 1999, the lodge nearly burned to the ground, but the Harringtons are restoring it to its former glory.

"Places like this are getting harder and harder to find," says Linda. "My husband and I used to own a motel in St. Pete until we got to the point where we couldn't take the traffic and congestion. There's inconveniences here, sure. The *no see 'ums* [biting bugs too small to be seen], for one thing. Then there's the lack of an adequate library. But that's more than made up for by the serenity of the setting and the kind of guests we get. People who are fed up with heavy traffic and crowded beaches and want to see the real Florida before it disappears."

But you'd better hurry . . .

On a recent evening at December's, a middle-aged realtor said to his female companion, "So let her split. She'll never find anyone else who's making six figures or better in real estate."

Across the road at the Captain's Pub, a Cracker hangout, a woman said to her husband, "If you was to sell some of that acreage on the Withlacoochee, we could afford us a pool like the one Laverne and them got."

The scent of money is everywhere, and the sharks are beginning to circle.

To get to Yankeetown, follow U.S. 19 north from St. Pete until you reach Inglis on the banks of the Withlacoochee River. Turn left on State Road 40 and head west toward the Gulf of Mexico.

The Island Hotel is the oldest building in Cedar Key, having been a boarding house, dry-goods store, makeshift hospital, saloon, and brothel throughout its history.

Cedar Key

The village of Cedar Key is at the tip end of a long string of desolate keys with cracker names like Stump Cay and Bugger Ridge, 120 miles north of St. Pete. My grandfather was born near here on a summer's day more than a century ago. Even today, it resembles a turn-of-the-century Florida village with white clapboard cottages (many with porches and rockers) and drawling inhabitants, possessors of a quiet dignity unique to the region.

Not that so-called progress hasn't made inroads. There have always been three or four moderately good seafood restaurants running the length of the concrete pier, but two tasteful Key West–style condominiums have sprung up, with a third in the works. Not to mention the old bank building that has been converted into a gourmet restaurant called the Heron, and another, the Blue Desert, on the road into town. There's even talk a large corporation wants to buy the Island Hotel and, heaven forbid, turn it into a museum.

The Island Hotel is the oldest building in Cedar Key. Constructed in 1859, prior to the Civil War, it has served as boarding house, dry-goods store, makeshift hospital (following the Spanish-American War), saloon, brothel, and hotel. Aside from its verandaed second story and a lobby right out of the movie *Key Largo*, it has a popular bar that hosts an eclectic mix of fishermen, college professors from nearby Gainesville, artists, and New Age psychics, with an occasional run-of-the-mill tourist thrown in for leaven. Through the years the hotel has played host to such notables as President Grover Cleveland, Nobel Prize–winning novelist Pearl Buck, singers Frances Langford, Vaughan Monroe, Tennessee Ernie Ford, and Jimmy Buffett, and actors Myrna Loy and Richard Boone. In addition to renting rooms, they run a state-of-the-art gourmet restaurant and referee any arguments in the bar. A beer-stained portrait of an amorous King Neptune, with a decades-old bullet hole between his eyes, hangs behind the long wood bar.

TWENTY YEARS AGO I was seated at the bar when the bartender mentioned that the local historical society had opened a museum. Curious, I walked over. The exhibit was housed in a newly remodeled turn-of-the-century building on Second Street. When I mentioned my grandfather was born here, the woman in charge produced a yellowed photograph of my great-great-grandfather, James S. Turner, one of the area's original settlers. In the photo, taken sometime during the 1870s, he's attired in a black frock coat and high white collar. An unruly white beard accentuates high, Indian cheekbones, but the feature that struck and held my attention was the deep-set, piercing, and rather sad eyes.

Fascinated, I went to the county courthouse at Bronson to pore over the court records yellowing with age, looking for information about Turner. From 1853 to 1865, James S. Turner was involved at least once yearly in a court action. In 1853 he assaulted "one Edmund D. Hogan" in what appears to have been a barroom brawl. In 1863 he was sued for libel by Nicholas S. Cobb, "said language being too profane to herein be recorded." Then this, from 1864:

108

Salt flats at Cedar Key.

Photo by Keith Bollum.

Aforesaid [James S. Turner] not having the fear of God in his eyes on 13th day of June, 1864, a Thursday, with force of arms upon Joseph B. Haskew, James S. Turner with a certain shotgun which he then and there held in his right hand, the said James S. Turner did discharge upon the body of Joseph B. Haskew, said gun being loaded with buckshot. Then and there with gun aforesaid and the buckshot aforesaid did inflict one mortal wound on the body of the said Joseph B. Haskew. Joseph B. Haskew did die in the county, circuit, and state aforesaid.

Signed this 14th day of June
Elias P. Turner
Clerk of the Court

Elias was Turner's brother. Figuring Haskew's death was the result of another barroom brawl, I put aside the records and returned to the Island Hotel for a drink. A local named John was pumping the bartender for information about a rumor the hotel was to be turned into a museum. When the bartender pleaded ignorance, John insisted he and his buddies would burn the place down rather than allow it to suffer such an indignity at the hands of Yankee interlopers!

LATER THAT EVENING I drove across town to the local "knife and gun" club, the Sundance, and ordered a beer in the rough, wood-boothed and jukebox-lit interior. I'd been drinking for fifteen minutes when a per-oxide blonde rushed in and grabbed the arm of a deeply tanned and aging commercial fisherman sitting next to me at the bar. She screamed, "You been out fishing for over a month and don't even bother to come home for supper your first night home!"

The fisherman shook loose her hand and returned to his beer.

Again the woman screamed, "And don't you be leaving this here bar with no damn sluts neither!"

This was highly unlikely since the only other woman in the joint was the barmaid who, as it turned out, was his daughter.

Said barmaid jumped into the fracas, screaming, "Don't hit her, Daddy!"

Which Daddy did, anyway, a quick jab to the side of the head. The woman scarcely felt it, so intent was she on telling him in no uncertain terms not to dare return to the trailer that night—which I'm sure he had no intention of doing, anyway.

When the disturbance adjourned to the outside, the barmaid-daughter rushed to the phone and dialed the law, enunciating "Domestic disturbance" into the mouthpiece as if it were the commonest expression in the world, next to "hello" or "goodbye." Slamming down the receiver, she rushed over to the screen door and peered out into the dark, screaming, "I knew it. Mama done brung along the .45! Watch the bar a minute, would ya, Jed?"

So Jed, who had been sitting quietly in the corner, moved over behind the counter while the barmaid stepped outside to referee the fight.

Just then the police arrived. They confiscated the gun and sent the woman home, and the fisherman came back in to finish his beer.

On leaving, I got my car tires stuck in the sand while attempting to back out of the drive. I went back in and asked a booth of "good ole boys" for assistance in getting it out. "Sure thing, Narc," said the largest of the three. Like most isolated stretches of Florida coastline, the area around Cedar Key was a prime unloading spot for boats carrying dope. Since I wasn't a regular and had been sitting alone in the joint for more than an hour observing, I must therefore be a narc. His logic was undeniable.

Eventually the three of them left the bar and freed my car by rocking it from side to side while I mashed down on the gas. The big one led the way in his pickup back to the main road. The last I saw of him, he was fishtailing the truck about in a 180-degree turn to head back to the club.

THE NEXT MORNING I returned to the courthouse at Bronson where I continued to delve into the history of Turner. In 1847 Turner, a farm boy from Tifton, Georgia (according to rumor, he killed a man in an argument over a woman), arrived in Cedar Key with a wagon load of calico for sale. Cedar Key was a village of less than a hundred people from Georgia and the Carolinas, many of them fugitives from the law.

Over the next fifteen years, Turner carved out an empire that, by the start of the Civil War, included some of the choicest cotton land in the state, along with 140 slaves and more than 1,000 head of cattle. He early recognized the economic advantage of Sea Island cotton, a long-staple cotton grown only in Florida and along the south Georgia coast. Sea Island cotton was selling for four or five times the price of short-staple cotton grown elsewhere. The demand for Sea Island cotton created a demand for slaves, which Turner bought from Zephaniah Kingsley, a well-known slave trader with a plantation on Ft. George Island at the mouth of the St. Johns River.

On January 15, 1862, the *Hatteras*, a Federal gunboat, sailed into Cedar Key harbor. Just offshore on Seahorse Key, a Reb contingent had been formed to maintain navigational markings and a lighthouse. They would travel to Cedar Key in skiffs powered by poles and *sweeps* (paddles). When they saw the gunboat approaching, they panicked and ran for the skiffs. In their haste they left behind the sweeps. Poling toward shore through the shallow oyster beds, they eluded capture for a time. But once they reached deep water the poles were useless. A strong tide swept their skiffs back in the direction of the *Hatteras*, where the entire group was captured without a shot being fired.

The next Turner entry in the courthouse records dealt with his killing Haskew. Then, according to an 1865 entry, he was involved in a business dispute with Nicholas S. Cobb, a former colonel in the Confederate army, over the ownership of a cow. Turner had killed Haskew in 1864. How could Turner kill him and be free a year later? It was a question that needed answering.

I recalled an elderly relative, second cousin to my grandfather, who lived in the area and whose name was, fittingly, Jim Turner. He was born and bred at Otter Creek, within twenty miles of Cedar Key. Judging by his name, he must have been christened after my great-great-grandfather. I called Jim and arranged a meeting that afternoon.

Jim lived at Fowler's Bluff, a tiny community bordering the Suwannee River. When I arrived around one o'clock, he met me at the side door in heelless brown slippers and led me to a screened-in back porch. We took seats in cane-backed rockers overlooking the muddy river. After the customary courtesies, I asked Jim if he knew anything about James Turner.

"You mean *Uncle* Jim," said Jim with a soft Southern drawl. "Uncle Jim was my daddy's uncle. His father and James Turner were brothers."

"Ever hear of anyone named Joseph B. Haskew?"

"Haskew?" repeated Jim, looking puzzled.

"James Turner shot and killed Haskew in June of 1864."

"That must have been the Union lieutenant who tried to confiscate Uncle Jim's heifer."

Finally I was getting somewhere. "Haskew was a Union lieutenant?"

"That's right. It was during the time when Cedar Key was being occupied by the Federals. He was in charge of requisitioning supplies for the troops. Uncle Jim told him he could have one of the steers, but not to take a heifer. A heifer was for milk. The lieutenant took a heifer, and Uncle Jim kilt him."

"What did they do with Turner after he shot Haskew?"

"Sent him to Federal prison at Savannah," said Jim, warming to his story. "He was incarcerated for over a year in a dungeon before the truce was called. Then they turned him loose, along with the rest of the political prisoners."

"But Turner never joined the Reb forces, did he?"

"No, sir. But he killed a Yank. That made him political in them days."

I thanked Jim for the information and he led me back to the door.

"Would you like to see where he's buried?" he asked as an afterthought.

"I sure would."

"Come back tomorrow, and I'll take you."

That evening, back at the motel, I had a strange dream. I'm young James Turner arriving at Cedar Key for the first time. I step off my calico-loaded wagon, and there it is, the Gulf. Stretching silent and implacable clear to the horizon. I gaze amazed at the watery immensity of it, while behind me stirs the tiny frontier village, so similar to the one I left behind in Georgia. Suddenly a clawlike hand grasps my shoulder. "What's'a matter, boy?" asks Nicholas S. Cobb in a harsh, nasal drawl, "Ain't never see'd water afore?"

EATING BREAKFAST at Richburg's the next morning, I study the people seated around me. These are fisherfolk, a throwback to the America of more than a century ago. They abide by their own schedules, live their own lives. Often it's not a pleasant life. The sun blinds; the lines twist and distort. One of the men seated at the table next to mine is blind in one eye. His bad eye resembles a cold hard marble with a pinprick in its center through which the sight has escaped. Still and all, these are some of the only free people left. They don't often take to outsiders. Outsiders throw up condos and spoil the waters for fishing. The people around these parts are strong believers in government, especially the military, provided it leaves them be. Leaves them to their boats, their babies, and their occasional forays into violence. Leaves them to be their own men. Dependent on no thing and no one. And if death comes early or violently, so be it. Each man must die, but it's the nature of his living that matters.

WHEN I ARRIVED at Jim's place, he got in the car and we drove twenty miles inland to just east of Chiefland, where the county seat of Levyville had stood. We got out and walked along a narrow dirt path until we reached a sagging metal fence that circled a graveyard. Jim produced the key to the rust-encrusted lock and swung open the gate.

Turner's grave was in between those of his two wives. The tombstone read: *Born August 7, 1818, Died August 17, 1904.* And beneath that the inscription: *Here Rests the Husk of a Man Gone to Glory.*

Curious, I examined some of the surrounding tombstones. Directly below Turner's was that of Joseph B. Haskew. *Born April 7, 1843, Died June 13, 1864. A Wayfarer There Was . . .*

I rubbed my eyes in disbelief. What possessed Turner to have himself buried above the man he murdered forty years earlier? Was it strictly coincidence that Haskew was buried at his feet? I pointed out Haskew's tombstone to Jim.

"Well, I'll be damned!"

After I dropped Jim home, I was driving back to Cedar Key when a scene flashed through my mind.

I'm James Turner standing in the pasture when Haskew demands I turn over the heifer.

"Nah, Suh," says I evenly. "Take one of the steers if you must, but ye'll not be taking ary heifer."

"James Turner," says Haskew. "I command you in the name of the United States government to turn over the heifer."

I bend down to pluck a blade of grass. "Take a steer." I place the blade between my teeth and chew slowly and evenly. "Steer's good eating."

"Nonetheless, I must . . . "

"Touch the heifer and ye're a dead man," says I in the manner of one acknowledging a given. My right hand caresses the barrel of the shotgun resting against my thigh.

"Private Reynolds, step forward," commands Haskew.

Reynolds extracts himself from the crowd of Union soldiers milling about the pasture and trots over with a rope in his hand. "Yes, Sir," he says, drawing up in front of Haskew and giving him a salute.

"Round up one of Mr. Turner's heifers and fetch her back to camp with us."

At that instant, I realize Haskew is a dead man. As Reynolds walks toward the heifer, I raise my gun and point it at Haskew. Damn him to hell, anyway, I think, as the mouth of the gun flashes once in the harsh sunlight and Haskew drops dead at my feet.

Absorbed in reflection, I came to, only to discover I was lost. I followed the road ten miles out until it dead-ended in a cow pasture. My tires were coated with the ghosts of cow turds, while my mind was beclouded with the ghosts of Turner and Haskew. Suddenly I experienced an epiphany. Perhaps the road had led me to a destination after all. A sacred place to which only the elect are permitted access.

POSTSCRIPT: I recently visited Cedar Key, and the development I saw coming twenty years ago has arrived. There are three condominium complexes on the bayfront, and a seventy-two-unit condo, with marina and clubhouse, in the planning stages. Not to mention a couple more gourmet restaurants. A recent article on Cedar Key in the travel section of the Sunday *New York Times* proves the place's newfound popularity. On a cold bleak January weekend, I had trouble finding a room, since all but one of the motels and condos were booked solid.

The Island Hotel is no longer the rough-and-tumble establishment it used to be. Under the ownership of three succeeding owners, it has become a haven for New Age thought. The rough-hewn bar has been replaced by a tiny, unobtrusive counter to one side of an open, airy room, and the metal bar stools have been replaced by comfortable stretch-cloth chairs. For a time the restaurant served strictly vegetarian dishes, and the tags on the cars parked alongside the hotel are almost as likely to read California or New Mexico as Florida or Georgia.

Then there's Cap'n Mac, a globetrotting wholesale seafood salesman from Tampa who spends weekends at his house on Cedar Key, where he fishes for the evil-eyed tarpon. The first time I met Cap'n Mac was at the Island Hotel bar, where he was spinning elaborate fish yarns to a wide-eyed audience. Thrusting forth a meaty paw, he introduced himself as "world-famous Cap'n Mac." In days following, we drank and fished—to no avail; I'm a Jonah where catching fish is concerned—and became bosom buddies. Cap'n Mac is a delightful character with a roving eye for *womens*, as Papa Hemingway called them. As Cap'n Mac puts it, "Any girl who goes fishing with me is guaranteed to come back with a red snapper."

Times have changed indeed.

To reach Cedar Key, take U.S. 19 north from St. Pete past Inglis and Gulf Hammock. Turn left on State Road 24 at Otter Creek and follow it twenty-four miles across a string of islets and pearl-gray water, until it dead-ends at the Gulf.

Steinhatchee

The name Steinhatchee (*Stein* rhymes with *bean*) means "dead man's river" in Creek Indian language, and it was the magical sound of the name itself that first drew me there. That and the fact it's as far removed from Miami and the Gold Coast as one can get and still be in Florida. Steinhatchee is, after all, in the middle of nowhere. The closest real town is Cross City, some twenty-five miles to the east, and even that isn't much of a town.

Imagine my surprise when I looked out the window of a three-room motel and saw the most beautiful girl I ever laid eyes on. She was pinning laundry on a clothesline, and the sensuous sway of her waist-length blonde hair and her long, languorous movements were something to behold.

"Come look at this!" I marveled to my buddy, who was stretched out on one of the twin beds.

"I meant to tell you earlier," he said, rolling over on his side and grinning broadly. "She's our maid."

Nancy, the maid, was driving a new model Mercedes with a Palm

Beach license tag. A long line of fashionable outfits was strung on a metal rod in back. To make a long story short, Nancy and I wound up living together in Sarasota. Yet she remained as much a mystery to me as the morning I first saw her. She claimed to have been a model in south Florida. Tiring of the fast-paced lifestyle, she opted for Steinhatchee as a place to cool out. Whether her story was true, I never found out. She was all but penniless when I met her and she was living with the proprietor of the motel, a fishing guide named Bill who, she claimed, was a platonic friend. Like some damsel in distress in a John D. MacDonald novel, her past was as mysterious as her future.

One morning, following an argument, I awoke to find her gone. I went back to Steinhatchee to search for her.

STEINHATCHEE CONSISTS of a long line of bait shops and marinas lining the muddy banks of the tannic-stained Steinhatchee River, with its cypress and pine-studded shoreline. Shrimpers and "bird-dogs"—flat-bottomed, extra wide skiffs with the engine and steering wheel in the center for easy maneuverability in shallow water—crowd the rickety wooden docks, with here and there a forlorn-looking pleasure cruiser, a rich boy amid poor country cousins. Cooey's, a famous seafood restaurant, sits on cypress pilings over the river. Behind it are several recently constructed cottages, called condominiums here.

A haven for loners, Steinhatchee is a natural habitat for persons with no discernible past. Gray-bearded hermits nest in abandoned shacks without running water or electricity and occasionally drop into town for supplies. Then there's Nancy's friend, Bill. Fifteen years earlier he left the industrial Northeast to become a fishing guide and hasn't been north of the state line since. Bill was out on the Gulf fishing when I arrived. So I quizzed Bud and Bett Hanks, the owner-operators of a tackle shop/saloon, as to Nancy's whereabouts.

Bud is a former professional wrestler who was raised here and recalls a time when you could toss a stone from one end of town to the other. Now it would take at least half a dozen tosses. Bett, his wife, serves as ministering angel to any passerby in need of a home-cooked meal and a warm place to sleep. Their place of business is a wooden shack next to a muddy creek that empties into the river. The inside resembles a Depression-era general store, with a pot-bellied wood-burning stove and posters of hunting scenes and scantily clad women on the walls.

I ordered a beer and Bud told me everything I wanted to know—and more besides, as Jim Turner would say—about Steinhatchee, occasionally turning to Bett for verification of a worrisome point.

When I eased the conversation around to Nancy, he nodded his head knowingly. "Palm Beach lady . . . Her and Bill are some kind of kin."

"What kind of kin?"

Bud's face went deadpan. "Just kin . . . "

"Know where I can find her?"

Bud regarded me suspiciously. "Can't say. Up and left with some stranger, I heared."

I'd come up against a brick wall.

NANCY FREQUENTED a seafood restaurant at the end of a rickety wooden pier at Dekle Beach (the restaurant has since been demolished by hurricane Andrew). It's thirty miles by river from Steinhatchee, a meandering course that leads to an especially shallow stretch of Gulf. By road, it's twenty miles through piney wilderness, punctuated by sawgrass-filled swamp and palmetto-studded hammocks. Occasionally an abandoned shack with a tin roof the color of dried blood materializes out of nowhere, a phantom in high grass.

Dekle Beach consists of several dilapidated shacks, a filling station, a beer joint with two threadbare, lopsided pool tables and a cigarette butt–littered concrete floor, and the restaurant. The tide was so low it was a half-mile walk across knee-deep mud flats to the Gulf. A narrow manmade canal had been dredged through the mud, and a couple of determined fishermen in knee-high rubber boots were dragging a wooden skiff to open water. The restaurant was closed for remodeling, a Florida euphemism for going out of business, and no one in the bar had seen or heard of any beautiful blonde. Or maybe they weren't talking.

"Where're you from?" asked the teenaged and pregnant girlfriend of a pool player.

"Sarasota."

I might as well have said Singapore, to judge by the uncomprehending look on her face.

In desperation, I asked three elderly crackers seated on a faded green wood bench next to the gas station if they'd seen a blonde in a new-model Mercedes.

There was no immediate reply, as the three pondered the possible ramifications of my question. Finally the one in the center volunteered, "Girl like that's liable to wind up in Perry [a moderate-sized town to the northeast]. A fella can get rude, screwed, and tattooed in Perry!"

I never found Nancy. Perhaps she moved back to south Florida to resume modeling. Or maybe she's fishing the Gulf with her kinsman, Bill.

To get to Steinhatchee and Dekle Beach, follow U.S. 19 north from St. Pete to Cross City. Continue ten miles north and turn west on State Road 358.

In recent years, Steinhatchee has become less isolated. It now sports the luxurious Steinhatchee Landing Resort—marina, canoes, bicycles, tennis courts, heated pool, gourmet restaurant, and Victorian, Georgian, and cracker-style villas with screened-in front porches. Former President Jimmy Carter often vacations here with his family.

Panacea

Panacea: A healing . . . A haven . . . A refuge . . . "Far from the madding crowd" . . .

Founded in the late 1800s, where the Ochlockonee River flows into an arm of Apalachee Bay, this Big Bend community was named for its healing sulfur springs, well known to the Indians and early settlers. Completion of a railroad from Tallahassee to Carrabelle in 1893 brought Panacea within a pleasant stagecoach journey. A resort hotel, opened in 1898, remained popular up to the 1920s. Today, Panacea is to crabs what Apalachicola is to oysters.

St. Marks and Panacea mark the eastern boundary of what writer/marine biologist Jack Rudloe calls the Wilderness Coast. In his book of the same name, he writes:

> Save for occasional storms, the waters along the shelf are placid, not like the north Atlantic or Pacific, where the deep ocean slips into the depths a little way offshore. Here the submerged shelf drops off at the rate of

only one foot per mile. Fifty fathoms is at least seventy miles from most . . . shores . . .

The area, with its endless submarine sea grass meadows and sand flats, is . . . one of Florida's best-kept secrets. Spotted sea-trout, redfish, drum, and bluefish concentrate in . . . mud holes and creeks. Sometimes acres of mullet move along the shallows in two feet of water, throwing a wake, and commercial fishermen . . . [haul] them in. Meanwhile sports fishermen in small boats cast four-pound test lines around oyster bars and are often rewarded with a big catch of redfish.

Towns like Panacea were founded by farmers of the poor sandy soil of west Florida, who augmented their meager diets and income by fishing. To again quote Rudloe:

In the late 1800s, fishermen stayed in primitive camps, usually just a shack where a few men had a fire to keep from being devoured by . . . clouds of mosquitoes . . . and yellow flies . . . They stayed in isolation for weeks, waiting for the fish to run. There were no highways, only rutted sand roads that went down to the coast. And though some [fish] . . . were sold fresh, most were salted in wooden barrels and shipped by mule-drawn wagon or railroad.

The outboard motor and the automotive age changed everything. Rural counties along the boundless west Florida swamps and coastline started putting in roads . . . access became easier, and the fishermen no longer had to live in total isolation . . . Truckers and fish peddlers, who carried the catch back over dirt roads to Georgia and Alabama, eagerly awaited the fish . . .

[T]he salted fish were loaded into boats and hauled to Cedar Key, Apalachicola, Carrabelle, and other fishing villages [with] a railroad spur, and their catches were shipped north by rail.

Things are not so different today. When hunting season arrives, the men and many of the women retire to hunting camps. And fishing is a full-time occupation. Crabbers plant traps, with narrow openings suitable for entering, but not leaving, in the grassy shallows and jealously guard their

124

territory from encroachment by other crabbers' and shrimpers' dragnets.

Livelihood depends on the season's moods, and people become a part of their environment—fierce, moody, and violent, or by turns warm and passive—to an extent unknown to their landlocked brethren. Depending on the weather, one spends one's days at sea, at dock mending nets and traps, at country cafes drinking bottomless cups of coffee, smoking endless cigarettes (the surgeon general's message has not penetrated the consciousness here), and shooting the breeze, or in the *jooks*, drinking up one's pay and fighting. Like the life of a wild creature, it would be a monotonous existence to one versed in the ways of the intellect and the city. But for one who seeks communion with the elements, it's a life like no other.

To reach Panacea, follow Highway 98 west at Perry and drive sixty miles.

Rudloe's Gulf Specimen Marine Laboratory, at 300 Clark Drive, supplies live marine fish and invertebrates to universities and colleges in the U.S., Canada, and Europe. To quote from its brochure: "At Gulf Marine Laboratory, you get a better sense of the enormous diversity of life on earth. Unlike most large public aquaria that emphasize porpoises and big fishes, we focus on sea horses, hermit crabs, emerald-eyed spiny box fish, red and white spotted calico crabs—all endless living treasures of the North Florida Wilderness Coast."

Florida shrimpers at dock.

Photo by Debra Force.

Carrabelle

The drive west on U.S. 98 from Panacea, over the long curving concrete bridge that crosses Ochlockonee Bay to Alligator Point, and thence to Lanark and Carrabelle, is like entering a time warp. No crowds, few signs, no pollution . . . A practically deserted two-lane road skirts the Gulf, offering up enchanting vistas of blue-green water. And the only sound is the wind sighing through the Spanish moss–draped live oaks and pines that line both sides of the road.

Carrabelle, with its drying fish nets and rusty trawlers glimmering in the late afternoon sun, is a quiet fishing village twenty miles east of Apalachicola. Here the Carrabelle River empties into St. George Sound and the Gulf of Mexico. Quaint, rustic, slow-moving . . . It's a place where all the small-town clichés apply. Natives meet in the mornings at the post office to pick up mail and chat. The men mostly fish. During hunting season the town practically folds up, as everyone heads into the woods to track game.

It's that kind of town . . .

CARRABELLE, OR RIO CARRABELLE, dates back to the late 1700s when it was a Spanish fur trading post. In 1766 a French vessel named *Le Tigre* wrecked on a reef off Dog Island, 7.5 miles long and 1.5 miles wide, three miles off the coast. Fifteen survivors made it ashore, where Native Americans were living. Three survived; the others died from drowning, illness, or cannibalism. One of the survivors related the tale in a notorious book that was fraught with untoward sexual activity and shocked Europe. *The Shipwreck and Adventures of Monsieur Pierre Viaud* is a recent account of their adventures.

In the late 1800s, Carrabelle became a seaport where virgin pine, juniper, and cypress were shipped out on sailing schooners headed for Europe and South America. The ships would anchor off Dog Island, and the timber would be floated out on barges.

The Great Hurricane of 1898 wiped out most of the town, but it was soon rebuilt. Much worse was the effect of the Great Depression. Carrabelle, like much of the nation, fell on hard times. Since most of the lumber had been cut away, locals smuggled contraband liquor from Caribbean ports and stashed it in the woods. Turpentiners, adept at the art of distilling, manufactured moonshine.

When World War II broke out, Camp Gordon Johnston was established at Carrabelle and points east, including the village of Lanark (today retirees inhabit houses that once served as officers' quarters). The camp held three divisions of troops, more than 60,000 men. There was also a prisoner-of-war camp.

The beach on Dog Island was used as a facsimile of a tropical Pacific island, and troops were off-loaded for "practice" military maneuvers. According to Carrabelle historian Leo Hance, "In the fall of '43, several landing craft filled with troops embarked from Lanark just before daylight in a driving squall. The landing craft struck a sandbar between Lanark and Dog Island, and the officers in charge—thinking they were on the beach— ordered the men ashore. Over 250 soldiers were drowned when they leaped, with full packs, into the treacherous waters. For days afterwards, floating bodies were recovered from points as far east and west as Alligator Point and Port St. Joe. But the incident was hushed up by the authorities."

Following the war, Carrabelle turned to the sea, with its harvests of shrimp, crabs, mullet, red snapper, scallops, redfish, and oysters, to eke out a precarious living. Today commercial and charter fishing are the major industries.

LIFE IS A SERIES of good-byes. Fortunately it's also a series of hellos. Consider scallops, for instance. A migratory species and a trademark for Shell Oil, they appear off Carrabelle every five or so years. News of the bonanza brings as many as fifty boats, a few with their own processors aboard, from all around the Southeastern coast. For days, sometimes weeks, the seafood houses process the catch. Then the scallops vanish as mysteriously as they appeared.

One evening I was drinking beer in a local joint when I ran across some literary scallop fishermen from Melbourne, Florida. It was a welcome change from the usual Carrabelle conversation, which consists of fishing, fighting, hunting, and beating the old lady. It's funny how things happen. You meet a stranger, and suddenly you *connect!* In no time at all, I was conversing with new friends about mutual writer acquaintances—John Hersey, Bill Manville, David Wolkowski, Peter Taylor, Nancy Friday, John Ciardi—whom I met in Key West twenty years before. There is a heightened reality about such meetings. Things don't happen by accident.

Naturally enough, we discussed the local women. In Carrabelle, one encounters the type of women described by Ernest Lyons, editor for the *Stuart News*, in his short story "A Blade of Grass":

> Women who bloom like moonflowers that fade overnight . . .
> [T]hey have hope at the start . . . life will be something better than
> a palm-thatch roof, a canvas fly, maybe a strip of old metal for

one wall [substitute rusted trailer and broken-down shack]; that their men will settle down instead of spending in the juke joints everything they make.

In Carrabelle, which was pioneered by four families, as in many small cracker towns, the genetic mix is not of the highest order. It shows in the often dull-eyed, slack-jawed descendants of the founding fathers. It's a town where new blood is desperately needed, but the natives' fear and mistrust of strangers is dictated by generations of hillbilly inbreeding. It's a town that recalls a time when people seldom traveled outside a fifteen mile radius of home.

Carrabelle is the home of the *reverse-yuppie*. In Carrabelle, one eats fried, greasy food and plenty of dead animals, not health food. Fire-and-brimstone fundamentalism, not New Age, is the religion of choice. One never jogs, seldom exercises (unless absolutely necessary), smokes incessantly, and drinks countless cups of coffee, while discussing the endless hard times and medical dilemmas of friends and family. One hastily downs cheap draft beer and rotgut whiskey, not premium wine. Atrocious grammar, bad taste in decoration and clothing—racist signs, plastic gimcracks, truckers' caps, torn dirt-streaked work clothes, white rubber boots, and dirty bare feet—are the accepted norm. Teenage and preteen pregnancy is a given, as is the ubiquitous sight of a pubescent mother, infant in arm, cigarette in mouth, dangling ashes on same. And political incorrectness—racism, ignorance, intolerance of any lifestyle save one's own—goes without saying.

Patricia Richardson, costar of the popular TV series *Home Improvement*, made the movie *Ulee's Gold* with Peter Fonda in Carrabelle. When she appeared on the *Rosie O'Donnell Show*, she let it be known that Carrabelle was the end of the earth. There were no locals with whom to share an intelligent conversation, and the nearest gourmet deli was seventy miles north in Tallahassee. (Still, it's nice to know some people in the world are still *enjoying* themselves!)

The literary scallopers and I ended our conversation with a joke: "What does a Carrabelle girl say the first time she has sex? 'Get up off me, Daddy. You're squashing my cigarettes!' "

WHEN THE SCALLOPERS left, I listened as the shrimpers next to me berated "niggers." It's a funny thing about racism. Its roots are often lost in the vagaries of time. These shrimpers had no logical reason for their prejudice. They had little or no social contact with blacks, much less ever been wronged by one. Generation on generation had fed one another a lie with no foundation. Hard times fostered a scapegoat, someone to look down on, someone whose skin color was different. The word "nigger" is spit rather than spoken, as if to rid the mouth of something unclean. In denying someone else's humanity, we deny our own.

As I listened to the shrimpers, I realized fear and prejudice weren't something willed, but the result of a form of mass hypnotism broadcast by the narrow world surrounding them. Hypnotism with a will of its own. Suddenly it was sad but understandable. I thought back to the many times I'd heard "nigger" flung into the void. Each time it boomeranged back on the sender, so it was he, not the target, who was diminished. You saw it in the flash of his eyes, the microsecond of fear and self-loathing that prompted the explosion. Racism is the crutch of a frightened man, a man incapable of dealing with reality. So he creates a bogeyman to bear the brunt of the world's ills. He's like a child blaming his own misdeed on some absent companion. The respite is temporary. He's found out in the end, made to suffer for his cowardly behavior. The world is to be enjoyed, not feared. But when we give in to our fears, they become our reality.

I walked out into the clear, frosty night. I got in my car and rolled down the window. I breathed in the pungent salt air and punched a Jimmy Buffett tape into my car stereo. To the accompaniment of my fingers drumming the wheel, I sang along:

Mother, Mother Ocean
I have heard your call
Wanted to sail upon your waters
Since I was three feet tall
You've seen it all; you've seen it all.

To get to Carrabelle, follow Highway 98 thirty miles southwest past Panacea. To one side of 98, in the heart of Carrabelle, is the "world's smallest police station." State and local law officers go there for news of any wrongdoing.

The restaurant Eula Mae's, across the bridge on 98, serves the kind of cracker cuisine written up in *The New York Times*. Its plastic-boothed and formica-tabled interior provides a scenic view of sea-grassy Florida wetlands.

Dog Island, accessible by boat or daily ferry, is a refuge for those who truly want to get away from it all. There are a hundred homes, along with dozens of salt-rusted cars left at the dock for transportation, but only twenty full-time residents. The only accommodation is the eight-room Pelican Inn. No phone. No television. But there's first-class bird-watching and shelling, and it's a surf-casters' paradise.

Harry's Bar

It's 7 A.M. on a Friday, and Jerry Adams, the owner/proprietor, is opening Harry's Bar for the 3,050th consecutive day in a row—not excluding holidays. The shrimpers have been hauling nets all night and seven is their happy hour. Then there's the occasional drunk, desperate for his sunrise alcohol fix. Jerry was a commercial airline pilot for twenty years, but now he's philosopher-in-residence at the town of Carrabelle, in the county of Franklin, in the state of Florida, in the country of America, in the world of the world, in the universe of the universe, in the Kingdom of God.

Aside from the winos who buy bottles to go, the first *real* customer to arrive is Sam, a retired marine sergeant with a thirst for early morning gin-and-tonics. Sam is as mad as a boil on the posterior of a junkyard dog because he bought a used camera in a pawnshop the day before and can't get it to work. Though he only paid seven dollars, he has used up twenty dollars worth of film in a vain attempt to produce a photo. Naturally enough, he doesn't get any sympathy from Jerry, who calls him several kinds of fool for buying the thing in the first place, when for a little more money he could have bought one that worked.

The camera debate has been going on for half an hour, with neither side asking or giving quarter, when two weary shrimpers enter and begin slamming down Natural Lights on special at a dollar apiece. It isn't long before they're engaged in a fierce argument—about hunting, fishing, trucks, and wayward women—that threatens violence. Jerry points at a wooden sign behind the bar: "The 'F' word will not be tolerated." The storm subsides for a time, but soon is raging again as fiercely as ever.

"I'm afraid you'll have to take it outside, boys," says Jerry in a diplomatic tone of voice. "You can take your beer with you if you like."

"We're sorry, Mr. Jerry," says Jethro, the larger of the two. "Can't we stay for one more beer?"

Jerry shakes his head no. "Head on down the road to Wet Willie's. They'll serve you there. No problem."

Jethro nods. "Whatever you say, Mr. Jerry. You're not mad at us, are you?"

Jerry swabs dry the bar where their beers were. "No, son, I'm not mad. Come back when you can behave yourselves."

The shrimpers depart, heads down, like corrected children.

Around noon, a Ma and Pa tourist couple enter and sit at the bar. "What'll you have?" asks Jerry.

The man orders a rum and coke, but the woman is uncertain.

"What kind of wine do you have?"

Clicking into auto-pilot, Jerry rattles off a dozen or so wines. When he's done, the lady is still uncertain. Finally she says, "A diet coke will be fine."

When Jerry returns with their drinks, the man says, "Well, Harry, we've seen the world's smallest police station. What else is there to do in Carrabelle?"

"Name's Jerry. And you can sit here and drink, or else go fishing."

The woman objects. "But the name of the bar is 'Harry's'!"

Jerry nods. "Name of the bar is 'Harry's.' My name is Jerry. Would you walk in a Wal-Mart and ask for Mr. Mart?"

"Go fishing, huh?" says the man. "What kind of fish do they catch around here?"

Once again Jerry clicks into auto-pilot and rattles off a dozen or so fish. The man nods disinterestedly. "I'm a freshwater fisherman myself. Not much salt water up in Indiana."

It's going to be one of those days, thinks Jerry.

As if to verify this, eighty-five-year-old Hook Talley enters, led by his baby boy, sixty-five-year-old Mr. Jimmy. Hook is the former High Kleagle of the Ku Klux Klan in Franklin County. He's nearly deaf and blind from cataracts, but refuses to have them removed for fear a vengeful black may be involved in the operation. So Jimmy serves as his guide and caretaker. Before they're seated, Jerry has two Natural Lights on the counter before them.

"That you, Jerry?" demands Hook, cupping his ear. Then, when Jerry doesn't answer immediately, "Is that Jerry, son?"

Mr. Jimmy leans over to shout in his ear, "Yessir. It's Mr. Jerry."

Hook sniffs the air suspiciously. "You're not smoking, are you, Jerry? That smoking will kill you!"

Jerry blows a puff of smoke at Hook and returns his attention to the Ma and Pa couple from Indiana.

Hook turns furiously to Mr. Jimmy. "Where's Jerry? Where'd Jerry go?"

"He moved on down the bar, Daddy."

A huge black woman enters with a paper bag. Inside are rolls of pennies totaling twenty dollars, with which she intends to buy a quart of Gilbey's Gin. She has no sooner opened her mouth than Hook screams.

"Is that a nigger I smell in here?!"

The black woman shakes her head resignedly and turns to Jerry, who has returned with her quart. "I sho' do feel sorry for you, Mr. Jerry. Having to put up with that old scoundrel all day long!"

Jerry nods. "Somebody's got to do it. Keeps him off the streets, I reckon."

"Whatever you says, Mr. Jerry." She departs with her quart.

JERRY PICKS UP the TV remote and switches on the set opposite the bar. There's a basketball game on.

"Just look at those black boys jump and run!" exclaims Jerry in a voice loud enough to be heard by Hook. "They're sure earning their thirty or forty million today!"

Hook is about to object when Mr. Know-It-All enters. Mr. Know-It-All, as he has been dubbed by the locals, hails from Wisconsin and claims to know a thing or two about any subject. Jerry has a Natural Light and a shot of Four Roses bourbon on the bar before he can sit down.

"What's that about thirty or forty million?" he demands, chugging the shot and chasing it with beer.

"We were talking about basketball players' salaries," explains Jerry.

Mr. Know-It-All delivers a dissertation on NBA salaries that covers everything from the highest-ranked players to the janitors who clean up after the games. When he's done, the others in the bar are nodding sleepily.

Typical Southerners with their brains on hold, thinks Mr. Know-It-All.

He turns to Jerry. "Another shot."

"Another shot, *please*," corrects Jerry.

Mr. Know-It-All smirks, but says nothing. Jerry moves on down the bar.

Damn stubborn rebs, thinks Mr. Know-It-All. But I can be just as stubborn as they are. Without so much as a word, he gets up and leaves. The bar heaves a collective sigh of relief.

The next to enter is Graham. Graham is fiftyish, a former member of the New York Stock Exchange who threw it all up a couple of years ago to move down to Carrabelle and go native.

There's a Natural Light waiting for him on the bar.

"Afternoon, Graham."

"Afternoon, Jerry."

"How's life on the other side of the bridge?"

"Same-old same-old." Then, following a brief pause, "What do you think about Early Cunningham's lot on the river?"

"How much is he asking?"

"Twelve-five."

"Sounds reasonable enough. But . . . "

"But what?"

"Those rock trucks are rolling by there on a daily basis now. That certainly isn't going to help the value any."

Graham nods grimly. "I know."

He lights a cigarette and mulls over the matter. He is still mulling when Rip enters. Rip is a tall, skinny stringbean of a man, a refugee from the Woodstock generation with a long white Mandarin beard and long silver hair in a ponytail. He's in town doing some work on a friend's house.

"Rum gimlet or a Miller?" asks Jerry.

Rip strokes his beard thoughtfully. "Rum gimlet." Then, following a brief pause, "Know where I can find some cheap two-by-sixes?"

"Tallahassee."

"No place close?"

Jerry delivers the gimlet. "No sir."

That out of the way, they discuss piloting and war. Rip is a Vietnam vet, former balloon pilot, and an armchair expert on military matters. He is also a connoisseur of fine art and literature. Jerry is none of these things, but is a good listener. Since Rip seldom listens to anyone but himself, he requires an appreciative audience.

Around 7 P.M., Odie enters. Odie is Jerry's surrogate son and relief bartender on the one night, Saturday, the bar stays open past eight.

Jerry greets him with an affectionate grin. "How's it going, son?"

"Rough day!" says Odie with a sigh. "Booger Matthews refused the load of block we had shipped in from Tallahassee because they sent a girl driver."

"Booger's never heard of the Equal Rights Amendment?"

"I guess not."

And so it goes . . . until eight when, for the 3,050th consecutive time in a row, Jerry calls it a day and hands the keys to Odie.

At the door, he pauses for an instant before leaving. "Night all."

"Night, Jerry."

The door swings closed and he is gone.

To get to Harry's Bar, follow Carrabelle's Main Street south of Highway 98 a block and a half. It's on the left.

Apalachicola

The drive west on U.S. 98 from Carrabelle to Apalachicola offers enchanting vistas of tiny white sand beaches, studded with cypress knees, and two pine-covered offshore islands, Dog and St. George. At Eastpoint, with its long row of fish houses and processing plants, and its tart, fishy aroma, you cross the five-mile causeway over Apalachicola Bay to Apalachicola . . . and into another century.

At the foot of the bridge sits the Gibson Inn, constructed in 1907 when Apalachicola was a booming lumber port. This four-story inn with its widow's walk (so called because a sea captain's wife would watch for his vessel's approach from the railed-in perch atop their house), tongue-in-groove wainscoting, window casings, trim work, and nautical bar, is a monument to a bygone era. Driving through town, with its one yellow caution light, four gourmet restaurants, a drugstore and soda fountain (that serves Cokes made thick with syrup and real limeade from freshly squeezed limes), and its charming Victorian mansions—with widow's walks, tin roofs, wrap-around porches, and lots of windows—I follow Route 98 to the Chesnut Street Cemetery and get out to look around.

It's a real Tom Sawyer/Huck Finn cemetery, with stunted magnolias oozing Spanish moss, and cracked, weathered tombstones dating back to the 1770s. It begins to rain, a soft mistlike rain, but the moss-draped branches shield you from all but the most persistent drops. Kneeling down, I examine a tombstone:

Born 1808. Died 1844. He was a pilot who brought ships safely
into the harbor. He died by drowning in a small boat.

Close by is a family plot that tells a sad but familiar story: Father, a doctor, born 1832, died 1875, age 43. Mother, a mother, born 1844, died 1920, age 76. Toby, a son, born 1865, died two months later. There are no other tombstones.

Less-anonymous persons are buried here. Dr. Gorrie, who invented the first ice machine in a vain attempt to cure malaria; Alvan Wentworth Chapman, the famous botanist; McQueen McIntosh, one of the South's leading secessionists . . .

I picture McIntosh with long, hoary locks waving about a domed head, spittle erupting in streams from thin, patrician lips as he harangues Congress. An Irishman like Scarlett O'Hara's father in *Gone with the Wind*. His first name the same as the last name of the black actress, Butterfly McQueen, who played the flighty house servant in the movie.

I leave the cemetery and walk over to Main Street. Taking a seat on a wooden bench underneath a metal awning, I watch the world go by. A covey of pretty, pregnant, teenaged girls stroll past—the lilting strains of their innocuous chatter drifting back like the gentle patter of springtime rain.

I check into the Rainbow Inn on the Apalachicola River. Behind the desk, an elderly, spectacled lady eyes me suspiciously. "You a commercial fisherman?"

"No, ma'am, I'm not," I say in my most polite Southern manner.

"I don't rent rooms to fishermen anymore. They get drunk and carry women into the rooms."

"Well, I'm not a fisherman."

Reluctantly, she hands me a room key.

BEFORE THE Civil War, Apalachicola was one of the three largest ports on the Gulf, after Mobile and New Orleans. Boatloads of cotton were shipped down the Apalachicola River from the fertile plantations of Georgia and Alabama, then transported in oceangoing vessels to textile mills in England. The city was laid out according to the plan of Philadelphia, with town squares every four or five blocks. Water Street, with its packing houses, runs along the Apalachicola River. Shrimp and oyster boats float at docks.

From the late 1860s to the 1880s there was sponge fishing. Greek sponge fishermen came to Apalachicola before they went to Tarpon Springs, and the old Sponge Exchange, built in 1832, is on Commerce Street at Avenue E. During the 1880s, cypress milling revitalized Apalachicola. In the 1920s it became the center of Florida's seafood industry, especially its world-famous oysters.

Oysters are pried off the ocean bottom with wood-handled metal pincers. On any given day, there are fifty to a hundred two-man skiffs out on Apalachicola Bay gathering oysters—unless weather or river pollution has temporarily shut down the industry. Fishermen work six to eight months out of the year. On a good day they make as much as $300. On a bad day they don't even cover their gas. Following a month or two at sea, a man wants to let off a little steam, and the Oasis bar is the modern-day equivalent of the Wild West. (As the saying goes: Never play cards with a man named Doc; never eat lunch at a greasy spoon called Mom's; and never, *ever* drink at a joint called the Oasis.)

The Oasis has been a local landmark for more than sixty years.

141

moon. The mournful moan of a tugboat pulling a long string of barges down the river is the only sound, as a disheveled seaman in shiny white boots—perhaps the ghost of some long departed sailor—appears out of nowhere, then vanishes in the fog.

Suddenly, the inscription on the tombstone I saw earlier leaps to mind: "He was a pilot who brought ships safely into the harbor. He died by drowning in a small boat."

THE NEXT NIGHT, an off-duty Hope and I meet at the Oasis. Hope is drinking Natural Light beer with shots of Jagermeister. She's none too steady on her feet and slurs badly. We haven't been there long before a boatload of shrimpers arrive. A herd of local girls who have a sixth sense where free drinks are concerned, including a lovely black prostitute and small-time drug dealer named Constance, arrive shortly thereafter. As the liquor flows freer and freer, the crowd gets rowdier and rowdier.

I excuse myself to go to the men's room. When I step back out, there's a great commotion and a crowd has gathered by the pool tables. Hope and another girl are wrestling around on the floor with the crowd egging them on! What is the dating etiquette for such an occasion, I wonder? Do I try to break it up or root for Hope? Since her opponent is at least fifty pounds heavier, she's wrestling way out of her weight class. Buddhist that I am, I opt for detachment and take a seat at the bar away from the main event. It isn't long before Hope's opponent has her pinned and is pounding her head against the floor. The cops arrive, and Hope and the other girl are hauled off in patrol cars.

Perhaps I should go her bail, I think to myself over several beers.

My mind hasn't been pondering this dilemma long when the phone rings and the bartender hands me the receiver. It's Hope, whom the kindly officers have dropped off at her trailer home in lieu of jail.

"Come and get me," she demands. "I'm gonna whip Betty Lou's ass if it kills me!"

142

Before that, as evidenced by its black and white, tiny-tiled floor, it was a barber shop. There's a long wooden bar separated by a blue partition, along with a juke box and two dusty pool tables. Behind the bar stands an attractive blonde bartender named Hope.

"What'll you have?" she asks as I enter.

Two pool-playing shrimpers are having a heated argument about the house rules for eight-ball.

"Bud Light."

Hope pops the cap with a metal opener and slams a cold one down on the splintered bar.

I sit down on a dilapidated stool. In front of me is a Mason jar with a handwritten sign requesting donations for Bobbie Lee Boeson's kidney transplant (most likely the latest in a series of similar entreaties). Hope and I engage in a long, convivial conversation. Eventually, we make a date for the following night.

At sunset I find myself at the Hut, a seafood restaurant and bar with a wooden deck overlooking the oyster-gray bay and the barrier islands beyond. The oyster cocktails and beers are plentiful and succulent, and the view from the deck resembles a Currier & Ives print with rusty trawlers, net-laden skiffs, and a blood-red sunset that rivals any in the state.

Rat, the bartender, a baseball-capped cracker, is the world's greatest complainer. He complains about customers wanting to use the phone behind the bar and the boss not letting customers use said phone, depending on whether he's talking to the customers about the boss or the boss about the customers. He complains about the money, or lack thereof, he makes working at the bar, and the long hours he worked at his last job driving a seafood truck. He complains about the scarcity of "kooty" (women), and the fights that are likely to break out if any *do* show up.

Around midnight I take a stroll along the gray foggy streets of Apalachicola. There are spirits here. Ghosts of the long-departed merchants and seamen who built the two- and three-story New England-style mansions that gleam like phantoms in the pale yellow light of a waning

"But Hope, I don't know where you live."

"You follow Dead Man's Curve past the old cemetery. My house sits on the right across from Johnson's Holler."

"If you *really* need to get back, why don't you take a cab? I'll pay the fare when you get here."

"I'm not taking no nigger cab at this time o' night! Come and get me, or I'll drive myself back."

"The cops will be on the lookout for you, Hope. Take a cab, and I'll pay the fare."

But Hope is not to be dissuaded. A half hour later she returns to the Oasis as full of piss and vinegar as when she departed. Ironically Constance, the black prostitute, has driven her over, and I'm on her shit list!

Oh, well . . .

The next morning, Hope's bout was overshadowed by two shrimpers who got in a fight at the Oasis after I left. When they carried it out to the street, one ran over the other in his truck and is under arrest for attempted murder.

I move over to the Gibson Inn bar, which has the look and feel of a huge stateroom on a luxurious oceangoing yacht—heavy wood shutters, walnut plank floor and ceiling, nautical decor. In the far corner, seated at a baby grand piano, is gnarly handed Ron, the world's only oyster-shucking pianist. I take a seat next to a distinguished-looking silver-haired gentle-man. His name is Mr. Ed, or so he has been christened by the women bar-tenders who dote on him like a favorite uncle, and he's the town philoso-pher. A thin-lipped, patrician New Englander, born and bred in New Hampshire, a member of the CIA in Vietnam and Asia, he has retired to the largest wetlands in the United States to collect and catalogue the flora and fauna. His knowledge is encyclopedic and not confined to internation-al intrigue and biology. At the drop of a hat, he will quote from Shakespeare, Dr. Johnson, or his personal favorite, H. L. Mencken. Like many cynics, his sardonic exterior masks the proverbial heart of gold.

So I spend the rest of the evening conversing with Mr. Ed. Citizen of New Hampshire, New England, the United States, Asia, the World, the Universe, the Kingdom of God. And presently Apalachicola, Florida . . .

To get to Apalachicola, follow Highway 98 twenty-two miles west of Carrabelle. Dr. Gorrie's house is now a state museum, and there's another nautical museum covering the history of the area. A large pontoon boat provides nature tours of the Apalachicola River, and the oldest functioning sailboat, the *Governor Stone*, built in 1878, takes passengers on sunset cruises. House and walking tours of the town can be arranged at the Gibson Inn, usually on weekends.

St. George Island

St. George Island, across the bay from Apalach, used to be the end of the world. It was a place where a speechwriter for the KKK and author of George Wallace's infamous "Segregation Forever" speech could change his name and become a critically respected and best-selling writer . . . and did. Where a millionaire counterfeiter and former cellmate of Watergate burglar Howard Hunt could retire to tend an elaborate garden . . . and did.

On my first trip here twenty years ago, there was only one bar, a ramshackle, wooden affair across from the beach where the locals, mostly fishermen and dope-smugglers, hung out. Entering it was like entering a Wild West saloon. Things have changed now. Newcomers from Tallahassee, Atlanta, and points north have moved in and built nice homes. The west end is a state park, and the east is a gated community of elaborate homes owned by celebrities like country singer Tom T. Hall and movie star Peter Fonda. Fonda received an Academy Award nomination for his starring role in *Ulee's Gold*, which was filmed in the area. But as the old saw goes: the more things change, the more they remain the same.

147

MARY DELL WALKER is a newcomer from north Georgia. She's left a carpet business, two grown daughters, and a forlorn husband to come to St. George and drink herself to death. She supports herself by waitressing and doing odd jobs at the Island Oasis, one of the island's four seafood restaurants.

Joe Hargreaves is a down-on-his-luck rancher from Oklahoma City who's in the midst of a disastrous divorce. He wants to open up a barbecue place on the island, away from his wife's greedy lawyers.

The two meet at Harry A's bar. Mary Dell has been drinking Natural Light since early morning and is falling-down drunk. Joe has just begun to drink Bud and is on the lookout for "stray kooty."

Joe: "You from around here?"

Mary Dell (slurring): "Could be."

Joe: "I'm serious."

Mary Dell: "You look serious, pardner. *Real* serious. Me, I'm silly."

Mary Dell tells Joe the tragedy of her recent life and Joe nods understandingly. *Here is a woman adrift,* he thinks, *one who desperately needs what I am about to give her.* When Mary Dell has finished, Joe suggests they go somewhere for dinner. Mary Dell isn't interested. She would rather drink. Joe says they can order drinks with their food. Mary Dell says eating will kill a good buzz. Joe settles the issue by ordering a cheeseburger and fries at the bar, and they continue drinking.

As the night wears on, Joe becomes increasingly irritated with Mary Dell for not going back to his motel room. But Mary Dell is in another world, back with her husband and kids before the need to drink became the most important thing in her life. Is it the island, with its ambiance of a *mañana* that never comes, or women in general, wonders Joe, as he experiences second thoughts about moving here.

Finally the bar closes. With no prompting, Mary Dell suggests they go to *her* apartment where there's a case of Natural Light in the refrigerator. Joe pays the healthy bar tab, and they leave.

ON THE WAY over in Joe's truck, Mary Dell begins sobbing heart-rending sobs. Joe places his arm tenderly about her shoulders and she buries her face in his shirt-front. There . . . That's more like it, thinks Joe. But when they get to her cramped garage apartment across from the beach, Mary Dell is distant, and huge studio portraits of her husband and daughters stand disapproving sentinel on the walls.

"Would you like a beer?" Mary Dell asks timidly, the gracious hostess at a party of two.

"Sure."

Mary Dell produces two Natural Lights from a droning refrigerator and hands one to Joe. She walks over to a cheap plastic radio and switches it on. A hillbilly lament engulfs the dimly lit room.

"Wanna dance?" she asks the far wall.

Joe moves over and takes her in his arms. They sway slowly, to and fro, to the heartbreaking lyrics. A man is losing his wife to his best friend. The keys attached to a loop of Mary Dell's jeans jingle time to the maudlin lyrics. Once again, Mary Dell begins to sob.

"What's wrong, honey?" asks Joe, feeling more and more in control of the situation.

When Mary Dell doesn't answer, he lowers his hands to caress her buttocks and maneuvers her toward the tiny bedroom. They are half-way there when Mary Dell objects.

"What the hell do you think you're doing?"

"Nothing."

"Nothing, hell? Get the fuck outta here!"

Joe is furious. Another hard-on and a headache. It's the island, he thinks. It's not like the solid red clay of Oklahoma. There's something about this island that gets to people; makes them moaning, sobbing, slobbering losers. It's like they've reached the end of the road and there's no place left to go.

Joe slams out of the apartment, vowing never to return—either to Mary Dell or this God-forsaken island. He fumbles for the radio dial.

Jimmy Buffett is singing "Changes in Latitude."

Joe settles back in his seat. To his left a full moon casts a silver thread across a purple sea. Maybe it's the full moon, he thinks. Not the island. The full moon will do that. They've proved it with scientific studies . . .

To get to St. George Island, head due south on State Road 300 at Eastpoint across the 4.25-mile causeway (a toll road). St. George Island is about twenty miles long by a half mile wide, and is home to wonderful beaches written up in numerous magazines, including *Time* and *People*. Jeanie's Journeys provides sailing and canoeing trips to nearby state-owned Little St. George wildlife sanctuary, where you can see an 1850s lighthouse and the lighthouse keeper's home.

Part 3
OLD FLORIDA

Home of Judge Bronson, built in 1854, Palatka.

Old Florida

Old Florida resembles the Old South, only more worldly and exotic. Florida is a stew of Scotch-Irish, English, Spanish, French Huguenot, Negro, Indian, Minorcan, South and Central American, Bahamian Conch, and Greek. Many prospered. Others didn't. The Seminoles, for instance. Three successive wars drove them south to their present home, the Everglades. Robbed of their homeland, all but stripped of their culture, many live on reservations and sell their native handicrafts to interlopers from the North.

For others, Florida was the land of opportunity. The Spanish were the first to arrive, searching for gold, riches, and a fountain of youth that never existed, unless you count the sunshine and warm climate. They settled at St. Augustine and Pensacola, establishing way-stations for the riches of the West Indies, South and Central America, and the resources of the North American continent. Then there were the buccaneers, freebooters, and privateers who used Florida's coves and inlets for a base of operations to prey on treasure-laden vessels.

Those who followed were dreamers, mostly. Often failures at home, they sought a newer, brighter dream in the Land of Eternal Sunshine. From the English remittance men who established some of the first orange groves in north central Florida, to the land speculators of the Twenties Boom, Florida has always appealed to those chasing the easy buck.

Often, like the Spanish, they failed to find the treasure trove they sought. But they remained, and their descendants live here today.

Here follow a few of their stories . . .

A bridge to history—the skyline of present-day St. Augustine, from the Bridge of Lions.

Photo by Debra Force.

The Other St. Augustine

The best approach to St. Augustine is from the south on A1A across the Bridge of Lions. It's like being in a time-warp and approaching the gates of an ancient Andalusian city. In the near distance is the centuries-old plaza and slave market. In the far distance, five-story Flagler College with its turrets and minarets, once the ultra-grand Ponce De Leon Hotel, the flagship of Standard Oil millionaire and railroad tycoon Henry Flagler's Florida vision. The architecture of St. Augustine's centuries-old buildings is Moorish, with red-tile roofs and cupolas, elaborate many-tiered fronts, and horseshoe-shaped entrances, windows, and columnades.

As resident St. Augustine expert David Nolan writes in *A Book-Lover's Guide to Florida*:

> St. Augustine, dating from 1565, is famed as the nation's oldest city—or more precisely the oldest continuous European settlement on the continental United States. That's a distinction . . . the casual tourist will not be likely to miss. Everything is at least old, if not *older* or *oldest*.

 . . . [Q]uite a bit of St. Augustine's history has more than a small amount of fiction in it. One should expect no less in a tourist economy. When criticized for some of the exaggerations he peddled, one local entrepreneur replied simply, "You can't tell a man how to run his business."

 In Ring Lardner's "Gullible's Travels," a '20s tourist recounts his day's itinerary: "First, we went to St. George Street and visited the oldest house in the United States. Then we turned the corner and went down St. Francis Street and inspected the oldest house in the United States. Then we dropped in to a soda fountain and I had an egg phosphate from the oldest egg in the Western Hemisphere."

THE AREA OF St. Augustine west of King Street, the main thoroughfare, is an oasis of peace and serenity compared to the hectic bustle of touristy St. George and similar streets to the east. Tourists are few and the natives are friendly. There's a cozy neighborhood feel; only parts of this neighborhood date back to the late sixteenth century. Marine Street skirts the bay, which is deep blue or pearl gray dependent on the weather, and winds past the old Spanish army barracks and military cemetery where graves date back to the late eighteenth century. Spanish-styled gardens in courtyards, plazas, and parks delight the eye—and birdsong, the ear—as one strolls narrow cobblestoned streets past the nation's oldest house (*really* the oldest, honest!) and the St. Francis Inn, built in 1765. The St. Francis has a resident ghost—a slave maid jilted by a colonial soldier. Occasionally, the steady clop-clop of a horsedrawn carriage, carrying tourists and a folksy guide giving the route's monologue, heightens the eighteenth-century reality of the centuries-old town.

 In Confederate General Edmund Smith Kirby's house on Aviles Street are the ancient city's archives. One enters through a tropical-flowered courtyard, then up a flight of ancient stone steps. In years past, I spent long afternoons here doing research, going over yellowing letters and papers piled up around me on a long wooden table, musty documents scenting the air.

For lunch, there's the A1A Ale Works on Marine Street, which specializes in Caribbean food. It's in the old Plaza Hotel building, circa 1888, across the street from City Marina, where the boat crowd hangs out. Inside, Captain Ron, a retired fireman from Atlantic City—and Travis McGee's boat-bum brother—recites his daily litany as he sips a noon beer at the zinc-covered bar. "One afternoon, Cap'n Nasty ran across a bale of 'square grouper' in Biscayne Bay. He'd no sooner separated the dry stuff from the rest and was headed south to the Keys in that ragamuffin skiff of his than a DEA seaplane landed light as a feather next to him. They were fixing to board when Cap'n Nasty stripped naked and waved at them! The next thing he knew, the seaplane powered up and took off, leaving him and the grass."

Then there're the cheapskate sailors, or "whistlers," as Cap'n Ron calls them. Every time they dock somewhere new, they query the dock master, "How much is gas?" Answer: Amazed whistle. "How much is dockage?" Answer: Longer amazed whistle. "How much for water?" Answer: Even longer amazed whistle. "How much for a six-pack of beer?" Answer: Longer still amazed whistle. "How far's the next dock?" Answer: Longest amazed whistle . . .

Or Cap'n Ron tells about the time he stumbled drunkenly on the dock and busted half his ribs, but was able to enjoy outrageous sex that same night . . . You get the picture.

Evenings catch Bobby Dee, St. Augustine's resident ivory-pounder, at one of the local watering holes. Dee puts on a full-fledged vaudeville act, donning appropriate hats and masks to accompany his Broadway-show and movie tunes, including a *Wizard of Oz* medley with Dorothy, the Scarecrow, the Tin Woodsman, and the Cowardly Lion. Or quaff a cold one at the Tradewinds, a St. Augustine tradition since the 1940s, with South Seas–style bamboo-studded decor, a simulated typhoon (flashing lights, recorded thunder, the relentless pounding of rain on a tin roof), and nightly entertainment that has included such Florida greats as Jimmy Buffett, Lynyrd Skynyrd, and Bertie Higgins of "Key Largo" fame. Or enjoy an after-dinner drink at the Conch House, a small octagonal building with a winding walnut staircase leading to the crow's nest at the end of a dock on the bay.

Or, if you must, there's always St. George Street, where tourists in shorts and black dress socks and shoes, with cameras strung around their necks, hang at the oldest school, the oldest jail, the oldest fort . . . et cetera . . . et cetera . . .

St. Augustine's Ghost Tour is the most popular historical tour in the state.

Kingsley Plantation

Zephaniah Kingsley was a nineteenth-century slave trader who married an African Princess, Anna Madgigaine Jai. They settled on a plantation at Ft. George Island above Jacksonville. According to family legend, my great-great-grandfather, the previously mentioned James S. Turner, purchased "Kingsley's Niggers." These slaves, having been trained in their native tongue by Anna Jai, were noted for their abilities as house servants, blacksmiths, and other specialized skills on a plantation.

The following is the preamble to Kingsley's will:

> Whereas I am of sound mind and disposing memory and know what I'm doing, and whereas I know perfectly well that it is against the laws and conventions of life to marry a colored person, and whereas this is my property and it is not anybody's damn business what I do with it . . . And whereas I have an African wife who is one of the finest women I have ever known and who has been true and faithful to me, and whereas I believe that the amalgamation of the white and colored races to be in the best interest of America, and whereas I know that what I am

about to do is going to bring down tremendous criticism, but I don't give
a damn. Now therefore I give my wife . . .

When Kingsley died in 1843, his will bequeathed most of his enormous estate to his black wife and their children, much to the consternation of collateral white relatives.

Today the Kingsley Plantation is a national historical monument on Ft. George Island, north of Jacksonville and across the mouth of the St. Johns River from the tiny fishing village of Mayport. One of the last car ferries in the state provides transportation to the island. A long, winding, oyster shell–filled road, canopied by Spanish moss and the sturdy branches of ancient oaks, leads to the plantation. A coquina wall with wooden gates guards a magnolia-scented yard and a modest, two-story, white-washed structure facing the deep blue river—Kingsley's home. The slave quarters consist of a line of twelve recently excavated twelve-by-twelve-foot coquina huts just outside the gates.

Tours start every hour on the hour, and there's a small museum to one side of the house that provides a brief illustrated history of the estate. The museum holds relics like the arm, leg, and neck braces worn by slaves being transported from Africa. A "whistling corridor"—so called because a well-trained house servant would whistle to himself while traversing its length, to prove to those seated in the dining room he wasn't sampling the food—connects the main house with the kitchen, with its wood-burning stove, hearth, and kettle. (The house and kitchen were separated for fear of a fire breaking out.) The dining room, with identical fireplaces at either end of the room, is circled by windows that offer a panoramic view of the swift-moving river. In the bedrooms upstairs are lowered ceilings and tiny beds indicative of the diminutive stature of early-nineteenth-century people.

On the day I toured the plantation to do research for a novel, I experienced a strange sense of deja vu. Only in my deja vu, instead of a manicured lawn, the yard was dusty topsoil and weeds. Later the tour guide

Kingsley Plantation on Ft. George Island, north of Jacksonville, home of Zephaniah
Kingsley, a nineteenth-century slave trader who married an African princess.

Photo by Debra Force.

explained that such, indeed, had been the case. What strange web of destiny had led me to this spot . . .

ZEPHANIAH KINGSLEY was born the second of seven children to Quaker parents on December 11, 1765, in Glasgow, Scotland. When he was seven, his family moved to Charleston, South Carolina, where his father traded with the West Indies. As an adult, Kingsley became a slave trader, importing slaves on ships from West Africa to Brazil and the West Indies. In 1803 he bought a large plantation near St. Augustine, where he and his African wife, Anna Jai, trained them for specialized professions.

A sea captain named Reuter operated Kingsley's fleet out of Mayport. At Dahomey on the African side, Gezo, an African chieftain, and his son-in-law, Lord George Russell, a former British Navy officer, provided the slaves. The price for a slave ran anywhere from fifty cents to fifteen dollars. Once trained at Kingsley's plantation, the same slave sold for up to fifteen hundred dollars. "Kingsley's Niggers" were said to be the finest stock available and were sold for up to three times the market value.

A visitor to Kingsley's plantation in the early 1800s remembers Kingsley seated at one end of a long wooden table, with Anna Jai at the other end. A manservant brought out the different courses. Anna Jai was the mistress of the household. Because of her aristocratic background and the fact she could speak several different African dialects, she was instrumental in training her husband's slaves.

In 1807 the importation of slaves into the U.S. was declared illegal by an act of Congress, and Kingsley was forced to smuggle his slaves into Georgia and the Carolinas from his home in Florida.

In 1813 Kingsley bought Ft. George Island, at the mouth of the St. Johns River, from Don Juan McQueen, an expatriate American. During this period, a band of renegade Americans under the leadership of McQueen tried to annex Spanish northeast Florida to the United States in a short-lived revolt known as the Patriots' Rebellion.

Accounts vary as to what role Kingsley played in the rebellion. According to Kingsley, he was held captive for more than a year while his plantation was used as the Patriots' base of operations for a series of skirmishes against the Spanish and their Seminole allies. Whether Kingsley was held captive or was one of the instigators of the revolt is uncertain. In later years, Kingsley sued the U.S. government for damages incurred to his plantation and in August, 1843, was awarded $73,222.

IN 1828, KINGSLEY'S *A Treatise on Slavery* was privately printed by Colombus Drew of Jacksonville. In it Kingsley argues that slavery is a necessary evil, since whites would die if forced to labor in the hot, subtropical sun. He views the Negro as "Safe, permanent, and easily governed . . . sober, discreet, honest, and obliging . . . [possessor] of a much better moral character than whites of similar condition." According to the pamphlet, Negroes who are Freedmen should be accorded equal treatment under the law. They should be allowed to vote, own land, and travel freely from place to place.

In 1839 Kingsley sent Anna Jai and their son, George, to Puerto Plata in Haiti, now the Dominican Republic. There he established a plantation where Freedmen, and those of his slaves who so desired, could "remove [them]selves and [their] properties to some land of liberty and equal rights where the conditions of society are governed by some law less absurd than that of color."

Just prior to his death in 1843, Kingsley met L. Maria Child, a noted New York abolitionist. Miss Child found his conversation "entertaining but marked by incongruity." Kingsley began by arguing that Negroes were the superior race. They were "more graceful, [had] softer skins, sweeter voices . . . were docile and affectionate . . . less prone to mischief [than whites]." When Miss Child asked that if such were the case, why must they remain slaves, Kingsley explained they were "kept in slavery by reason of their virtue." He claimed, "All we can do in this world is balance evils."

163

He justified his own past by explaining "to do good in the world one must [first] have money." Miss Child attempted to argue with him about fixed principles of right and wrong, but conceded "one might as well fire small shot at the hide of a rhinoceros." She lists Kingsley's virtues—perseverance, heroic candor, and kindly sympathy. At the conclusion of their conversation, Kingsley commented that once the terms of his will were made known, all hell would break loose.

Though Kingsley left a sixth of his estate to two white nephews, the rest went to Anna Jai and their two children and children of two black mistresses. According to the will: " . . . connubial relations [with Anna] took place in a foreign land where our marriage was celebrated and solemnized according to her African custom . . . [Y]et she has always been respected as my wife and as such I acknowledge her, nor do I think her truth, honor, integrity, moral conduct, or good sense will lose in comparison with anyone." None of Kingsley's slaves were to be separated from their families, and they could purchase their freedom for one half the common market value.

As might be expected, the will was contested by Kingsley's sisters. One, Martha Kingsley McNeill, was the mother of Anna McNeill, who was the mother of noted artist James McNeill Whistler and the model for his famous painting commonly called *Whistler's Mother*.

Anna Jai fled to Puerto Plata. Following the Civil War, she returned to Florida and lived out her life on the Ft. George plantation.

The ensuing court case lasted more than fifty years. At its close, the terms of Kingsley's will were upheld, though the estate was severely drained by lawyers' fees.

To get to the Kingsley Plantation, follow Highway A1A north of Jacksonville Beach to Mayport. Take the ferry across the St. Johns River to Ft. George

Island and drive four or five miles to a historical marker on the left-hand side of the road. Turn left and follow the oyster-shell road.

David Levy Yulee

State Road 24 leading into Gainesville is lined with shopping malls, condos, and partially constructed apartment buildings sprouting like concrete mushrooms on a hot, humid summer's day. There's even talk a large corporation is buying up land around Cross Creek to construct condos with tennis courts, swimming pools, and a thirty-six-hole golf course.

But the P. K. Younge collection on the fourth floor of the University of Florida Library is a peaceful sanctuary devoted to the history of the state. Here, amid age-worn letters and documents, I pieced together the following brief biography of David Levy Yulee, Florida's first senator, the first Jew in Congress, and one of Florida's premier land speculators.

YULEE'S GRANDFATHER was a financial advisor to the Emperor of Morocco until a change in regimes cost him his head. His grandmother fled to Gibraltar where his father, Moses, was raised. At an early age, Moses was shipped out to the West Indies. He used a legacy from his father to start a lumber business that earned him a fortune.

Moses lived on the Dutch island of St. Thomas where David was born. Four years later, Moses divorced his wife (in later years, David would claim his father was a widower, but recent evidence shows otherwise) and went to Florida to establish a colony for European Jews. He used money from European backers to purchase 500,000 acres of a Spanish land grant, the Arrendondo Grant, in present-day Alachua County. But the colony was never established.

David and his brother Elias were shipped over from St. Thomas. David was sent to Norfolk, Virginia, to attend military school. When he turned seventeen, Moses ceased his support, citing a Talmudic injunction that each man must earn his own keep. Returning to Florida, David assisted Elias in running their father's sugar plantation at Crystal River. Tiring of this, he fled to St. Augustine to work in the law office of Robert Raymond Reid, a prominent Democratic politician. David passed the state bar exam, then entered politics. In 1835 he was elected representative from St. Johns County to the territorial legislature. Shortly thereafter, Moses publicly disavowed his son for engaging in the two occupations he despised most, lawyering and politicking. In his will, he bequeathed David a hundred dollars of his huge estate.

The Whig party was the ruling force in Florida politics. Controlled by the aristocratic planter class, it manipulated the state's meager financial resources to its own advantage. Symbolic of the Whigs' control were the state-owned banks. They extended liberal credit terms to planters, but not small farmers (no substantial middle class existed). Reid and Levy, as members of the newly formed Democratic party, represented the small farmers and opposed the state-owned bank system. When Levy ran for Territorial delegate in 1840, the Whig-controlled press labeled him a "Jew and an alien" because he was born at St. Thomas. Despite the attacks of the press, Levy carried the election and was instrumental in getting Florida admitted into the Union.

"Fairbanks's Folly," the last home of Florida historian George Rainsford Fairbanks, editor of David Levy Yulee's newspaper. One of many restored buildings in the city of Fernandina.

Photo by Debra Force.

Racism was then prevalent in Congress. The following is a quote from New England abolitionist John Quincy Adams's diary: "Levy is said to be a Jew, and what will be, if true, a far more formidable disqualification . . . that he has a dash of African blood . . . which, sub rosa, is the case with more than one member of the House." ("African blood" presumably refers to Levy's Moroccan ancestry.)

FOLLOWING FLORIDA'S admission into the Union in 1845, Levy served as a U.S. senator, continuously except for one term, until the outbreak of the Civil War. He was a leader of the States' Rights movement headed by John C. Calhoun and Jefferson Davis. He was also associated with the Young American movement, which considered it America's manifest destiny to own Cuba and Mexico and to exercise control over the western hemisphere.

In 1846, at the insistence of his soon-to-be wife, Nancy Wickliffe, daughter of a former governor of Kentucky, Levy had his name changed to the less-Jewish David Yulee by a special act of the Florida legislature. Yulee was one of the names his grandmother dropped when forced to flee Morocco.

During his Senate years, Yulee's main concern was the construction of a cross-state railroad that would connect the east and west coasts of Florida. This would make the ports of New Orleans, Galveston, Mexico, and parts of the Caribbean easily accessible to the east. Merchandise could be transported by rail across the state, instead of ships having to circle Key West. Eventually he decided it would be to the state's advantage—and his own—if the railroad was constructed with private, rather than state, funding. He used his influence to secure backing from a group of wealthy New Yorkers and kept majority control of the corporation.

In 1855 the Florida Railroad began laying track at Fernandina on the east coast. It would head west through Gainesville to Cedar Key. Yulee got his brother-in-law, Nathaniel Holt, appointed postmaster general of the

U.S. That way, the railroad could procure the final leg of the mail route from Boston to Fernandina. On June 12, 1860, the track was completed as far as Cedar Key, where Yulee had purchased now-valuable land. His sugar plantation, called Marguerita, was a short distance down the coast on Tiger Tail Island in the Homosassa River.

ON THE BRINK of the Civil War, Yulee found himself in an uneasy position. For the benefit of voters back home, he favored secession; as head of a railroad financed by Northern backers, he pretended to favor reconciliation. Yulee's dilemma is shown in correspondence in which he assures his business partners of one thing, but the voters back home of another.

While serving in the Senate, Yulee wrote a letter to Governor Perry of Florida that would later surface to haunt him. In the letter, he wrote he would remain in Congress as long as possible to keep "[President] Buchanan's hands tied." He advised his constituents to press for the occupation of federal fortifications and concluded: "I shall give the enemy another shot before retiring. I say *enemy!* Yes, I am theirs and they are mine. I am willing to be their master, but not their brother." Following the Civil War, he referred to his mental state at the time of the letter's composition as one of "specific momentary excitement."

When Florida seceded from the Union, Yulee vacated his Senate seat and returned home.

At this point in my research, I left the library and walked across the street to the Holiday Inn for lunch. Seated at the table next to mine were two businessmen, an aging local and a young aggressive Northern salesman, a *bidness* man and a *bizznezz* man. They were arguing about interest rates. The Northerner was talking a mile a minute, with the Southerner occasionally throwing in a muted objection, as though arguing with a Yankee would be beneath his dignity. Underneath the Southerner's placid appearance, one could sense age-old resentment toward the victorious North.

I was reminded of David Levy Yulee. To the Florida natives of his era, he must have been an enigma. Being Jewish and a native of the West Indies, his Southernness could never be more than skin-deep. Still, as far as his Northern associates were concerned, he was a Reb. Yulee was a man poised between two opposing cultures, one agricultural, the other industrial. Yet he was a full-fledged member of neither.

Returning to the library, I continued my research.

ON JANUARY 15, 1862, the *Hatteras*, a Federal gunboat, sailed into Cedar Key harbor where, as I wrote earlier, the Rebs were captured without a single shot being fired. Among the casualties when the Federals came ashore was the Florida Railroad depot, which was burned to the ground. On hearing of the fall of Cedar Key, Yulee shot off an anxious letter to Confederate Commander-in-Chief Robert E. Lee requesting him to reinforce the Reb garrison at Fernandina. Before anything could be done, on March 12, 1862, a Federal gunboat entered Fernandina harbor. Warned of its approach, a crowd of citizens, along with whatever belongings they could muster, fled town aboard Yulee's train. The gunboat opened fire, and the rear car, with Yulee aboard, was hit, leaving one man "decapitated and mutilating another." Yulee escaped and was transported to the mainland aboard a rowboat.

This would be Yulee's sole exposure to enemy fire. He spent the rest of the war supplying sugar and other commodities at exorbitant prices to the Confederacy.

In the late fall of 1862, Jeff Davis issued an order to take up what remained of the Florida Railroad's iron railings for shipment north to Georgia, where they were badly needed for transport of supplies to Reb troops. When Yulee heard this, he obtained a restraining order that circled through the civil courts for two years. In 1864 a Reb lieutenant named Fairbanks (Florida's historian George Rainsford Fairbanks's brother) took matters into his own hands and commanded his troops to begin taking up

172

track. A posse from Gainesville was hastily dispatched to stop them, but thought better of the idea when confronted with the fixed bayonets of Fairbanks's troops. This instance of the military overruling civil authorities became a bone of contention between Yulee and his friend, Jeff Davis, and resulted in the dissolution of their friendship.

In the summer of 1864, while Yulee and his family were visiting friends in Gainesville, Federal troops sailed up the Homosassa River and burned Marguerita to the ground. With the belongings his slaves carried away, Yulee established a plantation at Archer that he christened "Cottonwood."

AT WAR'S END, Yulee was preparing to go to Washington to represent his defeated state when he ran across Northern journalist Whitelaw Reid. Reid was conducting a tour of the defeated South at Jacksonville. Far from being repentant, according to Reid, Yulee was "seemingly ignorant of the fact that . . . during the last four years anything had happened[;] . . . that Southern men were no longer heeded whenever they stamped their feet."

With Yulee away, nine men, who had been part of the group fleeing south with Jeff Davis, arrived at Cottonwood and beseeched Mrs. Yulee for shelter. Unknown to them, Davis had been captured a few days before by Federal troops in Georgia. They divided what remained of the Confederate treasury, $25,000 in gold. $6,250 was set aside for Mrs. Davis and her children. Davis's personal belongings were entrusted to Mrs. Yulee. She hid them in an unlocked storage shed behind the house. Since many political prisoners were being granted amnesty, they turned themselves over to Federal authorities in Gainesville.

Alerted by the Yulee's black coachman, black troops, under the leadership of Captain O. E. Bryant, marched to the Yulee plantation and located the baggage. According to Bryant's report:

The Palace Saloon on Centre Street in Fernandina. Close to the waterfront, "the oldest continuously operated saloon in the state" has served drinks since 1878.

Photo by Debra Force.

The property was found in a storeroom behind the house, unguarded even by a lock. To wit, a trunk full of letters along with articles of clothing, four pistols, smoking and plug tobacco, tooth brushes, a ring, some spectacles, six boxes of cigars, twenty thousand dollars in Confederate bills, portraits of Mr. and Mrs. Davis and General Lee, and a French musket—a most dangerous weapon.

Meanwhile, Yulee was arrested by Federal soldiers and charged with treason. Yulee's "traitorous" letter to Governor Perry resurfaced, along with some equally incriminating ones to his brother-in-law, Postmaster General Joseph Holt. He was labeled a traitor by Holt and the Radical Republicans in Washington. In a letter to Secretary of War Stanton, Holt wrote: "Yulee along with the rest of the traitors ought, if there is a God, to be hung by the neck until dead."

On May 15, 1865, Yulee was transported to Fort Pulaski in Savannah to begin serving a prison term. In a June 15 letter to his wife, he wrote: "Methinks it were Holt's intention to take the little [that] remains of my life. But it will have to be over my dead body." On his release a year later, he returned to Florida to raise funds for his crippled railroad. The railroad was reconstructed over the next few years, and a splinter branch ran south to Tampa.

Yulee spent his remaining years at Fernandina. He founded a newspaper and built a luxurious hotel, the Egmont, where he hosted a ball for former president Grant during his visit to Florida in 1880. The two former enemies even exchanged dances with one another's wives, though Mrs. Yulee insisted Grant danced abominably. On October 10, 1886, six months after his beloved wife's death, Yulee was visiting New York on business when he dropped dead of a heart attack in the lobby of the Gotham Hotel.

Among the pallbearers at his funeral were several former members of Congress and Confederate General Joseph Johnston.

HAVING COMPLETED my research, I drove twenty miles west to Archer to look for Yulee's plantation, Cottonwood. Archer is a cracker town of perhaps a thousand people. The main street consists of a half dozen faded storefronts and an ancient lumber mill. Sleepy-looking blacks and whites lean against the dented hoods of dusty pickup trucks and shoot the breeze. After several false starts, I pried information on Cottonwood's whereabouts out of a woman in a store that specialized in hand-woven cotton quilts. The spot where the plantation stood is now the site of a shopping complex named Cottonwood Plaza—a fitting monument to one of Florida's premier capitalists, David Levy Yulee.

To get to Fernandina, follow A1A north of Ft. George Island to Amelia Island. Or take the Fernandina exit off I-95 thirty miles north of Jacksonville.

Amelia Island, 2 miles wide by 13.5 miles long, is the only place in the U.S. to have flown eight flags: French, Spanish, British, American Patriots, Green Cross of Florida (more patriots), Mexican, Confederate, and U.S. The city of Fernandina has restored thirty blocks of buildings that date to the 1850s. "Fairbanks's Folly," the last home of historian George Rainsford Fairbanks, who served as editor for Yulee's paper, is among the restored buldings.

On Centre Street, close to the waterfront, is the Palace Saloon. Called "the oldest continuously operated saloon in the state," it has been serving drinks since 1878 to customers ranging from Vanderbilts, Morgans, Rockefellers, Pulitzers, Carnegies, and Goodyears to more modern celebrities like Pat Summerall, Jimmy Hoffa, Chris Evert, and Molly Ringwald. In 1957 the bar hosted Sam Goldwyn, Henry Ford II, and Miami Beach's premier developer, Carl Fisher. (The Palace is haunted by the ghost of a former bartender who lived upstairs and died in 1960.) Tourists and locals gather for drinks at the hand-carved, foot-railed bar, with wall murals of literary subjects—Long John Silver, Mr. Pickwick—copied from the illustrations of noted artists N. C. Wyeth and Maxfield Parrish, among others. Dress is casual; boiled shrimp is served at happy hour.

Fort Clinch, which saw action during the Civil War, is on the north tip of the island. The old Florida Railroad depot serves as the Chamber of Commerce.

To get to Yulee Sugar Mill, follow U.S. 19 sixty miles north of St. Pete to Homosassa. Look for the historical marker. The remains of the mill are on the left-hand side of the road.

Kate's Fish Camp, a cracker-style bar and boat rental that dates to the 1940s, is on Highway 24 just east of Gainesville. Every full moon in months with an R, there's an old-style oyster roast with a country band. Goerings Bookstore in Gainesville has one of the best selections of books—especially from university presses—in Florida.

Government buildings dominate the skyline of Tallahassee, Florida's only capital, founded in 1823.

Tallahassee

Twenty miles south of the Georgia border, Tallahassee was the only Confederate state capital never to be occupied by Union forces during the Civil War, and today the town retains much of its antebellum flavor. Tara-like mansions, a traditional old capitol building, and a restored downtown area vie for attention with the new capitol, a twenty-five-story skyscraper that stands right behind the old one. It's a modern, glassed-in building in the form of a tower flanked on each side by short domed wings, jokingly dubbed "Governor Askew's phallus" when it was built. According to author Gloria Jahoda in *The Other Florida*: "[Unlike other Florida cities, Tallahassee] has no orange groves . . . few bikinis, no porpoises . . . Tallahassee has never cared about jazzing up its antiquities. Its weathered 1840 houses are real enough to need paint . . . "

Before the Spanish came to Florida, Tallahassee, whose name means "old fields," was an Apalachee Indian village. The Apalachees grew corn, beans, and squash in the fertile soil of rolling clay hills and harvested oysters from the nearby Gulf of Mexico. In 1539 Spanish conquistadors, under the leadership of Hernando de Soto, celebrated America's first Christmas mass at present-day Lake Jackson, just north of Tallahassee, with "priests and soldiers to convert and conquer [the Native Americans]."

Until 1819, when Florida became a territory of the United States, the area around Tallahassee was occupied in turn by Spanish missions, the British, and various brigands including Andrew Jackson who, according to Jahoda, "swept down like a storm cloud in 1818, conquering what he had no authority to conquer." In 1823 Tallahassee was founded to serve as the state capital. Midway between the then population centers of St. Augustine on the east coast and Pensacola to the west, Tallahassee was selected as a compromise location. It's the only capital Florida has ever had. The town's first citizens, according to Ralph Waldo Emerson, who was advised not to go there by a Southern friend, were "public officers, land speculators, and desperadoes." Another New England tourist wrote home: "Not a house in Tallahassee is as fine as our father's barn."

Congress awarded thirty-six square miles of hilly countryside around Tallahassee to the Marquis de Lafayette in return for his services during the Revolutionary War. According to Diane Roberts, in her article, "Tallahassee: The Other Florida":

> The Marquis never found time to visit his Florida property, but, abhorring slavery, he sent some free Norman peasants (*citoyens*) to cultivate olive and lime groves on it, even though . . . [its] climate was completely unsuitable. The slaveholding cotton planters of Tallahassee—whose belief in *liberte, egalite, and fraternite* did not extend beyond their class and color—watched with undemocratic amusement as the groves withered, the Normans grumbled off back to France . . . and the noble experiment came to a sad end.

Frances Eppes, grandson of Thomas Jefferson, came to plant cotton, and his descendants still live here. Napoleon's nephew, Prince Achille Murat, established a plantation nearby. While attending a picnic, Murat met his future wife, Kitty Gray, a grand-niece of George Washington. Kitty objected to his chewing tobacco, so he acquired a St. Bernard dog to serve as a traveling cuspidor. According to Roberts: " . . . Prince Murat established a plantation and flourished, pursuing his hobbies, tobacco-chewing and preparing odd food. He would subject his guests at Lipon Plantation to cow's ear stew, whole rattlesnakes, or barn owls baked with their heads on. The one kind of north Florida wildlife he couldn't figure out how to cook was turkey buzzard. He tried roasting, frying, and broiling the bird, finally concluding . . . *Hee es no good.*" Murat died bankrupt in 1847, but Kitty lived to see Napoleon III gain power. His pension to her provided for many a needy Tallahassee family during the waning days of the Civil War.

THE GROVE, A HOME across from the governor's mansion, was built from 1825 to 1830 by Richard Keith Call. A protege of Andrew Jackson, Call came to Florida from Tennessee in 1814 while serving with Jackson against the British in Pensacola. To quote Jane Aurell Menton, his fifth-generation granddaughter, in *The Grove*: "When Jackson completed his brief gubernatorial assignment and returned to Tennessee in October 1821, Captain Call remained in Pensacola and . . . prepared himself for a professional future in his adopted homeland . . . Over the next several years, he built a legal practice . . . At age 30, he was elected the territorial delegate to Congress. "

On July 15, 1824, at Jackson's home, the Hermitage, Call married Mary Kirkman, an Irish girl from Nashville. He decided not to seek re-election and moved to newly established Tallahassee in 1825 to begin a law practice and to serve as a Receiver of Public Monies at the Federal Land Office.

To quote Menton:

> Serving as his own architect, General Call supervised The Grove's construction. Mary inspired her husband's careful design. He wanted their home to honor her and embody the refined lifestyle she left behind in

Nashville. . . . The majority of the building materials came from the property itself, including timbered pine and handmade brick. Slaves supplied labor. For a purposeful man, not known for his patience, Call found the slow, laborious construction process . . . an education and a test of character.

In February, 1836, during the Second Seminole War, General Call was preparing to sail out of St. Marks with his troops when Mary died. Devastated, he returned to the Grove to care for his infant daughter. Only two children were now living, out of seven born. A month after his wife's death, President Jackson appointed Call to a three-year term as Florida's third territorial governor. To quote Menton:

Following the despondent widower's appointment . . . Indian uprisings combined with a nationwide depression in 1837 to plunge many of Tallahassee's successful merchants and wealthy planters into financial ruin. Governor Call's frustrations with the federal government . . . put him at odds with President Jackson and the succeeding Democratic administration of Martin Van Buren . . . Van Buren asked Governor Call to relinquish the gubernatorial post, citing incompatible views . . .

Call switched parties and supported William Henry Harrison, the Whig candidate, in the presidential election of 1840. When Harrison was inaugurated in 1841, Call was rewarded with another appointment as territorial governor. To quote Menton:

In 1841, a yellow fever epidemic ravaged Tallahassee, inflicting a deadly toll . . . Governor Call himself contracted the deadly disease, but recovered. Two years later . . . a devastating fire swept through the Tallahassee business district, destroying nearly every building between the Capitol and Park Avenue, including Governor Call's office . . . Though some citizens packed up their families and moved away, most stayed on and set about rebuilding their lives and their businesses—this time using brick instead of wood.

When Florida became a state in 1845, its solidly Democratic citizenry defeated Call's candidacy for governor, and he turned his attention to agricultural pursuits.

When Florida seceded from the Union, Call, a staunch Unionist, delivered a tearful speech from the front porch of the Grove. "Ye have unleashed the floodgates of hell," he pronounced solemnly, "from which shall flow the curses of the damned which shall sink you to perdition." To quote Menton: " . . . despite his disappointment, General Call remained loyal to the state. He supported . . . the Confederacy to the point of volunteering himself for service, an offer that was not accepted." He also encouraged his namesake grandson and his son-in-law to serve in the Confederate military.

On the stormy afternoon of September 14, 1862, Richard Keith Call died at the Grove. In accordance with his wishes, he was buried beside his beloved wife in the family cemetery.

FLORIDA'S MAJOR ports were occupied by Union forces throughout most of the war, yet its interior served as a source of beef, fish, and salt for the beleaguered South.

In late February, 1865, Federal troops under the leadership of General John Newton landed twenty-five miles south of Tallahassee. They planned to march north through the sandy pinelands and capture the capital. Confederate troops burned the sole bridge over the St. Marks River and repelled the Federals with a blaze of gunfire. Newton marched his men upstream to Natural Bridge, a point where the river went underground, forming a bridge. He was met by General Clinton Miller heading the Gadsden Greys, a corps of elderly and infirm men, and the Baby Corps, apple-cheeked cadets from a local military academy. Miller's knowledge of the pinewoods and swamps served him well, and he was able to repulse the Federals on three separate occasions until reinforcements arrived. Newton retreated to the Gulf with Miller hot on his heels.

With the Baby Corps and the Gadsden Greys barely scathed, jubilant young bucks at Tallahassee and their lady friends celebrated the victory by taking picnic lunches to the battle site. According to an eyewitness: "the bloated dead floated face-down in the river, while onshore the corpses lay stacked in piles like cordwood with swarms of blue-black flies hovering about."

Today the roar of cannon and clash of infantry have been replaced by the swish of pine boughs on a windy day. Two small wood-framed signs commemorate the Battle of Natural Bridge. One is a map that shows troops and movements. The other lists the number of troops involved and the casualties. Of 893 Federal troops, 21 were killed, 89 wounded, and 148 were missing. Of 595 Confederates, there were 3 killed, 23 wounded, and none missing.

A week after Lee surrendered to Grant at Appomattox, Florida's Governor Milton delivered a speech before the state legislature in which he insisted death would be preferable to reunion. He then traveled to his family home at Marianna and shot himself.

Many freed slaves sharecropped on their former masters' estates. The remaining French peasants, who had been sent over by Lafayette to grow grapes, prospered by growing pines.

Reconstruction was fairly peaceful. Few carpetbaggers were able to cope with Tallahassee's torrid summers and with heavy death tolls from malaria, paratyphoid, and dengue fever. Those who remained were mostly dedicated men devoted to helping the black man and dealing fairly with the white. One such was a black named Jonathan Gibbs who was a delegate to Florida's constitutional convention. A native of Philadelphia, he was educated at Dartmouth and Princeton Theological Seminary, where he earned a degree as a Presbyterian minister. Eventually he was elected Superintendent of Public Education and was held in such esteem by formerly diehard Rebels that Gibbs Drive in a white section of Tallahassee was named after him. "The most cultured member of the convention," he was called by white observers.

THE PLEASANT winter climate of Tallahassee and north Florida, along with abundant wildlife, brought tourists from up North. During the 1870s, Tallahassee even threw a ball for world-famous abolitionist writer Harriet Beecher Stowe, author of *Uncle Tom's Cabin*, who was writing a series of articles extolling Florida. Though compelled by economic conditions to sell portions of the Grove and take in boarders, Ellen Call Long, General Call's daughter, published articles and a book, *Florida Breezes*, praising Florida and its unique history. She represented Florida at the 1876 Centennial Celebration in Washington and served as its commissioner at the New Orleans World Exposition of 1884.

North of Tallahassee, private hunting reserves were established by wealthy northerners, including heirs to United States Steel, the Pennsylvania Railroad, Wall Street, and Standard Oil.

In 1876, Florida returns became the pivot on which the presidential election depended. If Florida electors voted for Democratic nominee Rutherford B. Hayes, the South was promised an end to Reconstruction. This happened, by a narrow margin, and an era ended. "Jim Crow" laws went into effect, and segregation of the races ruled the day.

From then until the 1940s, Tallahassee was a quiet country town of tall stately oaks and around ten thousand people. Fain's drugstore and the F&D (Five and Dime) were gathering places for local gossip, and politicos made deals in the smoke-filled rooms of the Dixie and Leon hotels—until the Dixie burned to the ground in a tragic fire on October 12, 1925. On Saturdays, downtown Tallahassee was the setting for the Farmers' Mart where Tallahasseeans bought produce. Wilson's department store and Bradley's country store, where people bought fresh smoked sausage, were the closest thing to a mall. Though the town was legally dry, bootleggers were an old and abiding tradition, and brown-bag restaurants like the Silver Slipper (with its curtained-off dining alcoves where political deals were cut) and jooks like the Rendezvous on U.S. 27 thrived. Sheriffs realized that "Vote Dry, Be Wet" was the Tallahassee motto, and bootleggers were set free after they paid an occasional fine.

Reinette Long Hunt, Ellen Call Long's granddaughter, inherited the Grove. Though divorced from her wealthy New York–based husband, she received no financial settlement, and the Grove entered an era of benign neglect. Reinette was a bohemian eccentric who wore long flowing dresses and surrounded herself with an eclectic group of friends. She was an accomplished artist, and above her easel hung a portrait of a gypsy—a fitting symbol for its owner. During Reinette's reign, much of the Grove's land was sold as the basis for a future subdivision, and rooms were partitioned to make a rooming house/hotel.

IN NOVEMBER 1942, the Grove was purchased by future governor Leroy Collins and his wife, Mary Call, General Call's third-generation granddaughter, and restored to its former glory. As Collins wrote in *Forerunners Courageous*: "But Call's story . . . becomes more than the story of his . . . life and the lives of his descendants. It becomes the story of a beautiful and strongly built house . . . [This] may be regarded in the end as the true love story of a house, a tiny star in the civilization of its time."

Segregation of the races in Tallahassee and the South continued until 1954 when the Supreme Court outlawed "separate but equal" facilities in its landmark *Brown v. Board of Education* decision. Out of this turmoil emerged Leroy Collins, whom many consider the finest governor the state ever had. To quote Ed H. Price in his foreword to *Forerunners*:

> Florida was in turmoil when Collins became governor in 1955. The year before, the U.S. Supreme Court had discarded . . . state-enforced school segregation. The difficult times of Florida's rapid population

growth were just beginning. And state government labored under the iron hand of the most malapportioned legislature in the . . . United States.

Collins brought to the Florida of 1955 the ability to help people understand . . . they had more in common than their differences. He challenged Floridians to give their best and to expect the best from others. He gave them an example of courage in public office, a willingness to sacrifice momentary popularity for greater moral and ethical principal.

In 1953 Collins was a forty-four-year-old lawyer and legislator living with his family at the Grove. When his friend, Governor Dan McCarty, died in office, he ran to fill the unexpired term and won. Immediately he set about reapportioning Florida's Porkchop legislature—so called because the state's sparsely populated northern counties were vastly over-represented. To quote Collins's first inaugural address:

> I want the people of Florida to understand . . . progress in business, industry, and human welfare can only go so far with a ward-heeling, back-scratching, self-promoting political system . . . Governments must have qualities of spirit. Truth and justice and unselfish service are some of these. Without these qualities there is no worthwhile leadership, and we grapple and groan in a moral wilderness.

But it was Collins's race for re-election in 1956 that brought his toughest test. To quote Price:

> Under court pressure, racial tensions in Florida were high. The state was deciding the direction of its future. Some candidates shouted defiance. Collins calmly counseled moderation. He swamped five opposition candidates to become the only Florida governor to win a first-primary victory.

In his inaugural address of 1957, Collins, like General Call before him, advised against defying the federal government. He did not know "the ultimate answer" for school desegregation. But he did know it would do no good to defy the Supreme Court, "an essential institution

187

for the preservation of our form of government." He did know . . . violence and disorder [and hate were] . . . not the answer.

Collins closed his address with a quote from a hymn by New York abolitionist/poet James Russell Lowell:

> New occasions teach new duties,
> Time makes ancient good uncouth;
> They must upward still and onward
> Who would keep abreast of truth.

DURING THE Little Rock crisis in 1957, Collins reiterated his sentiments in a speech before the Southern Governors' Conference:

> I am convinced . . . the prevailing sentiment in this nation is not radical. It is realistic and understanding. It does not condone arrogance and the irresponsible forcing of issues. It believes . . . the decisions of the . . . Supreme Court are the law of the land. It does not sanction violence, defiance, and disorder. Above all, it abhors hate.

On March 20, 1960, during the violence of sit-in demonstrations in Southern cities including Tallahassee, Tampa, and Jacksonville, Collins delivered the following speech before a statewide TV audience, "As long as I am in . . . office, I will say what I think is right. I will not have on my conscience a feeling that, at any time the people needed my help, I ducked or dodged or looked the other way in order to follow the easy course."

Many Southerners recognized that racial strife damaged the nation, but believed no damage would occur, if only colored people would "stay in their place."

Collins addressed that:

> Now, friends, that's not a Christian point of view. That's not a democratic point of view. That's not a realistic point of view. We can never stop Americans from hoping and praying . . . this ideal that is embedded in our Declaration of Independence . . . that all men are created

188

equal, that somehow this will be a reality and not just an illusory distant goal . . .

Though civil rights demonstrators were beaten, bruised, and arrested—notably at St. Augustine, where (as previously mentioned) the elderly wife of Episcopal Bishop Malcolm Peabody of Massachusetts was arrested for violating a segregation law at a lunch counter—Florida remained relatively calm compared to the rest of the South. Within a few years of the 1964 Civil Rights Act, a black mayor, James Ford, was elected in predominantly white Tallahassee.

Collins chaired the 1960 Democratic Convention, which nominated John F. Kennedy for president, and served as president of the National Association of Broadcasters. He headed the Community Relations Service, which Congress created under the Civil Rights Act of 1964 to foster peaceful compliance with the law. He was present at the Selma March to represent the federal government and act as liaison between local authorities and Rev. Martin Luther King, Jr., and the demonstrators. But Collins's political career was dead, so far as his own state was concerned. In 1968 he ran for the Senate, but was roundly defeated by the mudslinging opposition.

Collins moved back to the Grove and resumed his law practice. He died in 1991, a visionary Southerner years ahead of his time.

Thanks in part to Collins, old-time politicians like my grandfather, James Turner Butler, came to see the light. Butler represented Jacksonville and Duval County for thirty years in the Florida legislature, serving one year as president of the state Senate and lieutenant governor. He originated the bill that consolidated the city and county governments of Duval County and made Jacksonville the largest city, in area, in the country. He drew up the legislation that culminated in Jacksonville's four bridges across the St. Johns River as well as Tampa Bay's Skyway Bridge. When the state wanted to name the Matthews Bridge in Jacksonville after him, he declined, declaring that monuments should only be named after dead people. Shortly after his death in 1969, James Turner Butler Boulevard, the main thoroughfare from Jacksonville to the beaches, was named for him.

One morning, Butler sat down to breakfast at his customary table at Jacksonville's Andrew Jackson Hotel. A black man was seated at the table next to his. "I looked at him and he looked at me," recalled Grandpops. "Then we nodded at one another and ate our breakfast. I couldn't help but wonder what all the fuss had been about all those many years."

To get to Tallahassee, follow I-10 west from Jacksonville or Lake City at the eastern edge of the panhandle.

The Florida State Museum, the governor's mansion, the Grove, the Florida State University campus, and the restored downtown section are within easy walking distance of the old capitol building. When the legislature is in session, Clyde's and Costello's Saloon downtown is a good place to watch the political animal in his natural habitat. Bellevue, the restored home of Achille and Kitty Murat, a modest clapboard cottage, along with a one-room schoolhouse and grist mill, is at the Junior Museum near the municipal airport.

Lake Jackson, where DeSoto and his troops celebrated the first Christmas mass in the continental United States, is just north of the city limits. North of Tallahassee and south of Thomasville, Georgia, around Lake Jackson and Lake Iamonin, are the quail-hunting preserves of many well known Americans, including Ted Turner.

The site of the Battle of Natural Bridge is ten miles southeast of Tallahassee.

Nearby Wakulla Springs Park, whose cool, crystal-clear waters bubble from an underground spring to form the Wakulla River, encompasses 4,000 acres of pine and hardwood forest donated by the late Ed Ball, a key figure in Florida politics. Ball's sister married into the DuPont family, and Ball turned his share of the estate into a two-billion-dollar Florida empire. Universal Studios filmed the classic horror film *Creature from the Black Lagoon* in this primeval setting. Portions of Johnny Weismuller's Tarzan films and Disney's *20,000 Leagues Under the Sea* were also filmed here.

Governors come in every size, shape, and form. Once on Bimini, I ran into Florida's first Republican governor, Claude Kirk. A woman and I were strolling on the beach and we walked past a gate marked Rockwell Tool Corporation. This technically made us trespassers, though I had done the same thing many times before, only to get a friendly wave from the Bahamian help. Suddenly a red-faced middle-aged white man in a golf cart, brandishing a .45, bore down on us. I assumed he was a security guard, but he identified himself as Governor Kirk and demanded to know what we were doing there. I recognized Kirk from TV and photographs. When I explained we were taking a walk, he called us dirty hippies and demanded we leave the premises immediately. "Ex-governor, isn't it?" I couldn't resist asking. There followed a long angry tirade. Later that evening, when I met Kirk and his son at a local restaurant, he appeared not to recognize me or to remember our earlier encounter—a model of civility and charm. What a trip!

Lake Helen, Fla.
Stevens Street, Camp Cassadaga

From years gone by, a postcard view of the main street of Camp Cassadaga.
Photo courtesy Florida State Archives.

Cassadaga

The tiny central Florida village of Cassadaga is like New England in appearance, with white clapboard cottages, neatly tended gardens, and narrow shaded streets. Reminiscent of the subtropics is the prolific Spanish moss bearding tall stately oaks. The first thing you notice is the quiet. Aside from the twittering of jays and rustle of squirrels, there's little to disturb the peace. Occasionally one passes groups of visitors, many of them elderly, with an almost equal number of middle-aged women, and a smattering of young couples chatting in low, subdued voices as though in church. The tags on the cars parked alongside the road proclaim most of them to be from up North, especially the Midwest.

The Spiritualist camp is laid out in a hilly square with four small tree-filled parks, with names like Healing Tree, around two dark green lakes, Lake Colby and Spirit Pond. Nine short roads at right angles to Stevens Street, the main drag, are lined with cottages inhabited by more than forty certified mediums. Small wooden signs out front list the names of the residents inside. Many of the names are preceded by the title

Reverend. Aside from the mediums' homes, the camp consists of the Cassadaga Hotel, a white stucco building with a long wrap-around porch, built in 1922. Its dimly lit lobby is decorated with a beshawled Victorian piano and photographs of famous mediums who have visited. An adjoining restaurant serves breakfast, lunch, and dinner. There used to be a bar—named Arthur's after the resident spook—where psychics and mediums gathered after work to watch TV and discuss such topics as where the criminals on *America's Most Wanted* are *really* hiding out. To one side of the hotel is the Andrew Jackson Davis meeting hall, a whitewashed, wood building resembling an army barracks, that contains meeting rooms and a wonderful bookstore that specializes in mystic and spiritualist literature, and where appointments with mediums can be made. Across the road is a similar bookstore.

Andrew Jackson Davis was known as the "Seer of Poughkeepsie." In 1844 he claimed that the noted but long-dead eighteenth-century mystic and mathematician, Emanuel Swendenborg, visited him and told him he had a mission to mankind. Three years later, at age twenty-one, Davis was living in luxury in New York on the proceeds of his mesmeric healing and had written—in trance—a book, *The Principles of Nature*, that described the spiritual and physical workings of the universe.

The Spiritualist movement began in March 1848 at the home of the Fox sisters in Hydesville, New York. To quote British writer/philosopher Colin Wilson:

> The Fox family, which included two teenage daughters, was kept awake . . . night after night by banging noises. One night, twelve-year-old Kate began snapping her fingers, and the bangs and raps imitated her. Neighbors were called in to witness the phenomena, and one of them began asking the invisible presence questions . . . [the presence] claimed to be the spirit of a peddler who had been murdered and buried in the basement. [In fact, when the basement was excavated in 1904, a skeleton and a peddler's tin box were found.] The children were separated and sent to live with relatives; the rapping noises followed them, and developed into [a] conventional "poltergeist" occurrence—objects fly-

194

ing through the air. Eventually on instructions from the "spirits," the first Spiritualist church was founded . . . [W]ithin ten years, Spiritualism spread all over the world . . .

Politically, Spiritualists were prohibitionists (the body is the temple of God), abolitionists, and women's suffragettes who, according to John J. Guthrie in an article in the *Florida Historical Quarterly* extended "a cordial invitation to all . . . regardless of caste or color."

CASSADAGA WAS founded on January 3, 1895, when the Reverend William Colby donated thirty-five acres of land in Volusia County to the Southern Spiritualist Camp Meeting Association. The seeds leading to this decision were planted twenty years earlier, when twenty-seven-year-old Colby held a seance in the home of S. D. Wadsworth of Lake Mills, Iowa. During this seance, Colby purportedly heard an urgent message from his Indian spirit guide, Seneca. Seneca told Colby he should immediately head for Eau Claire, Wisconsin, to meet with a fellow spiritualist named T. D. Giddings. The next morning, Colby traveled to Giddings's home at Eau Claire. Both men were told by Seneca to leave Eau Claire and travel to Florida, where a Congress of Spirits had decided a Spiritualist camp was to be established.

Colby and Giddings, along with Giddings's family, took the railroad to Jacksonville and traveled by steamboat up the St. Johns River to Blue Springs. Seneca had informed them the camp was to be established in the vicinity of Blue Springs "on high pine bluffs overlooking a chain of silvery lakes." In Blue Springs, Seneca made contact again and told them to follow his instructions. According to one account, the two men "followed a footpath for a little distance, then straight through the deep forest. They went for several miles, until at last . . . they viewed the promised land. The high bluffs, the lake, the lay of the land, everything was found exactly as it had been described by the Spirit Seneca before leaving Wisconsin."

For reasons unknown, Colby did nothing to establish the camp he was sent to create. Instead, for the next eighteen years he operated a dairy farm. In 1893 another spiritualist named Rowley attempted to establish a spiritualist camp in nearby Winter Park. A number of prominent spiritualists arrived from up North. Unimpressed with Rowley, they met with Colby. With his encouragement, they established the camp on his property. Since they didn't proselytize and were law-abiding citizens who contributed greatly to Volusia County's economy, Spiritualists were accepted locally. Soon theirs was the only Spiritualist assembly in the South, and the second-largest in the nation after Lily Dale in upstate New York.

Communicating directly with "ghostly presences" was a common occurrence at Cassadaga before the 1960s. According to an eyewitness account in Robert Harrold's *Cassadaga*:

> With the medium inside [a wooden closet] and the guard posted, all lights would be turned off . . . From out of the pitch darkness, a swirl would materialize. It would appear to come from the cabinet. Gradually it would form into a full-length human form. It would be white, yet appear to be almost transparent, ghostly . . .
>
> This materialized spirit would walk in front of [the spectators] and speak to them. Oftentimes the spirit would be personally known to someone in the room, a brother who had died, a husband, a sister. And more often than not, the spirit would have personal messages for all those present, either from the spirit itself or its companions in the World of Spirit.

Other spirits enlisted the aid of floating trumpets, through which to speak to the living. There were also photographic mediums, who took pictures of the deceased to show to their friends and relations.

Starting in the 1960s, the mediums of Cassadaga—perhaps put off by the accusations of trickery and attempted exposés—resorted to a more subtle form of communication with the dead. Today, the person seeking information sits in a dimly lighted room on a comfortable chair. A medium sits opposite and gives what is known as a "reading."

196

I HAD TWO READINGS at Cassadaga:

My first is given by Mr. X, a short nondescript man in his mid-forties. When we shake hands, I detect a vague odor of tobacco and alcohol about his person. His "reading room" is overheated, dimly lit, and furnished in early Sears Roebuck. We take seats opposite one another separated by a coffee table covered with different-sized "healing" crystals. He hands over a pen and a piece of paper and tells me to write something, anything. He then proceeds to chain-smoke menthol cigarettes.

I write: "It sure is hard to get a reading in Cassadaga since most of the mediums are booked up days in advance."

Mr. X looks over my sentence and smiles. "This exercise was merely meant to put you at your ease."

According to him, he can read my "vibrations" by interpreting colors he perceives as "auras" about my person. Leaning back on the sofa, he places his hands to his temples and delivers a series of generalizations that are, more or less, correct. I need to relax. In the future, I need to listen to women more and throw caution to the wind. I'm creative and artistic (I especially like this one).

His first direct hit is the fact I'm a writer—something I hadn't told him beforehand—and need to expand in the direction of computers and research. In fact, I'd recently purchased a good deal of computer equipment and planned to start a small publishing company of my own (the reading took place in the mid '80s before everyone was a computer geek).

He asks me a question: "You're planning a trip to Central America, aren't you?"

Since I had been considering a trip to Guatemala to see the Mayan ruins at Tikal, I nod my head yes.

"I'm not sure you'll be going. It could be dangerous. But if you keep your eyes and ears open, you ought to be all right. Wait! I'm getting a vision of you and your friends producing videos."

As it turned out, I never did make the trip to Guatemala, and I would have preferred a vision of my writing the Great American Novel, since my idea of videos at the time was what one saw on MTV. But he was right about the videos. A year or so later, some friends and I shot two unusual travel videos.

The rest of the reading consists of a long diatribe about local politics, a subject that doesn't particularly interest me. Some thirty or forty minutes after it began, the reading is over.

Mr. X charges me forty dollars and ushers me to the door.

His overall performance might not appear too impressive. But he did score three direct "hits," the fact I'm a writer, planning a trip to Central America, and would someday make videos. If all it takes is one white crow to disprove the notion that all crows are black, perhaps there's something to this "reading" business after all.

MY SECOND READING is given by a Mrs. Y—in her mid-forties, like Mr. X, with a slight British accent. A sign above the front door reads "No Smoking." Her small reading room is tastefully decorated with Indian artifacts and paintings, including an oil portrait of an Indian maiden who is her spirit guide. A welcome fan blows a cooling breeze across my face, and a bookshelf against the far wall is filled with "occult" works, including such classics as Robert Graves's *The White Goddess* and Colin Wilson's *Mysteries*.

Mrs. Y asks me to place my palms on top of hers so she can feel my vibrations. She leans back in her armchair and appears to go into a trance. Several minutes pass during which the only sound is the steady swish, swish of the fan.

Finally, Mrs. Y opens her eyes. "The first image I had was of you astride a horse. You're crossing a prairie with no paths. At first, you're hesitant to proceed. Then the horse takes off at a gallop, forming its own path. This image symbolizes the fact that career-wise you're forging your own path."

Mrs. Y closes her eyes. In a matter of seconds, she reopens them. "I see you as a bull grazing alone in a field. You're content just to graze and not charge anyone. This image symbolizes the fact that relationship-wise, you're no longer leading with your heart. You've learned the virtue of patience and are awaiting the right opportunity. Does this mean anything to you?"

I nod my head yes.

It certainly does, I think. However, the skeptic in me can't help adding: *Me and about a billion other people!*

Again Mrs. Y closes her eyes. Opening them, she says, "I see two eagles, a mother and baby, on a branch overhanging a high cliff. The mother eagle is forcing the baby eagle off the branch so it can learn to fly. This image symbolizes a new beginning. Spiritually, you're beginning to grasp the big picture from a bird's eye view."

Amen. I think to myself. Then, the skeptic in me adds: *Obviously, I want to hear something about my spirituality. Otherwise, I wouldn't be here.*

There follows more of this imaging, a golf ball sailing straight down a fairway, a tightrope walker finding the correct balance, a man on a diving board making a big splash.

Then she gives me a rundown on what to expect over the next six months. At the end of the reading, she asks if I have any questions or if there's anyone passed on whom I would care to contact.

"Borden . . . See if you can contact him."

My friend Borden had died four years before.

Mrs. Y again closes her eyes. "I'm not getting any messages. Sometimes the spirits are busy elsewhere. They can't always be there for *you*, you know."

The way she says it makes me feel guilty for having imposed on my old pal that way. "Try Jim Turner, then."

Turner, my high-sheriff cousin, had died two years before.

"I see a 'good ole boy' leaning against a pickup truck drinking a beer. He's wearing some kind of uniform and has a badge. He says he's here to protect you, to make sure no one gives you any trouble. Does that make any sense?"

"Jim was an old man when I knew him, and he drank Scotch. But that might have been a somewhat accurate picture of him when he was younger, especially the part about the badge and uniform and his protecting me. After all, he was a sheriff."

"Hold on a minute!" Mrs. Y closes her eyes and places her hand to her forehead. "Someone else is coming through. She's a little old lady, less than five feet tall. She lived to be very old, late eighties or early nineties. And she's wearing a thick pair of glasses like she can hardly see. She claims she just wants to shake you sometime. 'Loosen up,' she says. Does that make any sense to you?"

"The lady you describe bears a striking resemblance to my grandmother on my mother's side. Especially the part about her height and the glasses. And the fact she wants to shake me. It was one of her favorite expressions when she was mad with me."

But, then, a lot of people have a grandmother who would fit that description, pipes up the skeptic in me. *Still, there's the part about wanting to "shake me." It was one of her favorite expressions when she was angry.*

After all, it only takes one white crow to disprove the statement all crows are black!

When the reading is over, Mrs. Y charges me thirty-five dollars and gives me a clean bill of health.

This reading, given the symbolism and the personal contact, is more impressive to me than the one given by Mr. X. Being a writer, I am partial to symbols and personal contact.

THAT NIGHT I have a strange dream. It's about 1900 and my great-great-grandfather, James S. Turner, is at Cassadaga to see a medium. He's an old man, about to die, and his eyes are heavy with the cares of the world. The lights are dimmed and he is seated across a round table from an elderly shawled lady with a faraway look in her eyes. "James Turner!" she cries out in a deep baritone voice, her eyes rolling back in her head. "It is I, Joseph Haskew, the man you condemned to death some forty years ago."

For an instant, Turner's face takes on the animation of a much younger man. "A steer's good eating. You should have taken a steer. A heifer's for milk."

"Nonetheless, to kill a man over a hunk of beef!" returns the medium in the same baritone voice.

"You're right." Turner reassumes the expression of an old man. "But I was younger then and certain of my so-called rights."

"And I an even younger man, and just as certain of mine."

"You forgive me, then?" asks Turner with a look of surprise.

"T'were nothing to forgive. We both done what it was in us to do. Such is the Law of Life."

Turner can hardly believe his ears. Once again his face assumes the expression of a much younger man. "I spent a year in a Federal prison at Savannah. It was a far from pleasant experience."

Haskew (the medium) chuckles. "But well deserved."

"Mayhap, it were at that!" Turner chuckles to himself. "Mayhap, it were at that." Then, following a pause: "At any rate, I don't hold it against you any. Your causing me to kill you, I mean."

Awakening from my dream, I see the phantomlike figures of Turner and Haskew hovering to one side of my bed. When I reach out to touch them, they vanish before my eyes. The trail has led me to a destination, shaking my skepticism to a degree that has probably won the approval of my dead grandmother.

Cassadaga is twenty-five miles west of Daytona or thirty miles east of Orlando off I-4.

Stetson University in DeLand, one of the oldest private universities in Florida, founded in the 1880s by the hat-maker from Philadelphia. Elizabeth Hall (bottom) built in 1892, Sampson Hall (top) built in 1908.

Photos by Keith Bollum.

DeLand and Orlando

DeLand was founded in 1876 by wealthy Northern industrialist Henry A. DeLand. He and John B. Stetson, inventor of the Stetson hat, financed Stetson University—stately, white-pillared president's mansion, Victorian red-brick buildings, and five-story carrillon chimes that toll the hour—in the 1880s. By 1896 DeLand was a bustling community of more than 2,000 people.

In Stetson University's Ed Ball Library, I found a cache of turn-of-the-century letters from James S. Turner to my grandfather Turner Butler. Butler, Turner's grandson, was attending Stetson Law School and graduated in the first matriculating class of 1904. In one somewhat hypocritical letter, given his own colorful past, Turner was berating the president of Baptist-supported Stetson for carrying on an alleged affair with the dean of women, a cause célèbre at that time. According to Turner: "Old Satan must have gotten into that Stetson crowd."

I FIRST VISITED DeLand twenty years ago and fell in love with the Muse Book Store on Main Street. A Dickensonian repository of antiquarian and newly published books, it's the pulsebeat of downtown DeLand. The proprietors, Janet and Keith Bollum (later divorced) from snowy Minnesota, were the brother and sister I never had and showed me the town through their eyes.

Our hangout was the Airport Bar across from a tiny hangar, headquarters for the municipal airport. Open parachutes draped the ceiling, and tasty cheeseburgers were served. I fell in love with a freckled, redheaded schoolteacher who, as Jim Turner would say, knew all about Florida history and more besides! We explored the tea-brown, water-lilied St. Johns River. On its fertile black banks, we ate at deep-fry fish camps in "grit" towns like Astor and Orange City and drank at cracker jooks. One afternoon we took the short ferry ride from DeLand Landing to subtropical Hontoon Island and followed a winding trail through huge grotesquely branched oaks to huge Indian burial mounds that could have served as the setting for Edgar Allan Poe's *The Gold Bug*. At trail's end, we climbed a fifty-foot wood tower with a panoramic view of river, marsh, and hammock— like a technicolor vision of old-time Florida.

There was a harness race track at Spring Garden where one could breakfast sumptuously while watching sulky horses and trainers round the freshly raked track in the crisp early morning air. And Lake Helen with immaculately refurbished houses on Euclid Avenue, where Arthur Jones, inventor of the Nautilus machine, wrestled alligators and had a private zoo. But love, if tightly grasped, has a way of vanishing like winter mist before the summer sun. And DeLand became a faint dream at the edge of a dim horizon . . .

OCCASIONALLY I VISITED Keith at the Plaza Hotel on Lake Eola in Orlando. Once Orlando's premier hotel, where Walt Disney and President Johnson stayed in the '60s, the Plaza is now an apartment building with two bars, a gourmet restaurant, and huge outdoor pool. To me, a lover of grand old hotels, it's the perfect place to live, with a panoramic view of Lake Eola—fleets of ducks, pedal boats, a multicolored fountain, and a half-mile walking track around the lake with a constant flow of people, including joggers and mothers pushing baby carriages. At the south end is a bandstand and a stone monument to Orlando Reeves, the first U.S. casualty in the Third Seminole War. Looming in the background are huge glassed-in skyscrapers that light up the city at night.

In the evenings we would meet in the Plaza's Manhattan-style basement saloon, with Sinatra on the Wurlitzer jukebox, and make forays down bustling Orange Avenue to eat at the latest hip restaurant or take in the bluesy nightlife. Or if we wanted to play tourist, we'd visit Church Street Station, the Disney World of nightclubs, where tourists from around the world drink exquisitely colored, sickeningly sweet, and terribly expensive drinks with cutesy names.

Then there was the night Mohawk John—an African American with a mohawk haircut—and I were stumbling home from an all-nighter on Orange Avenue when we spied an amorphous trio of Halloween-type characters with green and purple hair, ring-pierced body parts, and long, flowing, gossamerlike robes, hovering before us in the early morning mist. "Rebels without a clue!" exclaimed Mohawk as they vanished into the enveloping fog.

Keith married Sandra, a beautiful Haitian, and between his and her children and my constant traveling, we seldom saw one another. And so Orlando, too, became a faint dream at the edge of a dim horizon. Like ghost ships passing in the foggy night, we sail on through eternity . . .

DeLand and Orlando are west of Daytona and east of Tampa off I-4.

The Plaza, a nine-story apartment building, opened as the Eola Plaza in 1950 (it was later renamed the Cherry Plaza), and served as the Minnesota Twins' home away from home during spring-training camp. On

October 25, 1964, Lyndon Johnson spent the night, the first U.S. president to stay overnight in Orlando. On November 15, 1965, Walt Disney rented the hotel's Egyptian Room to announce plans for Disney World. Over the years, opera singer Robert Merrill, actress Gloria Swanson, and comedian Danny Thomas stayed here. The building was bought by the present owners in the early '80s. Today it's a funky downtown apartment building with beautiful views and a laid-back attitude toward personal renovation and decoration. Tenants include, according to an article in the *Orlando Sentinel*: " . . . the old and the young, the gay and the straight—artists, symphony musicians, entrepreneurs, lawyers, physicians, bankers, architects, writers, bartenders, ministers, bureaucrats, hairdressers, exotic dancers, ranch managers, aerobic instructors, body-building gym owners, and (safe behind the poured concrete walls) singing waiters."

Part 4
THE GLADES

Everglades hunting trip with Seminole guides in December 1936.

The Glades

The Everglades don't appeal to everyone.

At first glance, they appear flat, desolate, forbidding—a mangrove swamp filled with gators and water moccasins. One can drive for miles down U.S. 41, the old Tamiami Trail, without apparent change of scenery. Occasionally there's a weathered sign advertising alligator wrestling, airboat rides, or a Seminole Indian Reservation. These attractions are usually housed behind sagging wooden fences, their ticket booths empty, the owners having moved elsewhere.

Still, if one has the eye for it, there is a brooding beauty here and a variety of wildlife unparalleled. In her ground-breaking 1947 book, author/naturalist Marjory Stoneman Douglas dubbed the Glades *River of Grass*. Its heart is a shallow, freshwater river, fifty, sixty, even seventy miles wide at places, no more than a few inches deep, that flows south from the Kissimmee River and Lake Okeechobee into Florida Bay, an 850-square-mile body of water whose depth ranges from three to six feet. Warmed by the hot subtropical sun, the Glades' shallow waters provide a natural breeding place and refuge for plant and animal life, including more than 300 species of birds, 1,000 varieties of seed-bearing plants, 120 species of trees, 25 kinds of orchids, and a variety of bromeliads. The Glades is also home to eleven endangered species, including the American crocodile, the Southern bald eagle, the West Indian manatee, and the Florida panther.

Here is a wealth of wildlife to be examined in detail by anyone with the least trace of adventure in his soul.

Lake Okeechobee

You're rolling down U.S. 27 south of I-4 and Haines City, through Avon Park and Sebring and Lake Placid. The retirees are thick as flies in the sawgrass, and the fast-food joints and motels and shopping centers of Anyplace, USA, are streaming past your car windows.

Damn, you think to yourself, *Am I really headed to the Everglades?*

Somehow it all seems too civilized.

But just past Lake Placid the highway clears and you find yourself alone for an instant. Not long, mind you. Up ahead there's a diesel. Off in the distance, another. Still, you've broken the tourist barrier and reached the other side. You're alone now, no matter an occasional car or truck—alone amid the buggy, buzzing solitude of the Glades . . .

LAKE OKEECHOBEE is 750 square miles, the largest lake in Florida and the second largest totally within the boundary of any state. For years it was known only to the Seminoles, who were driven steadily south into the Glades over the course of three Seminole Wars.

On Christmas Day 1837, General Zachary Taylor, future president of the United States, led 1,067 men, including 70 Delaware Indians, to a point near the present-day town of Okeechobee. He captured a Seminole brave guarding two or three hundred head of cattle. Under threat of death, the brave pointed to a dense cypress hammock a mile away where his compatriots lay poised to attack. The braves had obligingly cut a swath through the sawgrass, and General Taylor decided on a direct attack down the open lane.

The Indians held their fire until the soldiers were within range, then let loose with a volley that brought down a tenth of the troops. The soldiers continued to advance as though on parade. Indians were perched in trees and hidden behind logs and bushes. They raised their heads to fire, then ducked to reload.

The battle lasted from 12:30 P.M. to 3:00 in the afternoon. At its close, 26 soldiers lay dead, 112 wounded. The Indians, who totaled 380 warriors, counted 12 dead, including 1 Negro, and 9 wounded. Since the Indians had been driven out, Taylor claimed victory and gained the nickname "Old Rough and Ready."

According to a letter he wrote home, he had:

> . . . experienced the most trying scenes of my life. Besides the killed, among whom were some of my personal friends, there lay 112 wounded officers and soldiers who had accompanied me 145 miles, most of the way through unexplored wilderness and who had to be conveyed through swamps and hammocks without any apparent means of doing so.

TIRED FROM TRAVEL, you pull into Helen's Bar alongside State Road 78. Inside it's dim and smoky. In blatant disregard of the Surgeon General's warning, crackers wearing trucker's caps, with strings of keys connected to the belt loops of their jeans, are smoking up a storm at a horseshoe-shaped bar to one side of a deserted dance floor. A faded cowgirl is feeding quarters to the jukebox, while the country singer Hank Williams, Jr. croons "All My Rowdy Friends Have Settled Down." It's the sort of place you've entered hundreds of times before in "grit" towns like Chiefland, Williston, and Bronson.

You take a seat at the bar and order a beer from the tattooed, peroxide blonde. For an instant, everyone's attention focuses in your direction like the scene in many movies where the Easterner first enters the Wild West saloon. Having taken your measure, it's back to business as usual. Seated to your right before a beer mug is a weathered-looking cracker. Standing next to him, with a glass of Jack Daniel's, is a Seminole with a dusty black felt cap.

The Seminole proposes a toast, "Here's to George Wallace, Jefferson Davis, and Malcolm X." He waves his drink in the cracker's face.

The cracker smiles warily. "Whatever you say, Chief." He raises his beer and drinks.

You try to ignore them, but the Seminole catches your eye.

"How's it going, Preppie?" he asks with a mock friendly grin on his face. Then, to the barmaid, "Miss, let me buy this gentleman a back-up."

Perhaps it was your Lacoste shirt or your khaki pants or your topsiders that gave you away. Or maybe it was a combination of the three. At any rate, you admire a man who is able to pin you down that well. Though you don't *really* consider yourself a preppie, your dress and manner suggest it.

You are about to say, "Thanks, Chief." But think better of the idea. To address the Seminole as "Chief" suggests an unwarranted familiarity, a familiarity you haven't earned. You might end up dead.

"Thanks," you say instead.

"Are you an Ivy League man, sir?" asks the Seminole with mock formality.

"No, sir, I'm not."

213

"But might you have been?"

"Perhaps . . . "

If I hadn't been kicked out of an Eastern prep school, you think.

The Seminole returns his attention to the cracker. "You're a tiller of the soil, I take it, sir."

"Huh?"

"A farmer."

"For going on forty years . . . "

"But not a populist, I assume."

From the bewildered expression on his face, it's obvious the cracker has no idea what a populist is.

The Seminole enlightens him. "Did you vote for Jimmy Carter in seventy-six?"

"Hell, no!" growls the cracker. "I got no use for that damned peanut farmer!"

"Then you're not a populist," says the Seminole, in the manner of one addressing a young and not particularly bright child.

"If that's what it takes, I guess I ain't."

The cracker raises the beer mug to his lips in a quick, sullen motion. There's a flash of conflict like static electricity.

"Buy my friend here another drink, please, Miss." The Seminole motions with his glass at the cracker.

The cracker smiles a reluctant smile. "I like you, Chief. I wouldn't want you to go and tell *jest* anybody, but I like you."

"That's awfully considerate of you, sir. I find you less than offensive myself."

You finish your beer and the back-up and beat a hasty retreat.

The Seminole's ironic verbal sparring is the sort of subtle offensive that enabled his tribe to survive the bloody conflict in the Glades. Unlike "Old Rough and Ready," given his numbers, the Seminole can't afford a direct attack. Instead he fires a steady stream of lead from the shelter of tree limbs, stumps, and thickets, in hope some bullets will find their target.

Back in the car, you ponder the miracle of the Seminoles' survival in so inhospitable an environment. To your left are huge earthen dikes holding back the floodwaters of Lake Okeechobee.

THE HURRICANE that hit Lake Okeechobee on September 16, 1928, was one of the worst peacetime disasters in the history of the United States. There had been floods in '22 and '24, and the hurricane of '26 hit Moore Haven on Lake Okeechobee, killing three hundred people. But none of these disasters compared to the hurricane of '28.

The storm hit West Palm Beach on a Sunday, killing hundreds, then headed west for the lake. It wasn't the wind that killed. It was the water. Rains in August had raised the lake three feet. Its depth was 16.3 feet, much too high for safety. The telephone lines were down, and weather reports in those days before radar were often highly inaccurate. In any event, there was no place to run. There were no roads leading west, and anyone foolish enough to head east would be headed directly into the storm.

By 8:30 that evening, the gusts from the northwest were upwards of a hundred miles an hour and howled with the hollow roar only a hurricane can make. In no time at all, the dike gave way, in some places clean to the ground for a hundred yards at a stretch. Houses and trees were uprooted, and even the strongest of swimmers didn't stand a chance amid the floating debris. Air, water, and sky were pitch black. By ten o'clock, when the eye of the hurricane passed, the water was seven feet deep in the streets of Belle Glade. At South Bay, those not lost in the storm took shelter in the deckhouses of a quarterboat. Men down in the hold passed water up in buckets.

By storm's end, the lake's shores were wiped almost clean of settlements. One house, with thirty-eight people, drifted three-quarters of a mile. In all, more than two thousand people died. Naked bodies were doused in crude oil and burned, twenty or more in a heap. Many were Bahamian migrant workers, and there was no way to identify them.

As a result of the mighty storm, Congress authorized the Army Corps of Engineers to build an adequate levee around the lake.

YOU'RE CIRCLING Lake Okeechobee passing through "grit" and "wetback" towns like South Bay, Belle Glade, Pahokee, Canal Point, Okeechobee, and Buckhead Ridge. The land is flat, mosquito-ridden, covered with cypress, pine, and sawgrass whose razor-sharp edges kept the white man away for centuries. Occasionally you pass a trailer park or a Jiffy Mart or a dilapidated "knife and gun" club with mounted fish and game-covered walls, trucker-capped cracker clientele, and a crude, hand-stenciled, cardboard sign advertising a live band on Friday and Saturday nights. Once in a great while, an adjoining road leads atop the dike. Stretched out before you as far as the eye can see is the cypress and hyacinth-edged lake. At Canal Point, there's a historical plaque commemorating an ill-fated toll road.

DURING THE 1920s, W. J. Conners, a wealthy Palm Beach industrialist, bought four thousand acres of land around Lake Okeechobee. Conners's son-in-law was the cartoonist George McManus who created the strip *Maggie and Jiggs* based on Connors and his wife, who didn't approve of their socially un-prominent son-in-law.

At first Conners tried to farm the land. When that failed, he bought another 12,000 acres, including the townsite of Okeechobee, for $700,000. He went before the state legislature. In the record time of two hours and twenty minutes, they passed a highway bill that permitted him to construct a fifty-two-mile toll road from Palm Beach to his property at Canal Point.

Built at a cost of $1,800,000, the road was to attract potential buyers of his land, and Conners predicted Okeechobee would become the "Chicago of the South." On January 28, 1928, the first day the road was opened, Conners took in $8,200 in tolls at $.02 a mile. For a brief time, the

216

toll road averaged $1000 a day. The sale of small tracts of land brought in another million dollars.

Given the hostility of the setting—mosquitoes, saw grass, gators—and the Florida real estate bust, traffic and sales declined steadily. Conners was never able to recoup his investment, and the road was eventually sold to the state for $660,000.

YOU SPEND THE NIGHT at Buckhead Ridge.

The next morning you hire a guide to take you bass fishing. Heading out the pass, the tall grass and water hyacinths are thick enough to pass for dry land. When you look back, the trail cut by the outboard engine reveals dark, tannic brown water. The guide guns the engine and feathery, blurred flurries of brown ducks and cormorants scatter like buckshot to either side of the wake. It's amazing the guide knows where he's headed, so alike is the lakescape to the untrained eye. By day's end, you've caught more than thirty bass, several weighing in excess of five pounds.

You spend the night in Clewiston, a company town of 1920s crackerbox cottages built around the U.S. Sugar Corporation, the oldest and largest sugar manufacturer in the country. The company farms 175,000 acres in three counties on Lake Okeechobee's south side. There's a company whistle that goes off every afternoon at 4:30 to announce the end of the work day.

The Clewiston Inn, on the corner of U.S. 27 and Royal Palm Avenue, is Deep South in decor with a four-columned front entrance. It has a bird's-eye-cypress-paneled lobby and open-beam ceiling, and the terra-cotta tile floor is waxed to a glossy, smooth finish. Rooms are decorated '40s-style, and the restaurant serves some of the finest Southern cooking in the state. During World War II, the British Royal Air Force trained cadets at nearby Riddle Field, and the Clewiston Inn was their favorite hangout.

To one side of the lobby is the Bird Room Bar, a cozy, intimate lounge with an oil-and-canvas mural of local birdlife circling all four walls.

It was painted by J. Clinton Shepherd, who lived at the Inn for most of 1945. The 360-degree panorama is set in the early morning fog and depicts Glades wildlife. It contains many species of ducks, egrets, herons, and cranes. There are also owls, jays, ospreys, deer, opossum, a marsh hare, alligators, and a black bear with her cub.

To get to Lake Okeechobee, follow U.S. 27 south of Haines City past Lake Placid to State Road 78. Take a left on 78 and circle the lake. Follow it until it turns into 441 South.

At Buckhead Ridge, at the mouth of the Kissimmee River, there's a cruise ship that departs daily to cross Lake Okeechobee and dock at Ft. Myers.

Roland Martin, the world's most famous bass fisherman, host of his own TV show, and a top finisher in major bass tournaments, owns a combination marina, motel, resort, café, RV park, ship's store, and guide service on Lake Okeechobee at Clewiston, under his own name.

Flamingo and Everglades National Park

Flamingo . . .

The name of this frontier village, a tiny settlement at the tip end of the Florida peninsula, evokes an image of flocks of vivid pink flamingos circling grassy swamplands in the last magic moment of a vermilion-tinged Glades sunset. Nothing could be further from the truth. Flamingos were never native to south Florida, but migrated in large numbers from Cuba and the Bahamas. Once the most distinctive form of Glades wildlife, the population was reduced to several hundred by plume hunters during the late nineteenth and early twentieth centuries—bird feathers were then in vogue as decoration on women's hats—and flamingos were rarely sighted after that time. Today they're extinct in south Florida.

The first post office was established at Flamingo in 1893 when the famous birds could still be seen. After that, the town was a farming community, growing enormous squashes and other vegetables for market in Key West. Other sources of income were syrup derived from sugar cane and charcoal made from buttonwood. In 1908 the first fish company, the

Crossland, came to Flamingo. By 1947 two other fish companies were in business from mid-August to November during the fishing season. A commissary supplied the fishermen's needs, on credit. At the end of the season, the fishermen might be issued wages or be in debt for supplies.

In 1922 a road from Florida City reached Flamingo and cleared the way for local moonshiners to reach large markets in Florida City, Homestead, and Miami. The local product, "Cape Sable Augerdent," was described by a visitor in 1919 as "like drinking carbolic acid." When asked what difference the road into town had made, a Flamingo resident replied, "None. There were fewer people than ever . . . They had found a way to get out." Given its isolation, limited living area, danger of storm damage, and ubiquitous mosquitoes—another Flamingo resident is credited with the statement, "You could make a swing with a pint cup, and catch a quart of mosquitoes!"—Flamingo wasn't subject to much growth.

In 1926 pioneer environmentalist/writer Marjory Stoneman Douglas described Flamingo in a short story, "The Major of Flamingo":

> At the seeming end of the world . . . the . . . jumping-off place of the United States, there lies a wide dreaming country, flat as a painted floor. It is touched here and there with strange blanched thickets of buttonwood and . . . mangrove. It is spread with coarse salt grass and patched broadly with . . . thick saltweeds, which in . . . summer turn orange and canary and shell-pink and scarlet. The five occupied and the six empty houses of Flamingo, silver gray on . . . twelve-foot unpainted stilts, look to be wading in these shallows of color-shallows which melt at east and west horizons into silvery sun mirage, above which the tops of palm trees float detached. To the southward, away from which the trees and the coarse grass lean under the continuous beating of the wind . . . the weedy color stops . . . before a blistering white strip of beach tufted with occasional trees . . . [T]here . . . the lime green . . . Gulf and Atlantic merged . . . The tropic sun which dominates this country, whitening its light and its beaches, blanching its houses . . . burns . . .

In 1929, B. C. Perky, a fish camp owner on Sugarloaf Key, acting on the specifications of a Texas bacteriologist, Dr. Charles A. R. Campbell, constructed a bat tower. It had bat roosts and metal rat guards to cut down on the mosquito population. Unfortunately the smelly bat bait sold to Perky by Campbell failed to attract bats. A hurricane several months later washed the bait away. The tower, however, still stands.

Today, the tiny settlement of Flamingo has all but disappeared. In its place is a modern development that serves as headquarters for Everglades National Park.

THE IMPETUS behind Everglades National Park, the third largest U.S. park, goes back to the administration of our first environmentalist president, Theodore Roosevelt. In May 1901, William Dutcher, president of the Audubon Society, secured state legislation to protect non-game fowl. The National Audubon Society employed, at its own expense, four wardens to watch over endangered bird rookeries in the state. The cause of conservation suffered its first martyr when one of the agents, Guy Bradley, was killed in the Glades by plume poachers in 1905. Today, west of Flamingo at East Cape, a stone plaque commemorates Bradley. Three years later another agent, Warren C. G. Mcleod, was murdered near Charlotte Harbor.

In 1910 the New York legislature enacted a bill outlawing commercial use of American wild bird feathers. Since New York was the center for the millinery industry, this law acted as a great deterrent to poachers. Still, feathers were sold to foreign buyers who shipped hats into the U.S. Finally, an aroused public conscience, along with a change in fashion, made wearing bird feathers highly unpopular and resulted in an end to poaching.

Botanists ranging from David M. Fairchild, founder of Fairchild Tropical Garden at Coconut Grove, to John Kunkel Small, who came to Florida to collect plant specimens for the New York Botanical Garden, envisioned a federally owned park in the Glades as far back as 1916. In *Eden to Sahara*, Small wrote:

Here is a unique El Dorado . . . a tongue of land extending hundreds of miles into tepid waters reaching almost to the Tropic of Cancer, where . . . subtropic and tropic regions not only meet but mingle, where the animals of temperate regions associate with those of the tropics . . . [A]s much as possible of this natural history museum should be preserved . . .

The Everglades National Park Association was formed in 1928. Its first president was Fairchild; Ernest F. Coe was executive secretary. Coe, a newcomer, took up the project and, to quote one of his associates, "ran away with it." For nearly twenty years he hounded state and federal governments in support of the park. On December 6, 1947, President Harry Truman spoke at the opening ceremony for the 1.4-million-acre park: "Here is land, tranquil in its beauty, serving not as a source of water, but as the last receiver of it."

Establishment of the Park disenfranchised its former residents. There was a period lasting up to the late 1950s during which hunters and fishermen were legally reprimanded and told to go elsewhere. In the end, most agreed preservation of the Glades was in their best interest.

According to Glades old-timer Totch Brown, in his autobiography *Totch: A Life in the Everglades*:

This was one helluva blow to the people of the Everglades, especially along the southwest coast. There were (and still are) many that knew no other trade than the fisherman's and no other country than this one. The only fishing grounds left for them were the open gulf and Florida Bay, which are outside park limits . . . Many fishermen in the Chokoloskee Bay area and in the keys couldn't afford the expenses involved in gulf fishing, and gave up the one trade they knew. Some left the bay and went other places to fish, but only to their sorrow. Some hung on here doing anything they could (including smuggling) to exist.

According to Brown, establishment of the Park, though mostly beneficial, has introduced new problems that need to be faced. These include havoc caused to the environment by the deluge of visitors with cars, outboards, as well as dikes and canals built to drain away rainwater. There's a lack of brackish water in which Glades denizens breed. To quote Brown:

A big part of the problem has to do with the burning of the marshes. Before the park was established, we burned off the wet marshes once a year with the help of the Seminoles. This did not hurt the wetland and kept the mangroves, shrubs, and sawgrass from taking over. Shortly after the glades became a park . . . the authorities stopped all burning. Today, the marshes that were so filled with wildlife have grown up to nothing but a mangrove swamp, and the ponds and game are no more.

The Park contains a ranger station and marina on Chokoloskee Bay at the westernmost edge, and a more extensive park area with ranger station, museum, and nature trails at Flamingo to the east.

Western writer Zane Grey fished the nearby waters of Florida Bay. He described them in *Tales of Southern Rivers*.

Mystery hovers over this forbidden place, neither land nor water nor forest, yet a combination of all three. Though the sun shone brightly and the sky was azure and the breeze breathed off a summer sea, the wilderness of waterways and . . . mangrove forest did not . . . beckon to the adventuring soul. It repelled. It boded ill. It was of salt, hard, caustic, bitter. Never before had I seen a forest that did not lure. But this was not a forest; it was a sinister growth out of coral.

Myriad forms of plant and wildlife, many of them endangered, call the Glades home. The following quote from a plaque in the park will explain our relationship to the natural order and its dependence on nature's chain:

To produce 1/10 pound of human flesh requires one pound of bass meat, which requires 10 pounds of smaller fish, which requires 100 pounds of tiny crustaceans, mollusks, worms, insect larvae and copepods, which requires 1,000 pounds of microscopic plant and animal plankton and mangrove detritus, which requires the sun, unpolluted water, unobstructed flow of fresh water and protected estuaries.

The chain of life has been threatened in recent decades by the encroachment of southeast Florida and construction of ecology-threatening subdivisions and trailer parks. Seminoles and crackers alike feel threatened by the bureaucratic intervention of Everglades National Park. This conflict is shown in Randy Wayne White's novel, *The Man Who Invented Florida*. In it, an elderly cracker, aided by a descendant of the Calusas, Florida's original inhabitants, tries to stave off government intervention by claiming to have found Fountain of Youth–like mineral springs on his property. To quote from the novel:

> [O]ne by one, as he grew older, Joseph [the Calusa] saw the legends collapse beneath the weight of his . . . unworldliness. He realized . . . his grandfather was just another Indian drunk destined to die in an Immokalee flophouse, an empty wine bottle at his side. He learned . . . most people, no matter what color, stopped fighting long before their last heartbeat. Finally, he came to understand . . . Florida would be inherited by those who cared least about it: the concrete merchants and tourists and out-of-state rich people . . .

To get to Flamingo and Everglades National Park, follow U.S. 1 to Homestead, then take State Road 27 southwest through Everglades National Park.

For information concerning the Park, stop at the entrance ten miles southwest of Homestead. Things to bring include binoculars, bug repellant, and clothing that covers arms and legs as protection against the mosquitoes. Try to visit in the dry season, December through March, if you don't want to be pestered by bugs. Rooms are available at the 102-room Flamingo Lodge Marina.

An airboat—a common sight in Florida.

Photo by Debra Force.

Everglades City and
the Ten Thousand Islands

A half-hour drive east of Naples on the west coast, Everglades City and the Ten Thousand Islands are a world apart in pace and surroundings. No beaches. No bright lights. And the only nightlife you'll find is the occasional call of a heron or a mullet jumping in the moonlit river. In their place, you'll experience peace and quiet and the haunting beauty of the Glades themselves.

Everglades City's Rod & Gun Club on the Barron River has served as a refuge for four presidents—Herbert Hoover, Franklin D. Roosevelt, Dwight Eisenhower, Richard Nixon—and celebrities ranging from Zane Grey to John Barrymore. Constructed in 1883, the Allan house was home to the first settler in the area. In 1889 it, along with the acreage comprising present day Everglades City, was sold to J. B. Sorter for eight hundred dollars. Sorter added on to the main building and provided food and lodging to a steady trickle of hunters and fishermen.

Today this inn retains the charm of a late-nineteenth-century resort with whitewashed clapboard siding, canary yellow shutters, and a lobby paneled with knotty cypress. In the lobby are a five-foot-long sawfish bill, a gaping shark's mouth, heads of deer and wild boar, and an upside-down, open-mouthed gator overlooking a green-baized pool table and saloon piano. Framed clippings of magazine and newspaper articles and photographs of famous guests—including a grinning Eisenhower in a scruffy fishing hat, and his wife, Mamie, posed before a long row of fish—decorate the walls. A newer addition is the screened-in pool.

The manager, an attractive blonde in jeans, asks me to sign the register, then hands over a room key without asking to see either credit card or driver's license—wonder of wonders in this computerized age. My room is in one of three cottages to one side of the main building. It's decorated in early Sears Roebuck, with mismatched lamps and bedspreads and the sort of nautical painting common to cheap motel rooms everywhere. But then, how much time will I be spending indoors?

After I've finished unpacking, I head south to the headquarters of the state Park Service and buy a ticket for a cruise through the Ten Thousand Islands. They consist of countless tiny mangrove islands located off the southwest tip of Florida. The double-decker boat has no sooner left the dock than a pair of blubbery manatees surface briefly to study us forlornly before diving into the murky depths. Other wildlife pointed out by our guide include black skimmers, recognized by their long lower bill used to skim the water's surface for fish; anhingas, christened "snakebirds" by the Indians because of long, snakelike bodies and their ability to dive underwater to retrieve fish; pink roseate spoonbills, who can walk on top of lily pads without sinking; ospreys or fish eagles; white ibises; and terns. Red mangroves comprise more than 90 percent of the small islands and provide a natural barrier against hurricane-force winds. There are also such exotic imported plants as cabbage and coconut palms and tall, stately Australian pines.

THE FIRST PEOPLE to arrive were the Calusa Indians in 1500 B.C. They lived until around 1800, when the last survivors of their race were wiped out by smallpox and syphilis imported by the Spanish and their successors. Nearby 147-acre Chokoloskee Island, three miles south of Everglades City on State Road 29, is a monument to Calusa know-how. Constructed from discarded oyster shells piled up by generations of Indians, it's an engineering marvel that has been compared to the construction of the pyramids. Appropriately enough, Chokoloskee means "old abandoned house" in Seminole; it served as a haven for those driven south by the Seminole Wars.

The area was little known and hardly charted by white men until the end of the nineteenth century. In 1885, following a cruise of the islands, one visitor wrote of the current maps: "For general outline, they were superb, but for particulars all of them were signal failures. As we worked further south, they were quite useless." According to an article, "The Ten Thousand Islands," that appeared in London's *Blackwood* magazine in 1927 under the pseudonym Major L. A. M. Jones:

> The Islands, of which comparative few are inhabited, are separate from each other by a system of tortuous and shallow channels, which are more confusing than any maze. Only an Islander can find his way through them, and as each man discreetly confines himself to the immediate neighborhood of his own . . . island, there is probably not a single inhabitant to whom all the channels are known. The U.S. government once put up signposts to mark a channel for yachts. The islanders quickly rendered them useless by turning them in all directions but the right one.

Less than three hundred souls resided between Punta Rasa at the northernmost edge of the Ten Thousand Islands and Cape Sable to the south. Many of these men were refugees from the law, and it was the islands' isolation that attracted them. They hunted, fished, and killed birds and animals for their hides. To again quote Jones:

In the Ten Thousand Islands there are men whose lives of crime and adventure are equal in enthralling interest to anything . . . Joseph Conrad ever invented. Silent, bearded, and unkempt, they do not loiter, and they never talk. Their sole costume consists of an old shirt and tattered trousers, in the hip pocket of which can be plainly seen the outline of a heavy Colt—nothing more. Shoes are not known.

. . . The arrival of yet another fugitive from justice in these mournful solitudes spreads around in some mysterious way; but many will be the moons . . . before any sign is given . . . his fellow exiles are aware of his existence . . .

They have seven unwritten laws . . .

Suspect every man.

Ask no questions.

Settle your own quarrels.

Never steal from an islander.

Stick by him, even if you do not know him.

Shoot quick, when your secret is in danger.

Cover your kill.

And in another place:

To describe the fauna of the islands is a . . . simple matter. The coconut tree furnishes the Islander with house, furniture, clothing, table utensil, and drink. Panther, cabbage-bears, Florida beaver, and a very small species of deer provide him with his winter hunting, though there is little money to be made from it, as the pelts are very poor owing to the climate. The only exception to this rule is to be found in the case of raccoons, whose fur is of exceptionally good quality, and forms 90 percent of the islands' small pelt trade.

TED SMALLWOOD was developing Chokoloskee Island around the time W. S. Allan was developing Everglades City. He began farming in 1896 and turned the family home into a trading post that grew into a general store and post office. Built in 1917, the store is in a tin-roofed and -sided shotgun-style wood building that overlooks the water. Inside are the store's original furnishings, including an elbow-smoothed wooden counter running the length of one wall. Thousands of mud-dauber nests cover the ceiling.

The islanders retain a degree of self-sufficiency rare in this computerized age. The islands have provided food and shelter for any number of hermits through the years. Perhaps the most famous was Roy Ozmer, who lived alone on Pelican Key for more than twenty years before Hurricane Donna forced him to retreat back to the mainland. Totch Brown lived here for three-quarters of a century and made a living as a fisherman, gator trapper, and marijuana smuggler. I'm reminded of a story told me by Jim Turner. During the '40s, when he was a state conservation officer, he met a boy of six or seven living in the Ten Thousand Islands who had never set foot on dry land. His parents owned a general store constructed on wooden pilings above the water, and he had been born and raised there—never going to the mainland.

During the early '40s, Anne Morrow Lindbergh and her husband, Charles, the famous aviator, took two trips into the glades. In *War Within and Without,* she describes a boat trip they took via Shark River and down the coast to the keys from January 29 to February 5, 1940. They were accompanied by their friend, Jim Newton, and Audubon Society warden, Charlie Green. "One gets the sense of life—life in the air, life in the water, life on the banks—all the teeming life of a river . . . " On the same trip, quoting from her diary: "C[harles] takes up the oar and we drift soundless in the black night until we are part of that intense stillness—only an occasional splash of a bird or a fish and the hoot of an owl in the distance. I should always go when C. calls—break through my crust of inertia or fear because life lies behind it."

On March 7, 1941, the Lindberghs set out on a second boat trip from Ft. Myers Beach, through the Glades, to the Keys. This time, their boat was a sailboat with an engine and a small dory that Lindbergh describes as "sturdy, reliable, and a little perky." Their only companion was Newton. Lindbergh writes:

. . . we camped under the twisted seagrape trees on shore in a bugproof tent. We explored Shark River again . . . sailing before the wind with jib and jigger into the timeless world of wilderness and wild life. Pushing through the maze of streams and rivers opening up before us, between bare ghostly arms of mangrove roots, we scarcely made a ripple, occasionally startling a great white heron, or a pink ibis, or water turkeys. Swallow-tailed kites circled slowly above our heads. At sunset we put the sail down and poled through small bayous under arching branches.

MODERN-DAY Everglades City was founded by Memphis advertising magnate Baron Collier, who made his fortune buying up the overhead plac- ard rights for buses, subways, and trolley cars in major cities. He made Everglades City the nerve center for his extensive holdings in southwest Florida, 1.3 million acres of swampland, including most of present-day Collier County. He first came to the area on vacation in 1911. By the '20s, he was dredging and planting Everglades City. By '23, he owned more of the state than anyone else.

Writer John Rothchild gives a description of this process in his book, *Up For Grabs*:

> The Barron River had Collier's first name, the county . . . his last. [Everglades City was] . . . his company town, dug up and platted by his engineers, populated by his employees, financed by his bank. The old stucco buildings were all Collier buildings . . . the city sewer plant and the water plant were originally the Collier utilities, the older men [one saw] cleaning . . . traps along Collier's river were ex-Collier guides.

Collier envisioned a resort city to rival Miami Beach. Again, quot- ing from *Up For Grabs*:

> The Tamiami Trail was Collier's road; his dynamite crews blast- ed and loosened the oölitic rock, and his giant shovel machines

232

followed behind, scooping and piling the rubble into the two-lane passage, raised a few inches above the surrounding wetlands. It cost Collier several million dollars to complete the highway, a feat that was equated with the digging of the Panama Canal . . .

Anticipating the crowds, Collier's aides chartered a steamship company, a telephone company, the Trailways bus company, and a mercantile company. They designed a hub with boulevards of Parisian width, wide enough for all the traffic that could be enticed.

Later additions included a bank, a railroad station, a supermarket, and a theater.

Unfortunately for his heirs, Collier lost most of his fortune during the Depression, and his Florida development was terminated.

Today, one still sees the remnants of Collier's dream. A four-spoked hub is the focus of incoming traffic, and the central boulevard has a grassy median with Victorian-style street lamps down its center. Fading cracker-box company houses, constructed for Collier's employees, line the streets, and the abandoned courthouse with a pseudo-Grecian facade resembles, in Rothchild's words, a "dowager in high grass."

Collier acquired the Rod & Gun Club. He hired Kaiser Wilhelm's chef and added on new rooms to make it the luxurious resort it was for more than three decades. Today Collier's stern, Germanic portrait hangs alongside the upside-down alligator in the lobby. For years, according to former mayor Sammy Hamilton, practically everyone in town was either working at the hotel or charter-boating for guests. During the '50s, there were more than fifty-five charter boats in operation. In 1960 Hurricane Donna practically leveled the town, and East Naples became the new county seat. The hotel continued to operate, but the guests stopped coming. A fire in 1973 destroyed more than seventy rooms but, thanks to the pool, the main building remained standing. During the early '70s, there was talk of a jetport being built in the Everglades, and the lodge was filled with speculators and airline people. But conservationists put an end to that project, and the Rod & Gun Club entered a quieter, more relaxed era.

THE AFTERNOON of my arrival, I take a stroll along the town's raffish waterfront. With its concrete pilings, shrimp boats, crab traps piled ten feet high, and discarded engines, it resembles the montage in an oyster bar. The unreconstructed owner of one vessel displays a rebel flag flying above the skull and crossbones.

Following my walk, I have dinner in the high-ceilinged hotel dining room. Bathed in pale yellow light and surrounded by dark red, pecky cypress, I order the stone crab, since Everglades City provides 80 percent of the nation's supply, and they're excellent—and a conservationist's delight because the claws are removed without killing the crab, which grows a new pair.

The following morning, I walk across the street to Mama Dot's to have breakfast. Located in one of Collier's abandoned hotels, Mama Dot's has wooden booths, ceiling fans, and baby-blue trim. The menu is on a chalkboard behind the counter. The only other customer rests his gnarled fisherman's hands on the wooden counter and jokes good-naturedly with the motherly proprietress.

After a hearty breakfast of ham and eggs, I leave Dot's and walk across town to the Captain's Table Resort to sign up for a tour of the Everglades. Our guide is Ted House, who's descended from four generations of Glades inhabitants. His grandfather owned and operated a shrimp-processing plant at Flamingo, forty miles to the southeast. Interestingly enough, more than 70 percent of those born in Everglades City still live there. According to Ted, the Glades consist of countless mangrove islets dotting the area from U.S. 41 to the Gulf of Mexico. These islets form an intricate maze that only someone of his experience and savvy can negotiate.

Due to their remoteness and inaccessibility, the Glades have attracted numerous mavericks, including the notorious outlaw Mr. Watson. After

234

reputedly killing a black man in Columbia County, Florida, Watson escaped to Oklahoma Indian territory where he was rumored to have run with the James Gang and murdered the notorious woman outlaw, Belle Star. He fled to the Glades and homesteaded a sugar plantation at Cape Sable. He lured itinerant workers with the promise of good wages, then killed them in lieu of payment. One of Watson's intended victims escaped and told what happened. On October 24, 1910, when Watson boated to Chokoloskee Island for supplies, an angry mob surrounded and killed him. (For more on Watson, read Peter Matthiessen's award-winning trilogy, *Killing Mr. Watson, Lost Man's River,* and *Bone by Bone.*)

During the 1880s and '90s, steamboat-loads of tourists traversed the Collier River taking potshots at wildlife. The pink-flamingo population was devastated before the federal government cracked down and passed laws protecting wildlife. In the years since, the Glades have gained a reputation as prime smuggling territory, starting around 1900 with the illegal exportation of flamingo feathers for ladies' hats, then booze during Prohibition, and continuing up to the present with alligator hides, moonshine, and marijuana, or "square grouper" as the floating bales are dubbed locally. *Wind Across the Everglades,* a movie dealing with plume pirates, written and directed by Budd Schulberg and starring Christopher Plummer, Burl Ives, and Gypsy Rose Lee, was filmed here in the '50s. *Thunder and Lightning,* a moonshine saga starring David Carradine, was filmed in the '70s. No doubt, a marijuana-smuggling movie will be filmed in the near future.

If the marijuana-smuggling movie is filmed, its main character should be based on Totch Brown. Unable to support his family after two heart attacks, Totch took up smuggling and wound up serving twenty months in the federal pen for refusing to testify against his fellow smugglers. According to his account of his adventures, smuggling marijuana was mostly a series of misadventures with crooks outwitting crooks and nobody making much long-term profit. In August 1982, the government ran Operation Everglades, its biggest investigation ever on marijuana smuggling, in the area of Chokoloskee and Everglades City, and Brown was indicted for income tax evasion. To quote Totch, "[A]fter all the marijuana I handled, sat on, and smelled, I've never smoked a joint, and never seen cocaine. The home boys at Chokoloskee and Everglades City never hauled hard drugs. Nothing but marijuana."

THAT NIGHT, back at the hotel, I have a dream.

It's the late 1890s and a group of noted industrialists, including railroad tycoons Flagler and Plant, and James S. Turner, hire a paddle-wheeled steamer to do some shooting. Standing astride the wooden deck, they take pot shots at the local wildlife. Magnificent pink flamingos and bald eagles strike the brackish river with a sickening thud, as the boat continues on its course. No one bothers to retrieve the dead and dying birds.

When the boat pulls into Chokoloskee, there's a commotion at the end of the pier. A shot rings out and a local outlaw drops dead in the center of a vengeful mob. When the industrialists are told of the reason behind the shooting, they nod their heads sagely. "Frontier justice," they murmur in unison.

Behind them, in the Glades, the water flows blood-red as a result of their carnage.

To get to Everglades City, follow the Tamiami Trail twenty miles east of Naples. Turn south on State Road 29. The busiest time of the year is the third weekend in February when the Everglades City Seafood Festival takes place.

Part 5

CRACKER COUNTRY

Cross Creek, near Marjorie Kinnan Rawlings's house.

Photo by Keith Bollum.

Cracker Country

Compared to his counterpart in other Southern states, the Florida cracker is cosmopolitan. Consider Florida's history. It was inhabited by Native Americans, discovered by Spaniards, fought over by the French and English, bought by Americans, and overrun by tourists. There are Seminole Indians in the Everglades; Bahamian Conchs in Key West; Cubans, West Indians, and South and Central Americans in Miami; Greek sponge fishermen in Tarpon Springs; Minorcans (survivors of Andrew Turnbull's ill-fated colony at New Smyrna) in St. Augustine; and Yankees everywhere.

The Florida cracker has seen people and nationalities come and go and little fazes him. He remains as much a part of the Florida landscape as the cabbage palm or the palmetto scrub. He is tough, resilient, adaptable, highly opinionated yet strangely tolerant. A born teller of tales with an easygoing, though ironic, sense of humor.

Like the palmetto, the palm, and the state, he is a survivor.

A Brief Tour of Cracker Country

CROSS CREEK: Steve, the bartender at the Yearling restaurant, doesn't know a thing about Marjorie Kinnan Rawlings and couldn't care less. His wife reads books sometimes, but he has never cracked a book in his life and is proud of it.

A famous cracker novelist drove down once and wanted to rent one of the cottages out back to do some writing.

He handed Steve a fistful of money. "When this here gets used up, just let me know. There's plenty more where that come from."

The thing that impressed Steve most about the novelist, aside from his free-spending ways, were the tattoos of hinges on both his wrists. One was captioned "Open," the other "Closed."

Steve brightens visibly. "That writer fella was some character! If I hadn't of knowed better, I would've swore he was a trucker."

CEDAR KEY: Brooks Campbell has recently patented his "rheumatiz" medicine, and I'm examining the official-looking document from the Florida Department of Health. It reads: "Not to be taken internally."

"Has anyone ever drunk the stuff instead of rubbing it into his joints?"

"A half-blind eighty-year-old widder lady in Ocala mistook it for a diuretic once't and swallowed some."

"What happened?"

Brooks pauses to heighten the suspense. "She called me to the phone that evening, wanting to know if drinking it would kill her."

"Did it?"

"Hell, no! 'Cording to her, it worked near 'bout as good internally as externally."

UNIVERSITY OF FLORIDA, GAINESVILLE: In the center of the Quadrangle stands a Bible-thumper of indeterminate age. Beside him is a portable wood cross mounted on something resembling a golf cart with two spoked wheels. The preacher is berating a crowd of bored-looking college students for their sinful ways.

"Brothers and Sisters, we are all of us sinners . . . Only difference between you and me is I know it, and have sought my solace in the Lord."

"Why don't you be quiet so we can hear the birds sing?" yells someone in the crowd.

Aware of no other voice save his own, the preacher continues his relentless monologue . . .

CITRA, THE ORANGE BLOSSOM MOTEL: The vibration from the diesels roaring past on U.S. 301 is enough to rattle your teeth. Following a long sleepless night, I let the manager in on the secret.

"It gets some better once you've stayed awhile. I been here going on ten years now, and I hardly even notice anymore."

ORANGE LAKE: Columbus Cooney is the only licensed gator hunter in Alachua County. Whenever a gator becomes too familiar—makes threatening advances toward a pet or child or lazes too near a pool—the people involved call Columbus, who obtains a permit from the County Game Commission to eliminate the nuisance. He spears the gator with a harpoon connected to a Clorox bottle by a rope, then pulls him alongside his skiff and kills him with a bang stick. He dresses the gator out and sells the meat from the tail to local restaurants. Gator meat sells for $11.00 a pound, and a three-hundred-pound alligator has a *large* tail. Cooney also sells the hide and head for a tidy profit.

LIVE OAK: Tex spends his days seated on a wooden bench fronting the busiest intersection in town. His attire consists of western boots with spurs, faded jeans, a silver-buckled belt, and a western string tie. Pushed down over jug ears is an oversized white cowboy hat. A beatific smile lights up his face as he waves at motorists passing by.

Occasionally someone waves back.

WELAKA: Close by the St. Johns River, the Log Cabin is a long, narrow roadhouse dating back to the '20s. There's hardly space to squeeze past the customers' backs on the way to an end stool, but the lodgelike camaraderie of the place makes it worth the effort. On one evening, a man and his date fell backwards off their barstools without arousing so much as a whispered comment.

HAWTHORNE: I once asked the drunken proprietress at the local pizza place why she was slicing my pizza into irregular pieces.

"My Daddy owns the joint. I can slice it any damn way I please!"

MELROSE: I'm seated in a seafood restaurant listening to the world's fattest country-western band. The three male members must weigh in excess of a thousand pounds.

The boy seated at the table next to mine has mercurochromed scratches all over his face, and his father is berating him for it.

"How come you to let Rory hurt you thataway?"

"But, Papa, I bited him on the arm!"

"Hesh up now, son. Weren't ary teeth marks on Rory's arm what I could see. You hurt him some better next time, you hear."

CARRABELLE: Soliloquy overheard in a barbershop: "Lester Ray done got religion. He was up before Brother Bob . . . You 'member Brother Bob, don't you? Was him prayed over Festus Taylor after that there bad car accident, where his insides was all tore out and the doctors had done give him up for dead. But Brother Bob, he brung him back to life and the Spirit! Glory!

"Well, Lester Ray, he come up before the congregation and waved around a hundred-dollar bill what he had on him. Said he was gonna have spent that there money on crack when the Spirit up and moved him, and he come to the Good Lord instead! Hallelujah! He ain't cussed or nothing since. And he was a sho'nuff cusser! Hallelujah!

"Lester Ray's daddy, Earl, is eat up with lung cancer, and he never smoked a day in his life. Chewed plenty of tobacco, but never smoked it once't. They was gonna put him on the digitalis machine . . . But when he asked how much it was gonna cost him and they told him twenty thousand a year, that was the end of it. Said he'd as soon die and go to hell as pay the hospital folks that kind of money! Said he'd worked hard all his life for his money, and he wasn't about to throw it around thataway. Even if most of it did belong to the Blue Cross.

"Ole Earl, he had him some sure 'nuff hunting dogs. After I done found Jesus and quit the devil's ways, I took the money what I saved up from not drinking and smoking and raising the devil, and bought a dog off ole Earl. I'd spent near 'bout $350 on her when I heard somebody traipsing around my backyard fixing to steal her. I fired my shotgun after him, but he got clean away! I'd kill the man what messed with one of my dogs. But the sheriff, when he come, he told me to shoot him in the leg and wound him some instead. Wasn't nothing wrong to shoot a man what was trespassing on your land. Only wasn't no need to kill him, less he's a nigger. Just wound him some till the law can get there . . . "

Marjorie Kinnan Rawlings's house at Cross Creek, where she wrote *The Yearling*.

Cross Creek

"Cross Creek, Home of Marjorie Kinnan Rawlings," reads the sign on U.S. 301 headed north from Ocala. I had heard of Rawlings but considered her a children's writer, author of a book for boys entitled *The Yearling*. Following an impulse, I turned. A winding country road led past acre on acre of scrub pine and towering Spanish-mossed live oaks. Occasional breaks in the foliage offered up enchanting glimpses of lizard green, water-lilied Orange Lake. The sky was the palest of blues, and herds of somnambulant cattle grazed lazily in pea-green fields. Cross Creek consisted of two fish camps, a convenience store, and The Yearling restaurant, with cabins in back to either side of a narrow, muddy stream connecting Orange and Lochloosa lakes.

I stopped at the Jiffy Store to buy a pack of cigarettes and picked up a copy of Rawlings's *Cross Creek*. I took a seat on a wooden bench overlooking the black, tannic-stained creek that flows from Lochloosa to Orange Lake (I later learned by reading *Cross Creek* that the bridge where I sat was the community meeting place to socialize and settle disputes). I opened the book, which read: "Cross Creek is a bend in a country road by land, and the flowing of Lochloosa Lake into Orange Lake, by water. We are four miles west of the small village of Island Grove, nine miles east of a turpentine still, and on the other side we do not count distance at all, for the two lakes and the broad marshes create an infinite space between us and the horizon."

By the time I finished reading the first page, I was hooked. When next I looked up, two hours later, the setting sun had lent the now-vermilion creek and misty green foliage an opaque, dreamlike quality. As if on cue, a chorus of wildlife began their nightly chorus—the chirp of crickets mixing with the gruff croak of frogs and the lunatic hoot of a solitary loon.

To quote the closing words of *Cross Creek*: "It seems to me . . . the earth may be borrowed but not bought. It may be used, but not owned. It gives itself in response to love and tending, offers its seasonal flowering and fruiting. But we are tenant, and not possessors, lovers and not masters. Cross Creek belongs to the wind and the rain, to the sun and the seasons, to the cosmic secrecy of seed, and beyond all, to time."

Cross Creek . . .

The words denote a turning point, a line crossed. And the Creek was such a turning point for me. Here was a magical spot that was somehow strangely familiar—a place visited in a dream, perhaps, or during some previous life.

AS IT TURNED OUT, a relation of mine owned an orange grove at the Creek. Horace Drew, my mother's first cousin, inherited grove land from his great-great-grandfather George Rainsford Fairbanks, author of the earliest history of Florida. Horace's grove house was at the end of a twisting, turning dirt road that wound past several dilapidated shacks and an abandoned school bus that, I later learned, housed a cracker family. To either side of the road were fish ponds and fields planted in hay and alfalfa. Occasionally I spied a tractor, resembling a gigantic insect, in the center of a field. Horace was standing in the front yard of a nondescript red wood house fiddling with an outboard engine when I arrived.

Getting out of the car, I greeted him.

"I dreamt about you last night, David." were the first words out of his mouth. "Seems funny, since we hardly see one another."

Later that afternoon, Horace took me on a tour of the grove. Fairbanks's two-story wood-frame house, constructed about 1870, was still standing, a "shotgun" passageway through its center, so called because one could fire a shotgun at one end and the buckshot would exit at the other without harming anyone inside. The passage provided ventilation in summer.

We walked a mile or so down a sand road, past row on row of bare, leafless orange trees. Beside each tree was a rusty, fluted metal smudge pot for heating the grove during freezes. In Rawlings's day, as depicted in the winter chapter of *Cross Creek* and the movie of the same name, stacks of pine logs were used instead of smudge pots. The screech of a train whistle was their warning when the temperature dropped below freezing. Grove hands and neighbors would spend the night stoking the fires in a desperate attempt to keep the citrus warm enough to last the night.

The sun was setting as we walked, and a pale, thin, translucent wafer of a moon hung like a crescent-shaped pendant in the milky white sky. Eventually we reached the movie set where the movie *Cross Creek* was filmed on Horace's land.

The hollow-interiored sets for Rawlings's house and barn sat ghost-like amid tall grass and weeds. On the lookout for snakes, we waded through the undergrowth and mounted the sagging front porch. The view from the porch was eerily reminiscent of the film—a vista of bent, moss-covered palms, lily pads, and water hyacinths stretching out to an endless horizon.

Horace told me how actor Rip Torn, who stayed at the grove house during filming, researched his role as Marjorie's cracker neighbor by canoeing in the lake's frigid January waters looking for gators to kill and dress.

A month earlier, on a cold, blustery day, I'd seen the film in a practically deserted Manhattan movie house and experienced homesickness for a part of Florida I'd never seen. Now I was here.

OVER THE NEXT YEAR, I continued to visit the grove.

On one trip, I toured Rawlings's grove house, a Florida cracker building constructed around 1890 and now a state historical landmark. As Rawlings wrote: "It sat snuggly then as now under the tall old orange trees, and had a simple grace of line, low, rambling, and one-storied." Behind it is an outhouse. Around it are a duck pen, with ducks waddling in and out, and a vegetable garden. The house consists of three sections, with the back containing the kitchen and dining room. Here, Marjorie and her maids Geeche and later Idella prepared deep-fried, soft-shelled cooter (turtle) and blackbird pie, along with other cracker cuisine described in loving detail in *Cross Creek Cookery*. As Rawlings wrote: "Cookery is my one vanity and I am a slave to any guest who praises my culinary art." The other two sections of the house enclose a living room, an indoor bathroom (added five years after Rawlings moved in), and two bedrooms. But it's the front porch which is the most magical, for there sits Rawlings's old Royal typewriter with the first page of the *Cross Creek* manuscript half-typed.

Once again I had returned full circle to a mystical spot where time stands still.

Another time, I visited the nearby town of Micanopy, central Florida's oldest community. It was founded in 1821 and named Panton's Trading Post. Prior to that, the Spanish explorer De Soto passed through in 1539, and the Timucuan Indians inhabited this area as far back as ten thousand years ago. Collecting botanical specimens for his book *Travels*, naturalist William Bartram visited a nearby Seminole village in 1774.

Travels is the earliest reliable source about Florida's wildlife and plant life and the Seminole Indians.

Many of the battles of the first Seminole war, which roughly coincides with the War of 1812 and involved runaway slaves who joined the Seminoles, were fought nearby. A stone marker at Newnan reads: "This tablet marks the site of a battle between the forces of Colonel Daniel Newnan and hostile Indians and Negroes on Sept. 27, 1812, during which three or more soldiers and many of the enemy including King Payne were killed."

In 1833 Seminole leaders were coerced into signing a treaty that would result in their deportation to the Indian Lands of Oklahoma. An obscure half-white (his father was of Scottish descent) chieftain named Osceola showed his disgust by stabbing his knife into the treaty's center. In 1835 Chief Micanopy led an attack known as the Dade Massacre, instigating the Second Seminole War.

For three years, Micanopy, Osceola, and their followers conducted a successful guerrilla war against U.S. troops. To this day many of their Seminole descendants live in the Everglades, the only Indian tribe never to sign a peace treaty with the U.S. Finally, General Hernandez met Osceola under a flag of truce, surrounded his warriors and him with troops, and captured them with no resistance. Osceola was sent to Fort Moultrie at Charleston, South Carolina, where he died of malaria. According to legend, the attending physician cut off Osceola's head, a common practice at the time for famous individuals, and took it home to St. Augustine. The doctor's naughty children were punished by being locked in the bedroom with the head impaled on a bedpost.

Ironically enough, in 1835 the town's name was changed from Walton's Trading Post to honor Chief Micanopy, head of the Seminole Nation.

The first white man to plant oranges commercially in north central Florida was C. G. Edwards. In 1835 Edwards planted a 120-acre orange grove near Micanopy, and his son recalls growing up with Seminole playmates. In the 1870s and '80s, nearby communities like Melrose, McIntosh, and Evinston were founded by wealthy Northerners trying to get wealthier by harvesting "golden apples." The Great Freeze of 1894 drove many citrus growers further south, but today their homes are being lovingly restored by professional couples from nearby Gainesville and Ocala.

TO THE ROMANTIC, however, the importance of citrus is not its commercial value. It is, to quote from Gloria Jahoda's *Florida*: "the clouds of pale orange blossoms every year. It is the inland oceans of green in which golden orange, and yellow grapefruits are set like oversize pendants. It is the citrus lakes with their warm, low winds, and the high-pitched fatalistic laughter of black pickers . . . "

Downtown Micanopy is three blocks long and is an antiquers' and book lovers' paradise. Buildings dating back to the early nineteenth century are shaded by ancient oaks bearded with Spanish moss. The Herlong Mansion, a bed and breakfast, was built by a family of prosperous citrus farmers in the late 1800s. It's supported by four giant columns and has upstairs and downstairs verandas. The resident haunt is Inez Herlong, a kindly old lady who died while cleaning the mansion, and who to this day tidies up after guests. To the east of town, on Seminary Road, is Micanopy Cemetery, established in 1826, with ancient headstones and huge oaks whose massive canopy of branches and Spanish moss darkens the area beneath even at midday.

On yet other trips to the grove, I met the twin sons of actors Rip Torn and Geraldine Page, who spent a summer helping Horace tend orange trees near where their father acted in the movie. And I met Jake Glisson, artist, pilot, and architect, who appears in the book *Cross Creek* as J.T., the crippled and nature-communing son of Rawlings's neighbor, Tom Glisson (Rawlings later paid for an operation that restored Jake's legs). Jake is an author in his own right, with the publication of *The Creek*, his own account of life at Cross Creek.

Once Horace left me the key to his house, and I stayed alone for a week with a dog named Fluffy who accompanied me on long, rambling walks through the woods. At night I sat on the open-air back porch with the bug light on and read by the light of a solitary lamp.

One evening I was rereading *Cross Creek* when I happened on a reference to a Major Fairbanks, the same Fairbanks who was Horace's great-great-grandfather. As it turned out, it was one of Fairbanks's relatives who sold Rawlings her grove. At another point in the book, a ne'er-do-well relation of Fairbanks proposes marriage to Rawlings. Later I learned Rawlings had done research on Zephaniah Kingsley in preparation for a novel she never wrote. I, too, had been planning to write a novel based on Kingsley's life.

The seeming coincidences were piling up fast, and I was beginning to sense a strange kinship with this writer I'd only recently discovered. As if to verify my intuition, that evening I dreamt that Rawlings and I were sharing the same bed. I recalled Horace's earlier dream about me. Something strange was going on.

The next afternoon, I was walking through the woods when something prompted me to ask whatever powers there be whether I was on the right path. "If so," I spoke aloud, "let three deer appear before I reach the end of this trail." I'd no sooner said the words than, turning a bend, I spied three does grazing in a clearing to one side of the dirt path. Upon seeing me, they bounded off into the underbrush, their fluffy white tails twitching back and forth like signals from God. A wave of euphoria such as I'd never known swept over me, as tears of joy clouded my eyes. I was home.

To get to Cross Creek follow U.S. 301 or 441 north from Ocala to within twenty or thirty miles of Gainesville and look for exit signs.

Marjorie Kinnan Rawlings is buried in Antioch Cemetery near Island Grove, a few miles east of Cross Creek. The inscription on her flat granite tombstone reads: "Through her writings she endeared herself to the people of the world."

To get to Micanopy, take U.S. 441 twelve or so miles south of Gainesville until you see the sign.

Melrose, McIntosh, and Evinston are nearby. Rooms are available at the Herlong Mansion and at Merrily, a bed-and-breakfast, circa 1888, in McIntosh.

O'Brisky Books in Micanopy has one of the finest selections of Florida books in the state and has been featured in *Mama Makes Up Her Mind* by Bailey White of National Public Radio's *All Things Considered*.

The old colliding with the new—modern cars parked in old-fashioned downtown Micanopy.

Package-store entrance to the B&B club in Hawthorne, which the author often uses as his "post office" when away from home.

Photo by Keith Bollum.

The B & B

Nobody knows how the B & B got its name. Not the owner, W. C. Not his wife and chief bartender, Ann. Nor any of the old-time customers. It's a place shrouded in mystery and magic in the piney and live-oaked backwoods of north central Florida between Lochloosa and Hawthorne on U.S. 301.

W. C. was born at Hawthorne, a hunter and fisherman's paradise, sixty or so years ago. A big-hearted, large-souled, yet diminutive black man, he watches the human parade pass before his sparkling brown eyes like a compassionate Buddha. Though he lived and worked for a time in Connecticut, he is pure Florida through and through, a born leader with no need for the chicaneries of politics.

I first met W. C. seven or eight years ago when I entered his predominantly black establishment in search of liquid refreshment. It was some place close to home, away from the noise and chaos of cracker jooks. Immediately, I was made to feel at home, though at first a suspicious black lady accused me of being an agent with Florida Beverage Control.

The B & B's old-timey Wurlitzer has a Rhythm & Blues selection—
Sam Cooke, Bobby "Blue" Bland, Otis Redding, Clarence Carter, Al
Green, Tyrone Davis, Aretha Franklin—that's enough to send an affi-
cionado like myself into a state of religious ecstasy.

Elisa rushes over to feed quarters into the jukebox. "What's shaking,
Pops?" she asks W. C.

The song "Love and Happiness" by Al Green blasts forth, and Elisa
dances sensuously across the floor.

Buddy frowns. "Don't get too carried away now, girl. We've got several more calls to make before we call it a day."

"Hush up, you crazy old cracker, and finish your half-pint. I would-
n't go on this here boring-ass trip if I couldn't have me my fun."

Buddy takes a long pull of Scotch. "Go ahead and dance then. But
you won't catch me bailing you out of county lock-up the next time
around!"

They are about to break into their customary screaming match
when another customer drifts in and W. C. greets him.

"How's it going, Sammy? Half-pint of Crown Royal?"

Sammy doesn't even bother to nod as W. C. slides a bottle, a can of
coke, and a plastic cup filled with ice across the counter.

"Your wife called earlier looking for you."

Sammy feigns indifference. "What time?"

"You'll have to ask Ann. I wasn't in yet."

Within fifteen minutes, Sammy has downed his half-pint and left.

W. C. nods sagely. "You know how that go, don't you, Dave?"

And so it goes . . . Though compassionate toward his fellow beings,
the parade of life is a source of endless amusement to W. C., alias Doug,
alias Willie Nelson. Citizen of the town of Hawthorne, in the county of
Alachua, in the state of Florida, in the country of the United States. A part
of the world, the universe, and the Kingdom of God. Though W. C. seldom voices his spiritual convictions unless he senses a receptive audience,
he's a firm believer in the Ten Commandments and the Golden Rule. A

258

The B&B is unprepossessing from the outside, a small rectangular concrete block building with louvered windows and a tiny package store to one side. The *spell* of the B&B is apparent only when one enters the cool, dark interior with, thanks to Ann, a freshly scrubbed concrete floor and gleaming wood bar. Behind the counter stands W. C., huge cigar in mouth, smiling a faint, beatific smile. And beyond him on neat wood shelves are the magical elixirs he sells to customers who mix their own drinks straight from the bottle, one of the few "grandfathered-in" bars in the state allowed to do so. As W. C. knows, there are many paths leading to enlightenment. And his is that of compassion tempered with a firm hand. In short, though understanding and even-tempered, he takes no shit from anyone.

I draw up the stool across from him.

"How's it going, Dave?"

"Fine."

W. C.'s grin broadens. "Alright . . . Alright . . . " Then, following a brief pause: "Bud Light?"

I nod and Fifi, a full-sized white poodle, freshly permed and rib-boned, clickety-clicks around the counter on manicured nails to greet me. Aside from their two children and a granddaughter, Fifi, Fat Cat, and Clarence, an argumentative cockatoo, are W.C. and Ann's prides and joys.

Fifi lowers her ribboned head to be stroked firmly behind the ears.

"Anything new to Lochloosa?" asks W. C.

"A ten or twelve-foot gator passed by the dock this afternoon."

W.C. emits a hollow puff of cigar smoke and nods sagely. "That's a big one alright, but I've seen bigger."

He relates a story of a twenty-foot gator that would do Rudyard Kipling proud. By the time he's done, Buddy, the white jukebox conces-sionaire, and Elisa, Buddy's black chauffeur (Buddy has received one too many DUIs), sit down next to me at the bar. Buddy is having a half pint of Johnny Walker Red with a coke chaser and Elisa is having a coke.

Buddy hands Ann an updated list of 45s for the jukebox. "I've got some great new selections."

man of principle in an age (like most ages on the merely human level) of charlatans.

SATURDAY IS THE biggest-grossing day at the B & B, followed by Sunday afternoon when a blues singer performs. But weeknights, excluding Fridays, are my favorites. As often as not, there's just me, W. C., and a few talkative customers. Or, me, W. C., and a documentary on public TV. How many other bars have the set turned to PBS? Or, better yet, me and W. C.

How to describe our conversations? Sometimes intense; sometimes punctuated by long, comfortable silences. But always meaningful, at least to ourselves. For W. C. is brother to my soul. A physically diminutive black man born in backwoods Florida and an acne-scarred white man born to the upper reaches of Southern society, sharing little in common save an identical outlook on life, which is, in essence, everything. Like myself, W. C. knows the Kingdom of God is the Kingdom Within. Everything else is mere karma. Some good, some bad, some indifferent, but karma just the same.

On Saturdays, catfish and ribs are grilled out front by a local vendor, and blacks come from miles around to partake of the festivities. There's no music but that on the Wurlitzer, but there's plenty of soul and line dancing. If there's any trouble, W. C. is right in the thick of it, pouring the culprits' unfinished drinks on the concrete floor and himself hastily mopping it up, with the threat of dialing 911 as his trump card! But there's never any serious trouble because W. C. has the uncanny knack of nipping it in the bud with the steely calm of a zen master.

Almost any time, day or night, from eleven A.M. to an extremely flexible closing time, Ann, a statuesque beauty and fellow Sagittarian, presides over the proceedings at the B & B as though she were hosting a party in her own home. Without being intrusive, and with the greatest of tact, she manages to steer everyone at the bar into a lively group discussion on topics ranging from movies to music, sports, or politics, and back again. Like any good hostess, she never stoops to local gossip and is loved by all.

Especially Wes, who arrives at eleven sharp each morning for his first half-pint of the day. He does odd jobs for Ann—painting, fixing, mowing—between drinks. Then there's Al, poet, songwriter, and all-around creative genius who was a renowned chef in Miami, but has returned home to become another kind of artist. And Freddy, the musician, with the deep baritone voice and the ongoing monologue filled with joy and life and God. And Elsie with the soft brown eyes and kindly manner. And Ernestine, the former owner of the B & B, who accused me of being with Florida Beverage Control, bold and brassy with a heart of gold. And Bobby, W. C.'s cousin from Lauderdale, who knows the history of everything and everyone in Hawthorne. And Charles, the burly trucker with the dirty jokes and wily ways. And Lois, provider of love and discipline to the children of Hawthorne. And Cue, bon vivant and dancer extraordinaire. And Wolf, who knows everything about local wildlife and crops (*and more besides*, as Jim Turner would say). And Ann's beautiful daughter, Valerie, who works for the Society for the Prevention of Cruelty to Animals and provides the B & B with its ongoing menagerie of pets. And so on, and so forth, ad infinitum.

As for me, I prefer the nights when W. C. and I have the bar to ourselves, soul music playing gently in the background, discussing life, love, and the Kingdom of God, which is no place if not here.

The B & B is three miles south of Hawthorne on U.S. 301. On the last Thursday in June, black Hawthornians from across the nation and around the world gather here to celebrate Homecoming. Begun during the Depression as a harvest celebration for black farmers it has become a celebration of black pride with speeches and exhibits at Hawthorne High. The B & B is the nighttime center of festivities with soul food, music, and dancing to a blues band.

Pirate's Cove, a general store/gas station/bar on the Suwanee River at Fowler's Bluff.
Photo by Keith Bollum.

Fowler's Bluff

Fowler's Bluff is a community of less than a hundred souls. It has one gas station/general store/saloon. My elderly cousin, Jim Turner, lived there on the banks of the Suwannee River with his second wife and stepson. In the old days when Jim was High-Sheriff of Levy County, his house doubled as a hunting and fishing lodge. Friends and acquaintances, including a lot of high muckety-muck politicians, gathered there during hunting season.

On fall evenings, Jim and I used to sit on the back porch in twin rockers and watch the sun set over the slow-rolling river. Let's listen in on one of our conversations . . .

"EVER KILLED a bear, Jim?"

"No, sir, I reckon I ain't. Can't hardly eat a bear. Now, sailfish, them's good groceries. When I was State Conservation Officer, I hooked into plenty of sailfish and we'd cook 'em up on the boat."

"How 'bout Uncle Chauncey? What kind of hunter was he?" Chauncey, my great uncle, was one of the high muckety-muck politicians.

Jim chuckles dryly. "Chauncey Butler! Why, Chauncey was no kind of hunter *atall* [pronounced *ay-tall*]. Many's the time we'd be setting out on the front porch and Chauncey'd say, 'I ain't got nothing 'gainst no turkey or deer, Jim. So why should I kill one?' He was some kind of drinker though. Why, Chauncey spilled more whiskey than most men drink *enduring* a lifetime!"

Thus prompted, Jim begins a story about Chauncey.

"Once't your Uncle Chauncey was here hunting. Only there was more drinking than hunting going on, and a whole week passed without Chauncey setting foot out of doors. Then one morning a wire from Chauncey's wife, Marge, arrived at the Western Union to Chiefland: 'Stop drinking and come home—Stop—Your Loving Wife—Stop—Marge.' "

Jim pauses for dramatic effect. "When I handed Chauncey the envelope, he was setting out on the back porch with his feet propped up on the railing, drinking Canadian Club with a Lea and Perrins chaser. He didn't even need to open the envelope to know how it read.

"Chauncey tossed the unopened wire into a convenient trash can. 'Reckon it's high time we plugged us a gobbler, Jim! That way, I can claim to have been hunting all this time, and Marge will have one less bone to pick when I get home.'

"I said, 'But Chauncey, How on God's green earth are you going to bag a gobbler without setting foot off this here porch?'

" 'Tom Gilchrist! Is that boy still the hunter and tracker he used to be?'

" 'Yessir, he's still some good.'

" 'Then, he's our man. Tell Tom I'll pay him twenty-five dollars cash money if he'll fetch us home a gobbler.'

"This was during the Great Depression, remember, and twenty-five dollars was right smart of change. So it weren't no trouble *atall* to hire on

Tom. In fact, since Tom spent most of his time hunting anyways, paying him twenty-five dollars to do what come natural was a bonus.

"Sure enough, a day or two later, Tom showed up at the front door with a gobbler. Chauncey took it. 'This here is right smart of a turkey, Tom. How much you guesstimate it'll go?'

" 'Twenty-seven pound,' said Tom.

"Twenty-seven pounds was a pretty fair gobbler, even in them days when game was a heap sight more plentiful than it is today. So Chauncey and I had a drink to celebrate. In fact, we had several drinks. Then Chauncey decided to drive into town and wire Marge about the gobbler. On the way in, with him and me passing the bottle back and forth, he reckoned twenty-seven pounds wasn't big enough. A forty-seven pounder would be more like it!

"When the man at the Western Union office handed Chauncey the form to fill out, he scribbled acrost it: 'Dear Marge, bagged a 47-pound gobbler yesterday. Will be home on Friday. Your Loving Husband, Chauncey.' After he took another slug from his hip flask, he looked the message over and added a 1 in front of the 47. 'There! That ought to hold her till I get back!'

"Marge didn't know much about gobblers, but she knew a 147-pounder was a sho'nuff big 'un! When Chauncey come home, she had invited fifty or so dinner guests to help devour that turkey."

Jim chuckles his dry chuckle. "Chauncey got in a heap of conversation over that one."

HIS STORY FINISHED, Jim casts a practiced eye over the twilight river where two men in an aluminum skiff are casting for bass. A broken-down houseboat leans precariously against the opposite bank.

"What d'ya reckon they're up to?"

"Fishing?"

Jim leans over in his rocker and shields his eyes with his palm to get a better view. "Fishing? Not that far from the bank, they ain't." He smiles knowingly.

"Whatever happened to Chauncey?"

Jim leans back in his rocker. "Died . . . Called me from the hospital to Miamuh when he was on his deathbed. Said if there was anything I was doing wrong, anything I needed to change, he'd let me know once't he was gone, if it was humanly possible."

Jim takes a sip from one of the two scotch-and-waters he is allowed daily by his doctor and settles back contentedly in his rocker. "Never heard from Chauncey. Still waiting, though."

To get to Fowler's Bluff, follow U.S. 19 for 120 miles north of St. Pete and ask directions at Chiefland. Treasure Camp, a combination gas station/country store/bar, has local and good country music and a home-made buffet on Sunday afternoons.

A dozen or so miles west of Fowler's Bluff down the Suwannee River, in the grasslands skirting the Gulf, is the tiny village of Suwannee. According to Jim, Suwannee was a place of death and violence during the heyday of drug-smuggling in the '70s and early '80s. But things have quieted down considerably since then. Today, this idyllic setting, with picturesque houses on stilts, one marina and motel, and a lone seafood restaurant (open four days a week), is a great place to rent a houseboat and cruise the river, or simply chill out away from the pressures of the so-called real world.

To get to Suwannee, follow U.S. 19 thirteen miles north of Chiefland to Old Town. Turn left on County Road 349 and drive twenty-two miles west.

The Yearling Revisited

Sitting in the stained-glass dining room of the Sprague House Inn at Crescent City, you can practically hear the long, low, mournful whistle of an 1880s river boat—the *Crescent City*, perhaps, or the *Escort, Comet, Star, Georgia,* or *Governor Stafford*—chugging down Crescent Lake, fifth largest lake in the state. The two-story inn, white-washed and blue-shuttered,was constructed during the boom of the 1880s and '90s as a school for domestics to practice their housekeeping and culinary skills on guests. Boatloads of Northern tourists traveled the length of the St. Johns River—there were half a dozen hotels in Crescent City alone.

As the proprietor of a general store in Marjorie Kinnan Rawlings's novel *The Yearling* put it, "I'll swear those city folks traveling up and down the river—Hollering for venison, and 'tain't half as good as pork, and you and me, we know it."

During the 1980s the inn was restored by Barry and Elaine Nord, artists who had a glassmaking studio in back, and is presently run by Terry and Vena Moyer. It's the sort of place your grandmother *should* have had,

The Sprague House Inn in Crescent City, built during the late 1800s.

with nooks and crannies galore, assorted bric-a-brac, and the smell of fresh bread baking in the oven. Prominent guests have included Theodore Roosevelt, William Jennings Bryan, and Booker T. Washington, who worked for the Army Corps of Engineers to provide a pass between the St. Johns River and Crescent Lake.

The magnolia-scented streets of Crescent City are lined with "Steamboat Gothic" mansions that bring to mind a time when tourism and citrus were king. From 1870 to 1894, the citrus industry grew and prospered. Orange and lemon groves surrounded the lake, and packing houses lined its shore. The Great Freeze of 1894 was the first of a series of disastrous freezes that drove the citrus industry further south. Grove land was converted to ferneries on the outskirts of town.

Today Crescent City is known as the Bass Capital of the World, and fishermen come from near and far to hone their skills in the choppy gray waters of Crescent Lake. The river port where the Baxters go to trade in *The Yearling* bears a better-than-passing resemblance to Crescent City. There's the public dock, a rickety wood T-shaped pier a block from the inn on the town's main street, where sun-bonneted cracker ladies and long, lanky black men fish for bream with cane poles. And the barber shop where elderly crackers while away long summer afternoons spinning elaborate yarns about days past. And Hap's Diner where, as in the stereotypical western, all eyes turn to follow the progress of any stranger who chances to enter.

EIGHT MILES WEST of Crescent City on State Road 238 is Fruitland, where you can rent a skiff at one of several fish camps and explore the St. Johns River and Lake George. Across the river from Fruitland on Drayton Island is Fort Gates, a three-story, many-gabled, copper-roofed Victorian mansion with a widow's walk and an indoor bowling alley. There are servants' quarters to either side and a gingerbread dock house. In *The Yearling*, Fort Gates was where the Baxters' no-account neighbors, the Forresters, went to trade, having alienated the good Christian folk of Volusia by their wild and woolly ways. A mile east down the St. Johns is Salt Springs, named after a freshwater spring where fishermen stand in the bows of skiffs, with bows and arrows, on the lookout for bass in the gin-clear water.

It was here that Penny Baxter in *The Yearling* wounded the renegade bear, Slewfoot:

> The growth dissolved ahead into the grasses. [Slewfoot] was going like a black whirlwind . . . The bright swift waters of Salt Springs Run shone beyond. The bear splashed into the current and struck out for the far bank. Penny lifted his gun and shot twice . . . Slewfoot was clambering out on the opposite shore . . . The black rounded rump was all that was visible. Penny seized Jody's muzzle-loader and fired after it. The bear gave a leap.
>
> Penny shouted. "I tetched him!"

Today a single-car ferry provides transportation between Salt Springs on the west bank and Georgetown on the east. To summon it, park your car at the end of the concrete ramp on the Salt Springs side and blink your headlights on and off. A concrete barge, connected to a tiny tugboat by a free-swinging steel fulcrum, will appear and the skipper will help load your car for the trip across. This is a modern version of the ferry in *The Yearling*: "Penny shouted across [the river] to summon a ferry from the Volusia side. A man crossed over for them with a rough raft of hewn logs. They crossed back, watching the slow sweep of the river current."

Three or four miles south of the ferry is Lake George, a deep blue beauty of a lake, fourteen miles across. The Baxter family in *The Yearling* lived just south of here on the west side of the river in what is known as the Florida Scrub.

The Florida Scrub is as different from the swamp and hammock land that fringes the river as night and day. As Rawlings wrote in *South Moon Under*:

Cable ferry on the St. Johns River at Crows Bluff, 1913.

The two types of growth did not mingle, as though an ascetic race withdrew itself from the tropical one and refused to interbreed. The moisture along the rivers gave a footing for the lush growth of cypress in the swamp; of live oak, magnolia, hickory, ash, bay, sweet gum, and holly that made up the surrounding hammock . . . There was perhaps no similar region anywhere. It was a vast dry rectangular plateau, bounded on three sides by two rivers. The Oklawaha, flowing towards the north, bounded it on the west. At the northwest corner of the rectangle, the Oklawaha turned sharply at right angles and flowed due east, joining at the northeast corner the St. Johns River, which formed the eastern demarcation.

Within these watery lines the scrub stood aloof, uninhabited through its wider reaches. The growth repelled all human living. The soil was a tawny sand, from whose parched infertility there reared . . . so dense a growth of scrub pine . . . the effect of the massed trunks was of a limitless, canopied stockade . . .

In places the pines grew more openly, the sunlight filtered through and patches of ground showed, bald and lichened. The scrub was sparingly dotted with small lakes and springs. Around these grew a damp-loving hammock vegetation. Or a random patch of moisture produced . . . a fine stand of slash pine or long-leaf yellow. These were known as pine islands. To anyone standing on a rise, they were visible from a great distance.

It was on one of these pine islands, Baxter's Island, that the Baxter family in *The Yearling* homesteaded.

RAWLINGS WROTE *The Yearling* at the instigation of Max Perkins, the legendary editor of Hemingway, Fitzgerald, and Wolfe at Scribner's. Perkins suggested she try her hand at a boy's novel in the tradition of *Huckleberry Finn*. At first she was reluctant, fearing that being the author of a "children's" book might damage her reputation as a serious writer. But the idea stuck in her mind and was mentioned in several of her letters.

Over the years, the book took on a grander design until it became more than a simple juvenile about a boy and his pet fawn. In January, 1936, she wrote Perkins: "The feeling for the boy's book, the particular thing I want to say, came to me. It will not be a story for boys, though some of them might enjoy it. It will be a story *about* a boy, a brief and tragic idyll of childhood. I think it can not help but be . . . beautiful."

As planned, it would be an epic novel dealing with a way of life in the scrub that was fast becoming extinct. On July 31, 1936, Rawlings wrote Perkins: "I want to take all those pages and pages of a book to say it . . . But the short narrative I had in mind will make my culminating point—my climax and my point, and a very stirring point it is, too. . . . now I feel free to luxuriate in the simple details that interest me, and that I have been amazed to find interested other people . . . "

Rawlings used two elderly crackers as source material for her novel, Barney Dillard and Cal Long. To quote from one of her letters to Perkins: "I found old man Long, the hunter, still alive, and his wife very reproachful because I hadn't come two years ago to stay with them as I promised. I am going over next week to stay as long as necessary to get what stories I need from the old man. I hope you can see this place some day—in the very core of the scrub, where he has lived since 1872—falling into decay under the exquisite mantle of flowering vines. They are hard put to make a living, principally because the deer and foxes eat their crops almost faster than they can raise them." This sentence is a foreshadowing of the action in *The Yearling*. Jody Baxter's pet fawn, Flag, must be sacrificed so the family can survive.

The Yearling was published more than sixty years ago in February, 1938, to almost unanimous acclaim. The Book of the Month Club chose the novel as its March selection. Movie rights were sold to MGM for $30,000 and it topped the bestseller list for months. At year's end it won the Pulitzer Prize. Marjorie Kinnan Rawlings had become a national celebrity and deservedly so. Over the years, her novel about a boy and his pet fawn coming of age in the Florida scrub has become a classic.

To quote from its final paragraph: "Somewhere beyond the sink-hole, past the magnolia, under the live oaks, a boy and a yearling ran side by side, and were gone forever."

To get to Crescent City, follow Interstate 4 thirty-five miles east of Orlando to DeLand, then take U.S. 19 thirty miles north.

North Florida mosquitoes drove out an earlier film production of *The Yearling* with Spencer Tracy, but the 1946 version of the movie starring Gregory Peck, Jane Wyman, and Claude Jarman is an enduring family film classic. In 1994, there was a remake starring Peter Strauss.

Hyacinth Drift Revisited

In a closing chapter of *Cross Creek*, Marjorie Kinnan Rawlings describes a trip she and a friend took on the north-flowing St. Johns River during the '30s. Recently a friend and I took a similar trip.

MARCH 23, 1999: Cap'n Ed and I cast off from the Holly Bluff Marina at DeLand Landing, just west of DeLand, at 1:30 P.M. and head north. Our vessel is a forty-four-foot houseboat with three beds and a couch, a tiny head and galley, and a sundeck on top. Buffett, Sinatra, and Motown CDs are playing as we cruise past Astor and dock for the night in a cut, which was once part of the river bed before dredging by the Army Corp of Engineers in the 1930s changed the river's course. Following a delicious steak dinner grilled on the front deck, we retire around ten.

Marjorie Kinnan Rawlings and her woods-wise friend, Dessie, began their voyage in an eighteen-foot skiff, with two outboards, at Fort Christmas, the head of the St. Johns, "where the highway crosses miles of wet prairie and cypress swamp between Orlando and Indian City."

For Rawlings, it was a journey into her own heart, from being lost to being found:

> I loved the Creek, I loved the Grove, I loved the shabby farmhouse. Suddenly they were nothing. The difficulties were greater than the compensations. I talked morosely with my friend, Dessie. I do not think she understood my torment, for she is simple and direct and completely adjusted to all living. She knew only that a friend was in trouble . . .
>
> . . . The river was a blue smear through the marsh. The marsh was tawny. It sprawled to the four points of the compass; flat; interminable; meaningless.
>
> I thought: "This is fantastic. I am about to deliver myself over to a nightmare."
>
> But life was a nightmare. The river was at least of my own choosing.

MARCH 24, 1999: Cap'n Ed and I awake to a foggy morning and cross fourteen-mile-wide Lake George to Drayton Island and Georgetown on the north shore. On Drayton Island, accessible to Georgetown by a four-car ferry, is the previously mentioned Fort Gates mansion. Fort Gates is indicative of a time during the 1870s and '80s when land along the St. Johns was prime grove area, and Northern tourists made trips up and down the river on paddlewheelers out of Jacksonville. We cruise past Welaka—which means *chain of lakes* in Seminole—and San Mateo with tin-roofed cracker homes, rustic fish camps, and the mouth of the Oklawaha River. The Oklawaha runs west to world-famous Silver Springs. We dock at the Holiday Inn in Palatka. Here the river widens considerably on its trip north to Jacksonville. Appropriately enough, a convention of antique boaters is meeting, and the concrete dock is lined with meticulously restored wooden Chris Crafts from the '20s and '30s.

276

St. Johns River at Palatka.

Photo by Debra Force.

Marjorie and Dessie soon became lost. "The river was no more than a path through high grass . . . there would be neither lights, beacons, nor buoys for at least a hundred miles. Bridge and highway disappeared, and there was no longer any world but this incredible marsh, this unbelievable amount of sky."

A fisherman's wife tells them, "You just got to keep tryin' for the main channel. You'll get so you can tell."

"Young 'un," says Dessie, "it's mighty fine to be traveling."

Marjorie explains: "[Dessie] was born and raised in rural Florida, and guns and campfires and fishing-rods and creeks are corpuscular in her blood . . . She is ten years my junior, but she calls me, with much tenderness, pitying my incapabilities, 'Young 'un'."

They again became lost: "When we looked over our shoulders, the marsh had closed in over the channel by which we had come. We were in a labyrinth."

They circle the marsh looking for the main channel. Following a night fitfully sleeping in muck and mosquitoes, Marjorie awakens to find Dessie casting for bass.

> "Young 'un," she called, "where's the channel?"
>
> I pointed to the northeast and she nodded vehemently. It had come to both of us like a revelation . . . the water hyacinths were drifting faintly faster in that direction. From that instant we were never . . . long lost . . . [w]here the river sprawled in confusion, we might shut off the motor and study the floating hyacinths until we caught, in one direction, a swifter pulsing. . . . like all simple facts, it was necessary to discover it for oneself.

MARCH 25, 1999: This morning Cap'n Ed and I leave Palatka and return upriver, south to Dunn Creek, a tributary of the St. Johns that runs southeast through practically virgin forest to ten-mile-long Crescent Lake. And beyond that, Dead Lake. Having read "Hyacinth Drift," Cap'n Ed has taken to calling me "young 'un" due to my nautical incompetence, combined with my all-around incompetence in regard to *practical* matters.

Wood fences with nylon-mesh netting are sometimes found in shallow water close by the bank, to keep water hyacinths out of the main channel. Indigenous to Brazil, hyacinths were brought to Florida from the New Orleans Exposition of 1884 by a San Mateo woman to decorate her garden pool. They spread like wildfire until they became a menace to navigation on the St. Johns and throughout the state.

We spend the night in Crescent City at Tangerine Cove Marina. While I drink beer with locals at the bar, Cap'n Ed goes fishing off Bear Island, but only catches gars and junk fish.

Marjorie and Dessie pass wild cattle in the marsh. "They loomed startlingly above us, their splotches black and brown and red and white . . . "

Again they become confused and navigate Puzzle Lake under the impression they are navigating Lake Harney to the north. "[N]ot even the mistaking of whole lakes could lose us. Others of more childish faith were sure it proved the goodness of God in looking after imbeciles."

North of Lake Harney: "The character of the river changed . . . It was deep and swift . . . All its young torture was forgotten, and its wanderings in the tawny marsh. The banks had changed. They were high. Tall palms crowded great live oaks, and small trees grew humbly in the shadows. Toward sunset we swung under the western banks at one of those spots a traveler recognizes instinctively as, for the moment, home."

They spend the night in an abandoned cabin and Dessie comments, "Young 'un, Christopher Columbus had nothing on us. He had a whole ocean to fool around in . . . Turn that boy loose in the St. Johns marsh, and he'd have been lost as a hound puppy."

MARCH 26, 1999: This morning Cap'n Ed and I leave Crescent City and cruise to Astor, stopping off at Silver Glen Springs on the west shore of Lake George. As in Rawlings's day, herds of wild cattle free-graze in the marsh to either side of the river. Silver Glen Springs is crystal clear and bubbles up from an underground cave with a year-round 72-degree temperature. Numerous houseboats, including one with a pair of swimsuited lovers playing loud rock, dock overnight. Not relishing the raucous company, we leave the springs and finish crossing Lake George in late afternoon with the wind whipping up waves reminiscent of the sea. At Astor we eat at the Black Water Inn, the best and most popular restaurant on the upper river, and anchor in a secluded cut upstream. Cap'n Ed fishes for a time—again with no luck—while I listen to the bellow of the gators and the steady *peck-peck* of what turned out in the morning to be a rarely seen pileated woodpecker.

Marjorie and Dessie spend a lovely, almost mystic, night in the cabin by the river. "We had hot baths out of a bucket . . . and sat on the cabin steps in pajamas while the fire died down. Suddenly the soft night turned silver. The moon was rising. We lay on our cots a long time wakeful because of beauty. The moon shone through the doorway and windows, and the light was patterned with the shadows of Spanish moss waving from the live oaks. There was a deserted grove somewhere behind the cabin, and the incredible sweetness of orange bloom drifted toward us."

Dessie shoots a wild duck for breakfast and they spend all morning on the bank watching the mullet jump. They find their boat half-filled with water due to some loose caulking. They turn it upside down and stuff cloth from one of Dessie's shirts into the cracks. When they launch it, the makeshift caulking holds. They continue their journey.

MARCH 27, 1999: This morning Cap'n Ed and I head south past Hontoon Island with its Indian burial mounds, huge Spanish moss–festooned live oaks, and forty-foot wooden watch tower. Live oaks and magnolia give way to flat, swampy marsh between Hontoon and Lake Monroe, which is ten miles long and deep blue, the last stop for large-vessel traffic on the St. Johns. We dock for the night at Sanford City Marina—where the Sons of Norway are rowing replicas of Viking longships—and spend a riotous evening in the local bars with friends from DeLand.

Marjorie and Dessie reach Sanford on a Sunday, in need of a change of clothes and desperate for gas. When they tie up at the city dock, the owner of a pleasure yacht, "trim in double breasted blue," says all the gas stations are closed, save one that is opening for him. He offers to have his man drive them over with their gas tins in his car:

> There was a sound inside the yacht. There simmered up the companionway a woman, magnificent in [a] pink spectator sports costume. The crew jumped almost to attention and escorted her down the yacht's gangplank.
>
> The woman snapped over her shoulder, "I must have the car at once. I cannot be late to church for this nonsense."
>
> Our . . . man turned rosy and made a comradely gesture to us.
>
> He leaned over and whispered, "The car will be back in just a moment . . . "

Eventually, Marjorie and Dessie get gas and the New York Sunday papers and are off again.

> "Good luck!" called the yacht owner. "The very best of good luck!"
>
> He waved after us as far as we could see him, as though reluctant to break a mystic thread. His face was wistful.

"The poor b_____," Dess said pityingly and indignantly. "I bet he would give his silk shirt to go down the river with us instead of with Pink Petticoats."

MARCH 28, 1999: On a hangover morning, Cap'n Ed and I head back to DeLand Landing. He spends the afternoon fishing. He lands four freshwater rays, but nothing edible.

North of Lake Monroe, Marjorie and Dessie experience "right clare river":

> [N]ow the river life was indeed the finest of lives, and there was no hurry left in the world. We put up a golden-brown deep creek and fished all afternoon. A white egret fished companionably with us a few yards away . . .
>
> Beyond DeLand Landing we called at a houseboat tethered to the bank. Its owner had been captain of the old Clyde River Line, and he received our request for advice on crossing Lake George with the old-school graciousness of large craft meeting small . . .

In their small craft, they "would do best by taking neither [the main or west channels], and hugging the west shore."

Following a disagreeable encounter with a "sullen-faced" woman squatter and her "dirty" child in a hut on stakes over the water, they "retrace" several miles and camp on "a comfortable square of high ground."

"As we were making camp, three fishermen hailed us excitedly. Were we the women who had put in at Fort Christmas nearly a week before . . . Word had been sent down the river from other fishermen to watch for us and report our safety . . ."

The next morning they intended "to cross Lake George in the early morning before the wind rose . . . "

MARCH 29, 1999: Cap'n Ed and I awake to a mystical mist rising off the slate-gray river like the fog of heaven. Following a lazy day of fishing—again, no luck—we return to the Black Water Inn for dinner, then cruise back to DeLand Landing with the tape deck blasting '50s and '60s rock in the chill, fog-shrouded moonlight. Tomorrow morning, we return the boat.

At foggy dawn, Marjorie and Dessie cross Lake George. Rawlings writes:

> We had no intention of hugging the safe shore, so we compromised on the west channel. We left the great channel markers behind and a gust of wind twisted our stern. There was a half hour when the haze threatened to obscure all visible shore lines . . .
>
> Midway, the wind was blowing the whitecaps off the waves, but it was helpfully behind us. With both arms braced against the steering arm of the motor, Dess kept the boat headed when water that rolled like surf lifted our stern. The propellor churned high out of the water. When it dropped again the boat lunged and turned . . .
>
> The distant shore seemed stationary. We passed the north point of Drayton's Island, where the main channel joined the west, with the lake boiling after us . . . We had been some two and a half hours . . . crossing the lake.

They continue their leisurely journey:

> At Welaka one afternoon we . . . turned up our home river, the Oklawaha. I thought in a panic, I shall never be happy on land again. . . .
>
> But when the dry ground was under us, the world no longer fluid, I found a forgotten loveliness in all the things that have nothing to do with men. Beauty is pervasive, and fills, like perfume, more than the object that contains it. Because I had known intimately a river, the earth pulsed under me . . . I knew, for a moment . . . the only nightmare is the masochistic human mind.

Houseboats may be rented from the Holly Bluff and Hontoon Marinas at DeLand Landing just west of DeLand.

The Holiday Inn on the St. Johns River in Palatka has been called the best hotel in the country by Southern humorist Lewis Grizzard.

The Angel Diner in Palatka, the oldest diner in Florida, has served burgers, fries, and shakes since 1932.

Angel's Diner in Palatka.

Photo by Debra Force.

Zora and Keith

Zora Neale Hurston and Keith Bollum. A black woman from rural Florida, a Scandinavian from northern Minnesota. On the surface they seem to have little in common, but appearances can be deceiving. A spiritual thread connects and directs the two of them like a lodestar in heaven.

Keith is a newcomer to Florida, a Midwestern transplant who fell in love with the state and opened the Muse Bookstore in DeLand, specializing in Florida books, new and out of print. Like newcomer Marjorie Kinnan Rawlings before him, he has an innocent eye for things many natives miss. A soft-spoken Yankee, he is fascinated by Florida's black culture. Growing up in an all-white community in a practically all-white state, he had little exposure to blacks before moving here.

But he's rapidly making up for lost time. His fascination with black subjects, especially Florida author Zora Neale Hurston, is endless. What is it about this genius black lady that rings a common chord in so many people, male and female, black and white, rich and poor, Southerner and Northerner alike?

ZORA NEALE HURSTON was born in 1891 near Tuskegee, Alabama, though she later claimed to be ten or fifteen years younger. Shortly thereafter, her family moved to Eatonville, Florida, a tiny, isolated, all-black community seven miles north of Orlando. The seventh of eight children—six boys, two girls—she was a born traveler. As she wrote in her autobiography, *Dust Tracks on a Road*: "[O]nce I found the use of my feet, they took to wandering . . . I would wander off in the woods all alone, following some inside urge to go places. This alarmed my mother a great deal. She used to say . . . she believed a woman who was an enemy of hers sprinkled 'travel dust' around the doorstep the day I was born."

Following her mother's death, when Zora was about ten years old, her father, Rev. John Hurston, a one-time mayor of Eatonville, remarried. Zora and her stepmother didn't get along. To quote *Dust Tracks*: "That hour began my wanderings. Not so much in geography, but in time [and] spirit."

Zora found work as maid to an actress in a Gilbert and Sullivan acting troupe. In Baltimore the actress married, and Zora became a waitress. She was inspired to become a writer by a night-school reading of Coleridge's *Kubla Khan*. To quote *Dust Tracks*, she visualized: "all . . . the writer had meant for me to see with him, and infinite cosmic things besides . . . This was my world . . . and I shall be in it and surrounded by it, if it is the last thing I do on God's green dirt-ball . . . "

In 1918 Zora entered Howard University in Washington, D.C., and published her first story, "John Redding Goes to Sea," in Howard's literary magazine. In her sophomore year, she received a scholarship to attend New York City's Barnard College as its first black student. She received a bachelor of arts degree in 1928. In New York the Harlem Renaissance was in full swing, and "bold and brassy" Zora found herself among such literary greats as fellow Floridian James Weldon Johnson, Langston Hughes, Wallace Thurmond, and Arna Bontemps. She soon published short stories, including "Drenched in Light," "Spunk," and "Sweat." Due to her burgeoning literary ability, popular novelist Fannie Hurst hired her as a secretary. Hopelessly inept, Zora was fired but stayed on as companion and chauffeur. To integrate a restaurant in New Hampshire, Miss Hurst conferred on Zora the title of African royalty, "Princess," and the sobriquet stuck.

In *Twentieth Century Authors* Zora described herself as "a bright pupil, but impudent." An earthy beauty with a penetrating gaze, she used her considerable charm to gain favor and aid from mostly white sources. She was in a precarious position, shuttling back and forth between the white and black worlds to sell black culture to a white market.

A fast friendship between Zora and Langston Hughes ended when they quarreled over ownership of a collaborative effort, the play *Mule Bone: A Comedy of Negro Life*. Hughes wrote ambivalently of her in his 1940 autobiography, *The Big Sea*, "She was always getting scholarships and things from wealthy white people, some of whom simply paid her . . . to sit around and represent the Negro race for them . . . to many of her white friends . . . she was a perfect 'darky' . . . naive, childlike, sweet, humorous, and highly colored . . . " On the other hand, Zora was: "a student who . . . had great scorn for all pretensions, academic or otherwise. That is why she was such a fine folklore collector, able to go among the people and never act as if she had been to school at all."

In February 1927, Zora was studying anthropology at Columbia under Franz Boas, or "Papa Franz" as she affectionately called him, when he arranged a fellowship enabling her to return to Eatonville to collect black folklore. A later research trip was financed by her patron Mrs. R. Osgood Mason of New York, or "Godmother" as Zora and Hughes referred to her, an elderly white lady with an overriding interest in "primitive" cultures and mysticism. In 1935 this material would become the book *Mules and Men*.

Zora describes her collecting method in the introduction: "Folklore is not as easy to collect as it sounds. The best source is where there are the least outside influences and the people are the shyest. They are most reluctant to reveal that which their soul lives by . . . the Negro, in spite of his open-faced laughter, his seeming acquiescence, is particularly evasive . . . we are a polite people and we do not say to our questioner, 'Get out of here!' We smile and tell him . . . something that satisfies the white person because, knowing so little about us, he doesn't know what he is missing. The Indian resists curiosity by a stony silence. The Negro offers a feather-bed resistance . . . We let the probe enter, but it never comes out. It gets smothered under a lot of laughter and pleasantries."

TODAY THE SETTING of Eatonville that Zora so lovingly described no longer exists. It has been buried under commercial districts and housing developments. Joe Clark's General Store, the center of Eatonville society, where Zora listened to "the big picture talkers," is now the R&R Grocery Store, and the only indications of Zora's presence are a small plaque with a summary of her life and works in front of the Eatonville fire station, and the Zora Neale Hurston Museum, a small storefront establishment.

Little interested in politics or the black struggle with the white community, Zora's themes of self-discovery and African-American culture were held in little regard by her contemporaries. As she wrote in a 1928 magazine article, "How It Feels To Be Colored Me": "I am not tragically colored. There is no great sorrow dammed up in my soul, nor lurking behind my eyes . . . I do not belong to the sobbing school of Negrohood who hold that nature has somehow given them a lowdown dirty deal and whose feelings are all hurt about it."

Zora's territory was the phosphate, sawmill, and lumber camps where blacks entertained one another with folklore, a sort of shorthand novel. As Zora wrote in *Dust Tracks*: "I have memories within that came out of the materials that went to make me. Time and place have had their say."

In *Mules and Men* she describes Eatonville as " . . . the city of five lakes, three croquet courts, three hundred brown skins, three hundred good swimmers, plenty guavas, two schools, and no jailhouse." She gathered material by sitting and swapping lies with the menfolk on the front porch of Joe Clark's General Store.

Black folklore often deals with tricksters—small, weak animals who outwit stronger animals to reach their goals. Tricksters are born rebels who ignore society's laws and mores to wage a constant war of rebellion. In "Why Women Always Take Advantage of Men," Eatonville resident Matilda Mosely tells of an earlier day when the strength of Man and Woman was equal. Man persuades God to give him more strength so he can gain ascendency. Woman is then told by the devil to take from God "dat bunch of keys hanging by the mantlepiece." Thus she is able to keep Man out of the kitchen, the bedroom, and away from the cradle. Man must submit to Woman if he wants access to these essential areas.

To quote *Orlando Sentinel* writer John Hicks: "[This tale] depicts man and woman nearly on equal footing with God, wide awake to nature and integral, if small, parts of the cosmos . . . themes Zora Hurston would express again and again."

The last third of *Mules and Men* deals with Zora's studying to become a hoodoo, or voodoo, priestess: "I headed my toenails towards Louisiana and New Orleans in particular." Though written earlier, it was not brought out until after publication of her first novel, *Jonah's Gourd Vine*, in 1934.

Jonah's Gourd Vine was written when J. B. Lippincott inquired whether she was writing a novel, after seeing her short story "The Gilded Two Bits" in *Story* magazine, a showcase for new writers. Zora rented a house in Sanford, Florida, for $1.50 a week and wrote *Vine* "in about three months." It's the story of a Baptist minister with a weakness for women, and is based on her father's life.

In 1937 Zora followed *Vine* with *Their Eyes Were Watching God*, a novel that takes place at Okeechobee during the period of The Great Hurricane of '28. According to *Dust Tracks*, it was written "to embalm all the tenderness of passion" for a former lover.

Tell My Horse, a study of voodoo, was researched during seven weeks spent in Haiti and Jamaica on a Guggenheim Fellowship.

A later novel, *Moses, Man of the Mountain,* is told from a black perspective and deals with a hoodoo practitioner who uses his awesome power to force the Egyptian Pharaoh to let the Israelites go.

During the '30s and '40s, Zora was married twice but both marriages failed—court records show that her second husband accused her of using her voodoo powers against him—because she was married to her work, "the force from somewhere in space that commands you to write . . . "

DUST TRACKS, ZORA'S not very trustworthy, though highly poetic, autobiography was finished in 1942 while she was employed as a story consultant for Paramount in Hollywood. It was a critical success, though at the cost of her being less than candid. The following is one of the many passages excised by her editor: "[it] would be a good thing for the Anglo-Saxon to get the idea out of his head . . . everybody owes him something just for being blond. I am forced to the conclusion . . . two-thirds of them do hold that view. The idea of human slavery is so deeply ground in . . . [that] pink toes can't get it out of their system."

Zora was in demand as a spokesperson for blacks in lectures, magazines, and newspaper essays, but she only published one further novel, *Seraph on the Suwannee*, a depressing though well written book about poor whites with plenty of sensationalism and sex. It didn't sell particularly well.

During the '40s, Zora continued her wandering lifestyle. From '43 to '45 she lived on a houseboat in Daytona Beach. She sold it to help finance an expedition to Honduras in search of a lost Mayan civilization.

In September of '48, Zora was arrested on a morals charge in New York City. The charge involved a mentally retarded ten-year-old boy who accused her and two other adults of sodomy. Though the indictment was subsequently dropped, it did enormous damage to her literary career. To quote Larry Neal in his introduction to the 1971 edition of *Dust Tracks*: "All the evidence indicates . . . the charge was false since Zora was out of the country at the time of the alleged crime; but several of the Negro newspapers exploded it into a major scandal. Naturally, Zora was hurt, and the incident plunged her into a state of abject despair . . . "

In 1950 Zora was employed as a maid in a house on Revo Alto Island in Miami. According to her, she was working as a maid to gather material. But Mrs. Kenneth Burke, her employer, tells a different story, "She was down on her luck. She had pawned her typewriter and was living with some Puerto Ricans . . . she had been headed for Honduras. But an Englishman and another man were managing her money, she said. The Englishman . . . took the money to the racetrack to make a killing and lost it all."

In 1952 Zora emerged as a reporter covering the sensational Ruby McCollum trial for a black newspaper, the *Pittsburgh Courier*. The trial, in Live Oak, Florida, involved a black woman, mistress of a prominent white doctor and state-senator nominee, and wife of a wealthy black numbers-runner, who killed her lover. Zora brought the well known Southern writer William Bradford Huie into the case, and he subsequently wrote a best-seller, *Ruby McCollum, Woman in the Suwannee Jail*, with a chapter by Zora.

In the fall of '57, after Zora was dismissed from a job as a $1.85-an-hour librarian in the Pan American technical library at Patrick Air Force Base near Cocoa Beach, she retired to Fort Pierce to write full-time.

At Fort Pierce she worked at the *Fort Pierce Chronicle*, an African American weekly, and as a substitute teacher at the black high school, but neither position lasted long. According to Zora in a letter to the Florida Department of Education: "My name as an author is too big to be tolerated, lest it gather to itself the 'glory' of the school . . . the mediocre have no importance except through appointment. They feel invaded and defeated by the presence of creative folk."

Zora met Marjorie Alder, a white radio personality and newspaper columnist, and they became fast friends. Often she would dine at Mrs.

Alder's riverfront home. "I'm in my Zulu mood tonight!" she would exclaim, to test the reaction among Mrs. Alder's often conservative white guests. Leftovers from these parties would be distributed among the neighborhood children, to get them within listening range of her stories.

When Zora's ten-dollar-a-week rent became too much for her, she was befriended by her neighbor Dr. Clem Benton who provided her with a rent-free home. According to Dr. Benton: "She had no furniture or lights. She had a lamp, a table. She typed using an orange crate, with cushions for a seat. She had a small kerosene stove to do her cooking . . . I don't think the woman cared about money. *She cared only about writing*."

According to Mrs. Alder: "She made a desk and bookshelves out of fruit boxes. We provided some furniture. The things that were precious to her were her typewriter, her trunk full of letters, and her reference books. She spent her time at the typewriter. It had been a long time since she had been published, and she had lost contact with the publishing houses."

IN HER LAST YEARS, with the help of Mrs. Alder, Zora tried to peddle her last novel, *Herod the Great*, to New York publishers, but with no success. She took a stand against school integration in an article she was writing for *Atlantic Monthly* when she died. According to Mrs. Alder: "She was the first person to indicate to me . . . 'Black is Beautiful.' She thought Howard was just as good as Yale. She wanted all black kids to go to Howard and achieve their uniqueness. She believed . . . blacks had equal mental and philosophical resources they should develop as blacks . . . "

On October 12, 1959, Zora had a stroke. She was taken to Fort Pierce Memorial Hospital, then the segregated and welfare-operated Lincoln Park Nursing Home. She lingered for three long months, unable to write, and died on January 28, 1960 . . . aged anywhere from 52 to 69 years. Her literary effects were being burned when Patrick N. Duval, a black deputy with the county sheriff's department, armed with a writ from a county judge appointing Mrs. Alder as Zora's literary executor, put the fire out with a garden hose and saved what was left. In 1973, Pulitzer Prize–winning author Alice Walker placed a tombstone at the head of Zora's unmarked grave.

Zora wrote, in *Dust Tracks*:

> When the consciousness we know as life ceases, I know . . . I shall be part and parcel of the world. I was a part before the sun rolled into shape and burst forth in the glory of change. I was, when the earth was hurled out from its fiery rim. I shall return to the earth to Father sun, and still exist in substance when the sun has lost its fire and extinguished in infinity to . . . become a part of the whirling rubble in space. Why fear? The stuff of my being is matter, ever changing, ever moving, but never lost; so what need of denominations and creeds to deny myself the comfort of . . . my fellow men? The wide belt of the universe has no need of finger-rings. I am one with the infinite and need no other assurance.

Eatonville is just north of Orlando, off I-4 at the Lee Road exit.

Two other black Florida geniuses are James Weldon Johnson and Ray Charles.

Johnson was born in 1871 at Jacksonville, where his father was a porter at the elegant St. James Hotel. In 1894 he was the first African American admitted to the Florida Bar. In 1895 he founded a black newspaper, the *Daily American.* Following the trail of his brother, Rosamond, a popular composer of Broadway show tunes, Johnson left Jacksonville after the Great Fire of 1901 and moved to Manhattan. Together they collaborated on more than two hundred songs for the musical stage. Father of the Harlem Renaissance, he wrote a brilliant novel, *Confessions of an Ex-Colored Man* (1912), and a book of poems based on black sermons, *God's Trombones* (1927). One of these later became the NAACP's theme song, *Lift Every Voice and Sing.* He was serving as president of the NAACP when he and his wife died in a car crash in 1938.

Ray Charles, genius of the blues, was born in Greenville, near Tallahassee, on September 23, 1930. After the tragic death of his younger brother, which Charles witnessed, he went blind at age three when he contracted what doctors later guessed was congenital juvenile glaucoma. He attended the St. Augustine School for the Deaf and Blind, but dropped out at age fifteen to play music full-time. He lived in Orlando and Tampa, playing and composing for different bands, including a white country and western group, before moving west to Seattle in 1948. The rest is music history, and Charles is one of the most popular entertainers of all time.

Lochloosa Lake

Sixteen years ago, I decided I needed a quiet place to live and write. Tired of city life, where you can spend your entire life putting out brush fires, I drew a circle with a forty-mile radius around Gainesville. This encompasses some of the most beautiful country in the center of the state. Then I set out in search of my dream house. I found it at Lochloosa, a tiny fishing community on the shore of Lochloosa Lake, a huge marshy lake, five miles by water and twelve by land from Cross Creek.

Lochloosa . . . The first time I laid eyes on it, I knew I was home.

The first thing I noticed about the 6.5-acre lot at the end of a dirt road was the towering oaks with pale gray beards of Spanish moss fluttering gently in the afternoon breeze. Beyond that lay the pearl-shaped lake with its encircling halo of grotesquely shaped cypress trees and knees. Venturing out on the rickety wooden pier, I watched the setting sun transform the inky lake to an ever deeper shade of vermilion. As night fell, a chorus of crickets, frogs, and hoot owls commenced their nightly serenade.

Lochloosa Lake, the author's Florida home.

Photo by Debra Force.

In no time at all, I converted an old fish camp into a livable house and made friends with two neighboring dogs that I christened Yellow Dog and Blackie, not knowing their Christian names. The three of us took morning, noon, and evening walks along the half-mile-long dirt road that dead-ends at my house. In the proverbial "three shakes of a puppy-dog's tail," Blackie and Yellow Dog rousted out any "snakes that would have bit me."

Sometimes a fox materialized like a *haint* at the side of the road. Other times it was a coon or badger. Occasionally deer would streak across our path—a blur of brown with antlers and a flickering white stub of a tail. Once a huge gator raised its prehistoric head out of the lake. Quick as a flash it was up on the bank, its monstrous mouth opened wide, revealing rows of hideously sharp teeth, as it snatched a hapless goat wandering too near the shoreline. There was the pitiful bleat of the goat, followed by a relentless thrashing as the gator struck the murky water with its prey.

After that, silence.

Incidentally, a three-legged dog named Gator Bait lives nearby.

LIVING AT LOCHLOOSA, one participates in the changing of the seasons.

A hot, humid summer gives way to a prolonged Indian summer, followed by two or three months of on-and-off-again cold weather leading into an early spring. In spring and summer, the lush green landscape is reminiscent of a tropical rain forest. In late fall, the vegetation gradually assumes a burnt orange color. One morning, the lake is an oasis of silence; the next, there's the collective honk of thousands upon thousands of coots migrated from up north.

Lochloosa . . .

The name recalls Scotland. And the crackers hereabouts are mostly the descendants of Scotch-Irish who migrated from the mountains of

Appalachia to settle in the flatlands of Florida. One sees them out on the lake in flat-bottomed skiffs, fishing for bream with cane poles and bobbers. Plump, fair-skinned women in loose-fitting gingham dresses and sun bonnets, and pinch-faced men with pale blue eyes and thin bloodless lips, in checkered work shirts and worn jeans. The spitting image of their forebears in a faded daguerreotype retrieved from some long-forgotten chiffonier drawer. Then there are the blacks with loose-jointed arms and legs and polite Southern ways: "Morning, ma'am. Right pleasant weather we're having?"

Lochloosa . . .

Or perhaps it's an Indian name. Remnant of a time when Seminoles tended the longhorned Brahma cattle imported by the Spanish during the sixteenth and seventeenth centuries. Cattle whose descendants still free-graze the lake's marshy shoreline, occasionally winding up in my yard before the owners arrive to round them up.

Lochloosa . . .

The morning after a frost, there's a clarity to the air that's awe-inspiring. Greens are greener; blues, bluer. As though the Divine Artist had cleansed his brush and begun to experiment with clearer, sharper colors. God is consciousness, and consciousness forms matter, not vice versa.

The coots have fled to some point further south and the gators are in hibernation. A lone white egret is fishing at the edge of the deep blue lake, while an osprey skims the lake's surface on the lookout for an unwary fish to feed his family. The family awaits its meal perched securely in a huge stick nest in the highest branches of a tall cypress.

Lochloosa . . .

Mornings spent pen in hand, notebook in lap, gazing out at the brown-leafed expanse of lawn and Spanish-mossed oaks sloping down to the frosty blue lake, the pagoda dock, and the winter-treed opposite bank. Searching for the right, the only, word.

As Paul Brunton writes in *The Secret Path*: " . . . in such sacred moments one touches the infinite. Sentences form themselves from the ether, one hardly knows how; phrases disengage themselves from the skies and descend upon this subluminary world to feed one's pen. One must yield to these mysterious moods, and not resist them, thus does one render oneself worthy to become a mediator between the gods and frail forgetful man."

More prosaically, writing is like masturbation. If you *can* quit, you should.

MY NEIGHBOR Dekel Henry and I are walking along the dirt road.

Dekel: "Back in the old days, I counted two-hundred-odd squirrels on one tree alone. And talk about fish. Why, t'weren't nothing to catch a twelve-pound bass. Then a big construction company to Ocala bought up some of the land hereabouts and begun putting in subdivisions."

"What year would that have been?"

"I ain't for certain. But it was after one of them wars."

IT'S THE DEAD of night and I'm seated on my dock enjoying the peace and serenity. Suddenly a loud splashing shatters the stillness! Frightened out of my wits, I prick my ears to listen. The thrashing continues, and it's headed in my direction. I scan the full-moon-lit murky waters for a sign of what's approaching, my imagination running wild. Nothing . . . An unreasoning fear grips my heart. Leaping up, I am preparing to make a run for it when I spy a pair of antlers—phosphorescent in the glimmer of a full moon. Three or four feet from the dock, the buck attached to the antlers spots me and veers right, heading out across the five-mile-wide lake. I hear the dogs baying in the distance.

The buck has outwitted his pursuers.

To get to Lochloosa, take U.S. 301 twenty-five miles north of Ocala over rolling green hills and past luxurious horse farms. Fishing boats may be rented at the Yankee Landing.

EPILOGUE

As I think back over thirty years of wandering the length and width of Florida, the places don't stand out so much as the people, living and dead: My grandfather, the honorable Senator Butler . . . My illustrious and notorious great-great-grandfather, James S. Turner . . . My long lost cousin, High-Sheriff Jim Turner . . . Fisherman extraordinaire and womanizer, Cap'n Mac . . . My lost love, the mystery-shrouded Nancy . . . Writer/marine biologist, Jack Rudloe . . . The hate-spouting racists at Carrabelle . . . My incorrigible date, Hope . . . Lost and lonely, Mary Dell . . . Indomitable barkeep, Jerry Adams . . . Balladeer of the Florida cracker, Marjorie Kinnan Rawlings . . . Southern gentleman, lawyer, and keeper of the grove, Horace Drew . . . Florida's premier warrior/shaman, Osceola . . . Political animal and lovable rascal, Chauncey . . . Zen Buddhist black jook owner, W. C. . . . . Slave trader married to an African princess, Zephaniah Kingsley . . . Hip and ultra-sophisticated, Bob Plunket . . . Perfect arbiter of style and taste, Linda Roe . . .

And others: Florida's first congressman and the first Jew in congress, David Levy Yulee . . . Reluctant civil rights advocate, Governor Leroy

Collins . . . Black writer, Zora Neale Hurston . . . Florida writers, Ernest and Les Hemingway, John D. MacDonald, and Borden Deal . . . Playwright, Tennessee Williams . . . Beat writer, Jack Kerouac . . . Actor, Paul Reubens, AKA PeeWee Herman . . . Gun-toting governor, Claude Kirk . . . Wandering spiritualist, Reverend William Colby . . . Bookstore owners, Keith and Janet Bollum and my friends at DeLand and Orlando . . . Seminole at the edge of the Glades with his verbal ambush, descendant of Osceola . . . Florida's pioneer conservationist and Glades advocate, Marjory Stoneman Douglas . . . All-knowing Cap'n Ed . . . Assorted pirates, artists, and scoundrels . . . Ubiquitous realtors and drug smugglers . . .

And finally me, Florida's traveling bard and troubadour, revealer of its myriad mysteries and charms, its beauty marks and blemishes—not because I'm special, but because I'm here.

ABOUT THE AUTHOR

David T. Warner has written numerous articles and short stories for literary, New Age, regional, and national magazines. He has also been a contributing editor to *Gulfshore Life* and *Sarasota Magazine*. In 1986, the Florida Magazine Association awarded him a certificate of merit for his article "The Secret Life of Borden Deal," which is included as a chapter in this book. He has written and co-produced two unique travel videos, *Bimini-by-the-Sea* and *Cowboys and Indians and UFOs,* and is one of several authors of *A Book-Lovers Guide to Florida.* His book *High-Sheriff Jim Turner: High Times of a Florida Lawman* was recently published by River City Publishing under our Black Belt Press imprint. Warner lives in Lochloosa, the heart of *Vanishing Florida.*